WILLIAM SHAKESPEARE

AS YOU LIKE IT

William Shakespeare

AS YOU LIKE IT

[Edited with Complete Text, Background of Author, Study Questions and Select Criticism]

Mansi Sachdeva
B.A. English (Hons), Delhi University;
M.A., M. Phil. (English), IGNOU

ANMOL PUBLICATIONS PVT. LTD.
NEW DELHI - 110 002 (INDIA)

ANMOL PUBLICATIONS PVT. LTD.

H.O.: 4374/4B, Ansari Road, Darya Ganj,
New Delhi-110 002 (India)
Ph.: 23278000, 23261597

B.O.: No. 1015, Ist Main Road, BSK IIIrd Stage
IIIrd Phase, IIIrd Block
Bangalore - 560 085 (India)
Visit us at: www.anmolpublications.com

As You Like It

First Published, 2009

PRINTED IN INDIA

Printed at Mehra Offset Press, Delhi.

Contents

Preface

As You Like It is considered by many to be one of Shakespeare's greatest comedies, and the heroine, Rosalind, is praised as one of his most inspiring characters and has more lines than any of Shakespeare's female characters. Rosalind, the daughter of a banished duke falls in love with Orlando the disinherited son of one of the duke's friends. When she is banished from the court by her usurping uncle, Duke Frederick , Rosalind switches genders and as Ganymede travels with her loyal cousin Celia and the jester Touchstone to the Forest of Arden, where her father and his friends live in exile. Observations on life and love follow (including love, aging, the natural world, and death) friends are made, and families are reunited. By the play's end Ganymede, once again Rosalind, marries her Orlando. Two other sets of lovers are also wed, one of them Celia and Orlando's mean older brother Oliver . As Oliver becomes a gentler, kinder young man so the Duke conveniently changes his ways and turns to religion and so that the exiled Duke, father of Rosalind, can rule once again.

William Shakespeare never published any of his plays and therefore none of the original manuscripts have survived. Eighteen unauthorised versions of his plays were, however, published during his lifetime in quarto editions by unscrupulous publishers (there were no copyright laws protecting Shakespeare and his works during the Elizabethan era). A collection of his works did not appear until 1623 (a full seven years after Shakespeare's death on April 23, 1616) when two of his fellow actors, John Hemminges and Henry Condell, posthumously recorded his work and published 36 of William's plays in the First Folio. Some dates are therefore approximate other dates are substantiated by historical events, records of performances and the dates plays appeared in print.

Author

Chapter 1

Introduction

William Shakespeare, in terms of his life and his body of work, is the most written-about author in the history of Western civilization. His canon includes 38 plays, 154 sonnets, and 2 epic narrative poems. The First Folio (cover shown at left) was published posthumously in 1623 by two of Shakespeare's acting companions, John Heminges and Henry Condell. Ever since then, the works of Shakespeare have been studied, analysed, and enjoyed as some of the finest masterpieces of the English language.

It is all the more wondrous when one can study the works and see Shakespeare developing as a playwright right there upon the pages. *Love's Labours Lost* and the early comedies are the work of a gifted and clever author. Perhaps such plays alone would have earned him literary fame in later days. The grandeur of a *Hamlet* or *King Lear,* however, is the work of a master who learned from his own writing and long practice.

In his time, Shakespeare was the most popular playwright of London. As centuries have passed, his genius eclipses all others of his age; Jonson, Marlowe, Kyd, Greene, Dekker, Heywood—none approach the craft or the humanity of character that marks the Bard's work. He took the art of dramatic verse and honed it to perfection. He created the most vivid characters of the Elizabethan stage. His usage of language, both lofty and low, shows a remarkable wit and subtlety. Most importantly, his themes are so universal that they transcend generations to stir the imaginations of audiences everywhere to this day.

His plays generally fall into four categories:

- Pre-1594 (*Richard III, The Comedy of Errors*)
- 1594–1600 (*Henry V, Midsummer Night's Dream*)
- 1600–1608 (*Macbeth, King Lear*)
- Post-1608 (*Cymbeline, The Tempest*)

The first period has its roots in Roman and medieval drama—the construction of the plays, while good, is obvious and shows the author's hand more brusquely than the later works. The earliest Shakespeare also owes a debt to Christopher Marlowe, whose writing probably gave much inspiration at the onset of the Bard's career.

The second period showed more growth in style, and the construction becoming less laboured. The histories of this period are Shakespeare's best, portraying the lives of kings and royalty in most human terms. He also begins the interweaving of comedy and tragedy, which would become one of his stylistic signatures. His comedies mature in this period as well, portraying a greater characterization in their subjects.

The third period marks the great tragedies, and the principal works which would earn the Bard his fame in later centuries. His tragic figures rival those of Sophocles, and might well have walked off the Greek stage straight onto the Elizabethan. Shakespeare is at his best in these tragedies. The comedies of this period, however, show Shakespeare at a literary crossroads—moody and without the clear comic resolution of previous comedies. Hence, the term "problem plays" to describe them.

The fourth period encompasses romantic tragicomedy. Shakespeare at the end of his career seemed preoccupied with themes of redemption. The writing is more serious yet more lyrical, and the plays show Shakespeare at his most symbolic. It is argued between scholars whether this period owed more to Shakespeare's maturity as a playwright or merely signified a changing trend in Elizabethan theatre at the time.

William Shakespeare remains a mysterious figure with regards to personal history. There are just two primary sources for information on the Bard: his works, and various legal and church documents that have survived from Elizabethan times. Naturally, there are many gaps in this body of information, which tells us little about Shakespeare the man.

William Shakespeare was born in Stratford-upon-Avon, allegedly on April 23, 1564. Church records from Holy Trinity Church indicate that he was baptised there on April 26, 1564. Young William was born of John Shakespeare, a Glover and leather merchant, and Mary Arden, a landed local heiress. William, according to the church register, was the third of eight children in the Shakespeare household—three of whom died in childhood. John Shakespeare had a remarkable run of success as a merchant, alderman, and high bailiff of Stratford, during William's early childhood. His fortunes declined, however, in the late 1570s.

There is great conjecture about Shakespeare's childhood years, especially regarding his education. It is surmised by scholars that Shakespeare attended the free grammar school in Stratford, which at the time had a reputation to rival that of Eton. While there are no records extant to prove this claim, Shakespeare's knowledge of Latin and Classical Greek would tend to support this theory. In addition, Shakespeare's first biographer, Nicholas Rowe, wrote that John Shakespeare had placed William "for some time in a free school." John Shakespeare, as a Stratford official, would have been granted a waiver of tuition for his son. As the records do not exist, we do not know how long William attended the school, but certainly the literary quality of his works suggest a solid education. What is certain is that William Shakespeare never proceeded to university schooling, which has stirred some of the debate concerning the authorship of his works.

For the seven years following the birth of his twins, William Shakespeare disappears from all records, finally turning up again in London some time in 1592. This period, known as the "Lost Years," has sparked as much controversy about Shakespeare's life as any period. Rowe notes that young Shakespeare was quite fond of poaching, and may have had to flee Stratford after an incident with Sir Thomas Lucy, whose deer and rabbits he allegedly poached. There is also rumor of Shakespeare working as an assistant schoolmaster in Lancashire for a time, though this is circumstantial at best.

It is estimated that Shakespeare arrived in London around 1588 and began to establish himself as an actor and playwright. Evidently, Shakespeare garnered envy early on for his talent, as related by the critical attack of Robert Greene, a London playwright, in 1592: "...an upstart crow, beautified with our feathers, that with his Tiger's heart wrapped in a player's hide, supposes he is as well able to bombast out a blank verse as the best of you: and being an absolute *Johannes fac totum,* is in his own conceit the only Shake-scene in a country."

Greene's bombast notwithstanding, Shakespeare must have shown considerable promise. By 1594, he was not only acting and writing for the Lord Chamberlain's Men (called the King's Men after the ascension of James I in 1603), but was a managing partner in the operation as well. With Will Kempe, a master comedian, and Richard Burbage, a leading tragic actor of the day, the Lord Chamberlain's Men became a favourite London troupe, patronised by royalty and made popular by the theatre-going public.

Shakespeare's success is apparent when studied against other playwrights of this age. His company was the most successful in London in his day. He had plays published and sold in octavo editions, or "penny-copies" to the more literate of his audiences. Never before had a playwright enjoyed sufficient acclaim to see his works published and sold as popular literature in the midst of his career. In addition, Shakespeare's ownership share in both the theatrical company and the Globe itself made him as much an entrepeneur as artist. While Shakespeare might not be accounted wealthy by London standards, his success allowed him to purchase New House and retire in comfort to Stratford in 1611.

William Shakespeare wrote his will in 1611, bequeathing his properties to his daughter Susanna (married in 1607 to Dr. John Hall). To his surviving daughter Judith, he left £300, and to his wife Anne left "my second best bed." William Shakespeare allegedly died on his birthday, April 23, 1616. This is probably more of a romantic myth than reality, but Shakespeare was interred at Holy Trinity in Stratford on April 25. In 1623, two working companions of Shakespeare from the Lord Chamberlain's Men, John Heminges and Henry Condell, printed the First Folio edition of his collected plays, of which half were previously unpublished.

William Shakespeare's legacy is a body of work that will never again be equaled in Western civilization. His words have endured for 400 years, and still reach across the centuries as powerfully as ever. Even in death, he leaves a final piece of verse as his epitaph:

Good friend, for Jesus' sake forbeare
To dig the dust enclosed here.
Blessed be the man that spares these stones,
And cursed be he that moves my bones.

TIMELINE OF SHAKESPEARE

Shakespeare Timeline describes the many chapters in Shakespeare's colourful life. From humble beginnings in Stratford to his marriage to the older Anne Hathaway and popular acclaim for his works, Shakespeare Timeline follows the life of literature's most famous playwright.

1564: William Shakespeare is born in Stratford upon Avon to local tanner John and Mary Shakespeare. His actual birthday is unknown but assumed and celebrated today on April the 23rd, just three days before his baptism was recorded in the Parish register of the Holy Trinity Church on April the 26th.

1571: Shakespeare is likely to have begun his formal education. By local tradition, children in the Stratford area, entered the local grammar school at age seven.

1575: Queen Elizabeth pays a visit to Kenilworth Castle, just a short journey from Stratford. Legend has it that an impressionable eleven year old William saw the Queen's procession, and recreated it several times later in his historical and dramatic plays.

1582: Shakespeare is in love... At age 18, he marries the considerably older Anne Hathaway (26 years old) from Shottery on November the 27th at Temple Grafton, a village just five short miles (8 km) from Stratford.

1583: Susanna, William and Anne Shakespeare's first child who lives a full 66 years, is born just five months after Shakespeare and Anne Hathaway's wedding (May 26th). Illegitimacy was not uncommon in the 1500s.

1585-1592: Shakespeare is believed to have left his family in Stratford to join a company of actors as both playwright and performer, starting his career in theatre.

1585: Shakespeare's twins, Judith and Hamnet are born, (February 2)Hamnet living only eleven years whilst Judith lived 77.

1589-1590: Shakespeare is believed by most academics to have written his very first play, *Henry VI, Part One* in this year.

1590-91: Shakespeare is again believed to have written *Henry VI, Part Two* and *Henry VI, Part III.*

1592: Shakespeare begins to be noticed as a force within London theatre; Robert Greene's *Groatworth of Wit* famously calls Shakespeare an *"upstart crow"*. He attacks Shakespeare as lacking originality since he borrows ideas from other for his own plays. Academics see this criticism as proof that Shakespeare was in London at this time.

Theatres in London close because of the plague.

1592-93: Shakespeare is thought to have written the poem *Venus and Adonis* and the plays *Richard III* and *The Two Gentlemen of Verona.*

1592-94: *The Comedy of Errors* written in this time.

1593: Shakespeare begins to compose the first of what will amount to a 154 sonnet collection. His narrative poem *Venus and Adonis* is his first ever published.

1593-94: *The Rape of Lucrece, Titus Andronicus* and *The Taming of the Shrew* are thought to have been penned by Shakespeare at this time.

1594: The Lord Chamberlain's Men, a theatre troupe including distinguished actor Richard Burbage and comic Will Kemp performs with Shakespeare in their group.

1594-1595: Shakespeare pen's *Love Labour's Lost.*

1594-1596: *King John* is assumed to have been written.

1595: A busy year for Shakespeare as he is thought to have composed *Richard II* performed that very same year, *A Midsummer Night's Dream,* thought to be composed for a wedding and the greatest love story of all time, *Romeo and Juliet.*

1596: *The Merry Wives of Windsor* is thought to have been written. The Lord Chamberlain's Men lose their original patron, Henry Carey, Lord Hunsdon and Lord Chamberlain to be replaced by his brother George Carey, Second Lord Hunsdon, who succeeds his late brother.

1596-1597: *The Merchant of Venice* and *Henry IV, Part One* are thought to have been written.

1597: Shakespeare buys the New Place, one of Stratford's most preeminent homes. This fuels speculation today by some academics that William was really a successful businessman and not literature's celebrated playwright.

1598: William is thought to have written the play *Henry IV, Part Two* and Shakespeare's reputation as an actor is confirmed his performance in Ben Jonson's *Every Man in his Humour* which clearly lists his name as a principal actor in the London play.

1598-99: William writes the play *Much Ado About Nothing* in this year.

1599: The Major shareholders of the Lord Chamberlain's Men lease land from Nicholas Brend, The Globe theatre opening later that same year. *Julius Caesar* is performed at the Globe Theatre for the first known time on September the 21st according to German tourist Thomas Platter's diary. John Weever praises Shakespeare's *Romeo and Juliet, The Rape of Lucrece* and *Venus Adonis* in the poem *Ad Guglielmum Shakespeare.*

1600-1601: Shakespeare is thought to have composed arguably his greatest play, *Hamlet* at this time.

1601: The narrative poem, *The Phoenix and the Turtle* is thought to have been written.

1601-1602: *Twelfth Night or What You Will, All Well That Ends Well* and *Troilus and Cressida* are probably composed.

1603:*A Midsummer's Night* is performed at Hampton Court before Queen Elizabeth who dies later that year. James I originally James VI of Scotland proves to be an enthusiastic patron of the arts granting *The Chamberlain's Men* a patent to perform. In return the Company renames itself *The King's Men* to honour James I and they quickly become a favourite with the new king.

As You Like It is performed by the newly named King's Men before King James at Wilton. Acting-wise, Shakespeare is recorded as performing in Ben Jonson's *Sejanus,* Shakespeare's last recorded acting performance.

1604: *Measure for Measure* is believed to have been written in this year. It is later performed at King James I Court. Othello is also penned, being performed on November the 1st at Whitehall.

1605: *The Merchant of Venice* is performed twice at King James' Court earning a commendation from the King. King Lear is believed to have been composed in this year and as is Macbeth, the play's Scottish background and kind portrayal of ancestor Malcolm being intended as a celebration and honouring of King James Scottish ancestry.

1606:Antony And Cleopatra is believed to have been composed.

1607: *Hamlet* and *Richard III* are performed aboard the British ship *Dragon* off the west coast of Africa at Sierra Leone.

1607-1608: *Timon of Athens, Pericles* and *Coriolanus are composed.*

1608: The King's Men take on a twenty-one year lease of London's first permanently enclosed theatre, the Blackfriars Theatre in this year. Notes on stage directions, suggest *The Tempest* was penned with a performance at this theatre in mind.

The return of the plague forces a closure of all playhouses and theatres from the spring of 1608 through to early 1610.

1609-1610: Cymbeline is thought to have been composed.

1610: Othello is performed at Oxford College by the King's Men during a summer tour.

1610-1611: The Winter's Tale is written.

1611: The Tempest was written.

1612-1613: The King's men perform Othello and Julius Caesar amongst others in this year. Shakespeare is thought to have written Cardenio, his only lost play during this period and with John Fletcher as a likely contributor, composes Henry VIII.

1613: The Globe Theatre burns to the ground. The Two Noble Kinsmen is penned. A 1634 entry within the Stationer's Registry confirms that both William Shakespeare and John Fletcher composed this play.

1614: The Globe Theatre reopens.

1616: William dies on April 23rd, his burial being recorded in the Stratford Holy Church Register two days later.

1619: Hamlet is performed as part of Christmas celebrations at court.

1623: Shakespeare's wife, Anne Hathaway dies, the same year, and fellow actors John Hemminges and Henry Condell gather together and publish for the first time, 36 of Shakespeare's 37 plays in a collection known as The First Folio.

Chapter 2

Biography of Shakespeare

William Shakespeare Biography describes the life of William Shakespeare. From birth to death, Shakespeare Biography describes all that is known about Shakespeare's life from available documentation including court and church records, marriage certificates and criticisms by Shakespeare's rivals.

Shakespeare (1564-1616)

Though William Shakespeare is recognised as one of literature's greatest influences, very little is actually known about him. What we do know about his life comes from registrar records, court records, wills, marriage certificates and his tombstone. Anecdotes and criticisms by his rivals also speak of the famous playwright and suggest that he was indeed a playwright, poet and an actor.

William was born in 1564. We know this from the earliest record we have of his life; his baptism which happened on Wednesday, April the 26th, 1564. We don't actually know his birthday but from this record we assume he was born in 1564. Similarly by knowing the famous Bard's baptism date, we can guess that he was born three days earlier on St. George's day, though we have no conclusive proof of this.

William was the third child of John and Mary Shakespeare. The first two were daughters and William was himself followed by Gilbert who died in 1612 and Richard who died in 1613. Edmund (1580-1607), sixth in the line was baptised on May the third, 1580 and William's oldest living sister was Joan who outlived her famous playwright brother. Of William's seven siblings, only Judith and four of his brothers survived to adulthood.

From baptism records, we know William's father was a John Shakespeare, said to be a town official of Stratford and a local businessman who dabbled in tanning, leatherwork and whittawering which is working with white leather to make items like purses and gloves. John also dealt in grain and sometimes was described as a glover by trade.

John was also a prominent man in Stratford. By 1560, he was one of fourteen burgesses which formed the town council. Interestingly, William himself is often described as a keen businessman so we can assume he got his business acumen from his father. In the Bard's case, the apple didn't fall far from the tree at all...

William's mother was Mary Arden who married John Shakespeare in 1557. The youngest daughter in her family, she inherited much of her father's landowning and farming estate when he died.

Since we know Stratford's famous Bard lived with his father, John Shakespeare, we can presume that he grew up in Henley Street, some one hundred miles northwest of London.

Very little is known about literature's most famous playwright. We know that the King's New Grammar School taught boys basic reading and writing. We assume William attended this school since it existed to educate the sons of Stratford but we have no definite proof. Likewise a lack of evidence suggests that William, whose works are studied universally at Universities, never attended one himself!

A bond certificate dated November the 28th, 1582, reveals that an eighteen year old William married the twenty-six and pregnant Anne Hathaway. Barely seven months later, they had his first daughter, Susanna. Anne never left Stratford, living there her entire life.

Baptism records show that William's first child, Susanna was baptised in Stratford sometime in May, 1583. Baptism records again reveal that twins Hamnet and Judith were born in February 1592. Hamnet, William's only son died in 1596, just eleven years old. Hamnet and Judith were named after William's close friends, Judith and Hamnet Sadler. William's family was unusually small in a time when families had many children to ensure parents were cared for in later years despite the very high mortality rates of children and also their life expectancy in the 1500s.

Evidence that the great Bard was also a poet comes from his entering his first poem *Venus and Adonis* in the Stationers' Registrar on the 18th of April, 1593. The playwright registered his second poem *The Rape of Lucrece* by name on the 9th of May, 1594.

In 1609, the Bard's sonnets were published without the Bard's permission. It is considered unlikely that William wanted many of his deeply personal poems to be revealed to the outside world. It was not however the first time; in 1599, in a collection entitled *"The Passionate Pilgrim"*, two of his poems had been printed without William's permission.

Looking for work in London, just four days ride way from Stratford, William is believed to have left his family back home for some twenty years whilst he pursued his craft. He only returned back to his family in 1609, having visited only during the forty day period of Lent when theatres though open well into the start of Lent would later close in accordance with the traditional banning of all forms of diversionary entertainment around this important Easter event.

Records with the College of Heralds, reveal William applied for a coat of arms. Despite a lack of proof, he was granted his request. Later in 1599 he applied for his mother's coat of arms to be added to his own.

At age 15, William purchased the New Place. This was one of the most prominent and desired properties in all of Stratford being the second largest house in town. Given his father's known financial hardship from 1576, William must either have used his own money to buy this expensive property or his father had placed money in his son's name. It is possible William might have bought this prominent property with money from his plays. It is estimated that roughly fifteen of his 37 plays would have been written and performed by 1597!

Court records of a dispute between William's landlord Christopher Mountjoy and his son-in-law Stephen Belott confirm that William was living in London around 1601. The playwright's name is recorded in the court records when he gave testimony in 1612 concerning Mountjoy and Belott's dispute. Interestingly, in 1601, he bought roughly 107 acres of arable land with twenty acres of pasturage for 20 pounds in Old Stratford.

William made his greatest financial gain in 1605 when he purchased leases of real estate near Stratford. This investment of some four hundred and forty pounds doubled in value and earned him 60 pounds income each year. Some academics speculate that this investment gave the Bard the time he needed to write plays uninterrupted and we know that he was indeed thought of as a businessman in the Stratford area...

Yet another record confirming the Bard's existence was John Comb's will which bequeathed to the Bard the princely sum of just five pounds.

Records reveal that the great Bard revised his will on March the 25th, 1616. Less than a month later, he died on April the 23rd, 1616. Literature's famous Bard is buried at the Holy Trinity Church in Stratford. He infamously left his second-best bed to his wife Anne Hathaway and little else, giving most of his estate to his eldest daughter Susanna who has married a prominent and distinguished physician named John Hall in June 1607. This was not as callous as it seems; the Bard's best bed was for guests; his second-best bed was his marriage bed... His will also named actors Richard Burbage, Henry Condell and John Hemminges, providing proof to academics today that William was involved in theatre. The Bard's direct line of descendants ended some 54 years later until Susanna's daughter Elizabeth died in 1670.

Written upon William Shakespeare's tombstone is an appeal that he be left to rest in peace with a curse on those who would move his bones...

Good friend, for Jesus´ sake forbeare
To digg the dust enclosed here!
Blest be ye man that spares thes stones
And curst be he that moues my bones.
Translated this reads as:
Good friend, for Jesus' sake, forbear
To dig the dust enclosed here;
Blest be the man that spares these stones
And curst he that moves my bones.

The evidence above proves William existed but not that he was a playwright nor an actor nor a poet. In fact recently some academics who call themselves the Oxfords argue that Stratford's celebrated playwright did not write any of the plays attributed to him. They suggest that he was merely a businessman and propose several contenders for authorship, namely an Edward de Vere.

The earliest proof that William did indeed write 37 plays was Robert Greene's criticism of the Bard in his *Groatsworth of Wit, Bought with a Million of Repentance* which attacked Shakespeare for having the nerve to compete with him and other playwrights in 1592. Robert Greene made this quite clear by calling him *"an upstart crow"*. This criticism was placed with the Stationers' Registrar on the 20th of September, 1592.

Proof that William was an actor comes from his own performances before Queen Elizabeth herself in 1594 and evidence of William's interest in theatre comes from the Bard's name being listed in 1594 and 1595 as a shareholder (part owner) of the Lord Chamberlain's Company, a theatre company.

The Bard's reputation as a poet is again confirmed in 1598, when Francis Meres attacked him as being *"mellifluous"* and described his work as honey-tongued, *"sugared sonnets among his private friends"* in his own *Palladis Tamia* of 1598.

William's theatre presence is again confirmed by his name being recorded as one of the owners of the Globe theatre in 1599 and on May the 19th, 1603, he received a patent, titling him as one of the King's Men (previously called the Chamberlain's men) and a Groom of the Chamber by James I, the then King of England. This honour made William a favourite for all court performances, earned each King's man extra money (30 pounds each for a performance in 1603 alone) and made the Bard's name one rather above reproach. Macbeth which celebrates King James I ancestor Malcolm, is considered to have been written in part as appreciation for the King's patronage. And as a potent form of royalist propaganda (it warned of the dangers of killing a King appointed like James, by God).

The First Folio (1623): Conclusive proof that Shakespeare authored his plays.

The proof most often cited that Shakespeare authored his plays however, was the First Folio (1623) where Henry Condell and John Hemminges who were actors in the Bard's theatre company, claim in a dedicatory verse within the Folio that they recorded and collected his plays as a memorial to the late actor and playwright. In terms of value, the First Folio originally was sold for just 1 Pound in 1623. Today as one of just 250 still in existence, it would fetch nearly 3 million dollars (US).

Ben Jonson criticises and then praises William by name.

Further proof of authorship comes in the form of a poem by Ben Jonson, one of the Bard's more friendly rivals, which criticises the playwrights dramatic plays. It is contained within a work entitled Discoveries (also known as Timber) dated 1641. Despite his criticism, Ben Johnson paradoxically also said that Stratford's famous Bard's works were timeless, describing them as "not of an age, but for all time".

SHAKESPEARE'S ANCESTRY

As a brief introductory detail it should be mentioned that, during the sixteenth century, there were many families with the name Shakespeare in and around Stratford. "Shakespeare" appears countless times in town minutes and court records, spelled in a variety of ways, from Shagspere to Chacsper. Unfortunately, there are very few records that reveal William Shakespeare's relationship to or with the many other Stratford Shakespeares. Genealogists claim to have discovered one man related to Shakespeare who was hanged in Gloucestershire for theft in 1248, and Shakespeare's father, in an application for a coat of arms, claimed that his grandfather was a hero in the War of the Roses and was granted land in Warwickshire in 1485 by Henry VII. No historical evidence has been discovered to corroborate this story of the man who would be William Shakespeare's great-grandfather, but, luckily, we do have information regarding his paternal and maternal grandfathers.

The Bard's paternal grandfather was Richard Shakespeare (d. 1561), a farmer in Snitterfield, a village four miles northeast of Stratford. There is no record of Richard Shakespeare before 1529, but details about his life after this reveal that he was a tenant farmer, who, on occasion, would be fined for grazing too many cattle on the common grounds and for not attending manor court. There is no record of Richard Shakespeare's wife, but together they had two sons (possibly more), John and Henry. Richard Shakespeare worked on several different sections of land during his lifetime, including the land owned by the wealthy Robert Arden of Wilmecote, Shakespeare's maternal grandfather. Robert Arden (d. 1556) was the son of Thomas Arden of Wilmecote, Shakespeare's maternal great-grandfather, who probably belonged to the aristocratic family of the Ardens of Park Hall. He was catholic and married more than once (we know the name of his second wife — Agnes Hill) and he fathered no fewer than eight daughters. He became the stepfather of Agnes' four children. Robert Arden had accumulated much property, and when he died, he named his daughter (Shakespeare's mother) Mary, only sixteen at the time, one of his executors. He left Mary some money and, in his own words, "all my land in Willmecote cawlide Asbyes and the crop apone the grounde, sowne and tyllide as hitt is".

SHAKESPEARE'S PARENTS

Shakespeare's father, John, came to Stratford from Snitterfield before 1532 as an apprentice glover and tanner of leathers. John Shakespeare prospered and began to deal in farm products and wool. It is recorded that he bought a house in 1552 (the date that he first appears in the town records), and bought more property in 1556. Because John Shakespeare owned one house on Greenhill Street and two houses on Henley Street, the exact location of William's birth cannot be known for certain. Sometime between 1556 and 1558 John Shakespeare married Mary Arden, the daughter of the wealthy Robert Arden of Wilmecote and owner of the sixty-acre farm called Asbies.

The wedding would have most likely taken place in Mary Arden's parish church at Aston Cantlow, the burial place of Robert Arden, and, although there is no evidence of strong piety on either side of the family, it would have been a Catholic service, since Queen Mary I was the reigning monarch. We assume neither John nor Mary could write — John used a pair of glovers' compasses as his signature while Mary used a running horse — but it did not prevent them from becoming important members of the community. John Shakespeare was elected to a multitude of civic positions, including ale-taster of the borough (Stratford had a long-reaching reputation for its brewing) in 1557, chamberlain of the borough in 1561, alderman in 1565, (a position which came with free education for his children at the Stratford Grammar School), high bailiff, or mayor, in 1568, and chief alderman in 1571. Due to his important civic duties, he rightfully sought the title of gentleman and applied for his coat-of-arms in 1570 (see picture on left). However, for unspecific reasons the application was abruptly withdrawn, and within the next few years, for reasons just as mystifying,

John Shakespeare would go from wealthy business owner and dedicated civil servant to debtor and absentee council member. By 1578 he was behind in his taxes and stopped paying the statutory aldermanic subscription for poor relief. In 1579, he had to mortgage Mary Shakespeare's estate, Asbies, to pay his creditors. In 1580 he was fined 40 pounds for missing a court date and in 1586 the town removed him from the board of aldermen due to lack of attendance. By 1590, John Shakespeare owned only his house on Henley Street and, in 1592 he was fined for not attending church. However, near the very end of John Shakespeare's life, it seems that his social and economic standing was again beginning to flourish. He once again applied to the College of Heralds for a coat-of-arms in 1596, and, due likely to the success of William in London, this time his wish was granted. On October 20 of that year, by permission of the Garter King of Arms (the Queen's aid in such matters) "the said John Shakespeare, Gentlemen, and...his children, issue and posterity" were lawfully entitled to display the gold coat-of-arms, with a black banner bearing a silver spear (a visual representation of the family name "Shakespeare").

The coat-of-arms could then be displayed on their door and all their personal items. The motto was "Non sanz droict" or "not without right. The reason cited for granting the coat-of-arms was John Shakespeare's grandfather's faithful service to Henry VII, but no specifics were given as to what service he actually performed. The coat-of-arms appears on Shakespeare's tomb in Stratford. In 1599 John Shakespeare was reinstated on the town council, but died a short time later, in 1601. He was probably near seventy years old and he had been married for forty-four years. Mary Shakespeare died in 1608 and was buried on September 9.

SHAKESPEARE'S BIRTH

The baptismal register of the Holy Trinity parish church, in Stratford, shows the following entry for April 26, 1564:

Gulielmus filius Johannes Shakespeare. The actual date of Shakespeare's birth is not known, but, traditionally, April 23, St George's Day, has been Shakespeare's accepted birthday, and a house on Henley Street in Stratford, owned by William's father, John, is accepted as Shakespeare's birth place. However, the reality is that no one really knows when the great dramatist was born. According to the Book of Common Prayer, it was required that a child be baptised on the nearest Sunday or holy day following the birth, unless the parents had a legitimate excuse. As Dennis Kay proposes in his book *Shakespeare*

If Shakespeare was indeed born on Sunday, April 23, the next feast day would have been St. Mark's Day on Tuesday the twenty-fifth. There might well have been some cause, both reasonable and great — or perhaps, as has been suggested, St. Mark's Day was still held to be unlucky, as it had been before the Reformation, when altars and crucifixes used to be draped in black cloth, and when some claimed to see in the churchyard the spirits of those doomed to die in that year....but that does not help to explain the christening on the twenty-sixth.

No doubt Shakespeare's true birthday will remain a mystery forever. But the assumption that the Bard was born on the same day of the month that he died lends an exciting esoteric highlight to the otherwise mundane details of Shakespeare's life.

Shakespeare's Siblings

William Shakespeare was indeed lucky to survive to adulthood in sixteenth-century England. Waves of the plague swept across the countryside, and pestilence ravaged Stratford during the hot summer months. Mary and John Shakespeare became parents for the first time in September of 1558, when their daughter Joan was born. Nothing is known of Joan Shakespeare except for the fact that she was baptised in Stratford on September 15, and succumbed to the plague shortly after. Their second child, Margaret, was born in 1562 and was baptised on December 2. She died one year later. The

Shakespeares' fourth child, Gilbert, was baptised on October 13, 1566, at Holy Trinity. It is likely that John Shakespeare named his second son after his friend and neighbour on Henley Street, Gilbert Bradley, a glover and the burgess of Stratford for a time. Records show that Gilbert Shakespeare survived the plague and reached adulthood, becoming a haberdasher, working in London as of 1597, and spending much of his time back in Stratford. In 1609 he appeared in Stratford court in connection with a lawsuit, but we know no details regarding the matter.

Gilbert Shakespeare seems to have had a long and successful career as a tradesman, and he died a bachelor in Stratford on February 3, 1612. In 1569, John and Mary Shakespeare gave birth to another girl, and named her after her first born sister, Joan. Joan Shakespeare accomplished the wondrous feat of living to be seventy-seven years old — outliving William and all her other siblings by decades. Joan married William Hart the hatter and had four children but two of them died in childhood. Her son William Hart (1600-1639) followed in his famous uncle's footsteps and became an actor, performing with the King's Men in the mid-1630s. His most noted role was that of Falstaff.

William Hart never married, but the leading actor of the restoration period, Charles Hart, is believed to have been William Hart's illegitimate son and grandnephew to Shakespeare. Due to the fact that Shakespeare's children and his other siblings did not carry on the line past the seventeenth century, the descendants of Joan Shakespeare Hart possess the only genetic link to the great playwright. Joan Shakespeare lost her husband William a week before she lost her brother William in 1616, and she lived the rest of her life in Shakespeare's birthplace. Joan died in 1646, but her descendants stayed in Stratford until 1806. Undoubtedly already euphoric that Joan had survived the precarious first few years of childhood, the Shakespeares' joy was heightened with the birth of their fourth daughter, Anne, in 1571, when William was seven years old. Unfortunately, tragedy befell the family yet again when Anne died at the age of eight. The sorrow felt by the Shakespeares' over the loss of Anne was profound, and even though they were burdened by numerous debts at the time of her death, they arranged an unusually elaborate funeral for their cherished daughter. Anne Shakespeare was buried on April 4, 1579.

In 1574, Mary and John Shakespeare had another boy and they named him Richard, probably after his paternal grandfather. Richard was baptised on March 11 of that year, and nothing else is known about him, except for the fact that he died, unmarried, and was buried on February 4, 1613 — a year and a day after the death of Gilbert Shakespeare. Mary gave birth to one more child in 1580. They christened him on May 3 and named him Edmund, probably in honour of his uncle Edmund Lambert. Edmund was eager to follow William into the acting profession, and when he was old enough he joined William in London to embark on a career as a "player". Edmund did not make a great reputation for himself as an actor, but, in all fairness, cruel fate, and not his poor acting abilities, was likely the reason.

Edmund died in 1607 — not yet thirty years old. He was buried in St. Saviour's Church, in Southwark, on December 31 of that year. His funeral was costly and magnificent, with tolling bells heard across the Thames. It is most likely that William planned the funeral for his younger brother because William would have been the only Shakespeare wealthy enough to afford such an expensive tribute to Edmund. In addition, records show that the funeral was held in the morning, and as Dennis Kay points out, funerals were usually held in the afternoon. It is probable that the morning funeral was arranged so that Shakespeare's fellow actors could attend the burial of Edmund.

Shakespeare's Education and Childhood

Shakespeare probably began his education at the age of six or seven at the Stratford grammar school, which is still standing only a short distance from his house on Henley Street and is in the care of the Shakespeare Birthplace Trust. Although we have no record of Shakespeare attending the school, due to the official position held by John Shakespeare it seems likely that he would have decided to educate young William at the school which was under the care of Stratford's governing body. The Stratford grammar school had been built some two hundred years before Shakespeare was born and in that time the lessons taught there were, of course, dictated primarily by the beliefs of the reigning monarch.

In 1553, due to a charter by King Edward VI, the school became known as the King's New School of Stratford-upon-Avon. During the years that Shakespeare attended the school, at least one and possibly three headmasters stepped down because of their devotion to the Catholic religion proscribed by Queen Elizabeth. One of these masters was Simon Hunt (b. 1551), who, in 1578, according to tradition, left Stratford to pursue his more spiritual goal of becoming a Jesuit, and relocated to the seminary at Rheims. Hunt had found his true vocation: when he died in Rome seven years later he had risen to the position of Grand Penitentiary.

Like all of the great poets and dramatists of the time, Shakespeare learned his basic reading and writing skills from an ABC, or horn-book. Robert Speaight in his book, *Shakespeare: The Man and His Achievement*, describes this book as a primer framed in wood and covered with a thin plate of transparent horn. It included the alphabet in small letters and in capitals, with combinations of the five vowels with b, c, and d, and the Lord's Prayer in English. The first of these alphabets, which ended with the abbreviation for 'and', began with the mark of the cross. Hence the alphabet was known as 'Christ cross row' — the cross-row of Richard III, I, i, 55. A short catechism was often included in the ABC book (the 'absey book' of King John, I, i,).

In *The Merry Wives of Windsor*, there is a comical scene in which the Welsh headmaster tests his pupil's knowledge, who is appropriately named William. There is little doubt that Shakespeare was recalling his own experiences during his early school years. As was the case in all Elizabethan grammar schools, Latin was the primary language of learning. Although Shakespeare likely had some lessons in English, Latin composition and the study of Latin authors like Seneca, Cicero, Ovid, Virgil, and Horace would have been the focus of his literary training. One can see that Shakespeare absorbed much that was taught in his grammar school, for he had an impressive familiarity with the stories by Latin authors, as is evident when examining his plays and their sources. Even though scholars, basing their argument on a story told more than a century after the fact, accept that Shakespeare was removed from school around age thirteen because of his father's financial and social difficulties, there is no reason whatsoever to believe that he had not acquired a firm grasp of both English and Latin and that he had continued his studies elsewhere. The famous quotation from Nicholas Rowe's notoriously inaccurate biography of Shakespeare (written in 1709), where he claims that Shakespeare "acquir'd that little Latin he was Master of" and that Shakespeare was prevented by his father's poor fortune from "further Proficiency in that Language", should be read with an extremely critical eye.

There are other fragmented and dubious details about Shakespeare's life growing up in Stratford. He is supposed to have worked for a butcher, in addition to helping run his father's business. There is a fable that Shakespeare stole a deer from Sir Thomas Lucy at Charlecote, and, instead of serving a prison sentence, fled from Stratford. Although this surely is a fictitious incident, there exists a few verses of a humourous ballad mocking Lucy that have been connected to Shakespeare. "Edmond Malone records a version of two verses of the Lucy Ballad collected by one of the few great English classical scholars, Joshua Barnes, at Stratford between 1687 and 1690. Barnes stopped overnight at an inn and heard an old woman singing it. He gave her a new gown for the two stanzas which were all she remembered":

Sir Thomas was so covetous
To covet so much deer
When horns enough upon his head
Most plainly did appear
Had not his worship one deer left?
What then? He had a wife
Took pains enough to find him horns
Should last him during life. (Levi)

Shakespeare's daily activities after he left school and before he re-emerged as a professional actor in the late 1580s are impossible to trace. Suggestions that he might have worked as a schoolmaster or lawyer or glover with his father and brother, Gilbert, are all plausible. So too is the argument that Shakespeare studied intensely to become a master at his literary craft, and honed his acting skills while traveling and visiting playhouses outside of Stratford. But, it is from this period known as the "lost years", that we obtain one vital piece of information about Shakespeare: he married a pregnant orphan named Anne Hathaway.

Shakespeare's Marriage and Children

Recordings in the Episcopal register at Worcester on the dates of November 27 and 28, 1582, reveal that Shakespeare desired to marry a young girl named Anne. There are two different documents regarding this matter, and their contents have raised a debate over just whom Shakespeare first intended to wed. Were there two Annes? Was Shakespeare in love with one but in lust with the other? Was Shakespeare ready to join in matrimony with the Anne of his dreams only to have an attack of conscience and marry the Anne with whom he had carnal relations? To discuss the controversy properly we should look at the documents in question. The first entry in the register is the following record of the issue of a marriage license to one Wm Shakespeare:

Anno Domini 1582...Novembris...27 die eiusdem mensis. Item eodem die supradicto emanavit Licentia inter Wm Shaxpere et Annam Whateley de Temple Grafton.1

The next entry in the episcopal register records the marriage bond granted to one Wm Shakespeare:

Noverint universi per praesentes nos Fulconem Sandells de Stratford in comitatu Warwici agricolam et Johannem Rychardson ibidem agricolam, teneri et firmiter obligari Ricardo Cosin generoso et Roberto Warmstry notario publico in quadraginta libris bonae et legalis monetae Angliae solvend. eisdem Ricardoet Roberto haered. execut. et assignat. suis ad quam quidem solucionem bene et fideliter faciend. obligamus nos et utrumque nostrum per se pro toto et in solid. haered. executor. et administrator. nostros firmiter per praesentes sigillis nostris sigillat. Dat. 28 die Novem. Anno regni dominae nostrae Eliz. Dei gratia Angliae Franc. et Hiberniae Reginae fidei defensor &c.25.2 The condition of this obligation is such that if hereafter there shall not appear any lawful let or impediment by reason of any precontract, consanguinity, affinity or by any other lawful means whatsoever, but that William Shagspere on the one party and Anne Hathwey of Stratford in the diocese of Worcester, maiden, may lawfully solemnise matrimony together, and in the same afterwards remain and continue like man and wife according unto the laws in that behalf provided...

Three possible conclusions can be reached from the above records:

1. The Anne Whateley in the first record and the Anne Hathwey in the second record are the same woman. Some scholars believe that the name Whateley was substituted accidentally for Hathwey into the register by the careless clerk. "The clerk was a nincompoop: he wrote Baker for Barber in his register, and Darby for Bradeley, and Edgock for Elcock, and Anne Whateley for Anne Hathaway. A lot of ingenious ink has been spilt over this error, but it is surely a simple one: the name Whateley occurs in a tithe appeal by

a vicar on the same page of the register; the clerk could not follow his own notes, or he was distracted" (Levi). Moreover, some believe that the couple selected Temple Grafton as the place for the wedding for reasons of privacy and that is why it is recorded in the register instead of Stratford.

2. The Wm Shaxpere and the Annam Whateley who wished to marry in Temple Grafton were two different people entirely from the Wm Shagspere and Anne Hathwey who were married in Stratford. This argument relies on the assumption that there was a relative of Shakespeare's living in Temple Grafton, or a man unrelated but sharing Shakespeare's name (which would be extremely unlikely), and that there is no trace of this relative after the issue of his marriage license.
3. The woman Shakespeare loved and the woman Shakespeare finally married were two different Annes. Not many critics support this hypothesis, but those that do use it to portray Shakespeare as a young man torn between the love he felt for Anne Whateley and the obligation he felt toward Anne Hathwey and the child she was carrying, which was surely his. In *Shakespeare,* Anthony Burgess constructs a vivid scenario to this effect:

It is reasonable to believe that Will wished to marry a girl named Anne Whateley. The name is common enough in the Midlands and is even attached to a four-star hotel in Horse Fair, Banbury. Her father may have been a friend of John Shakespeare's, he may have sold kidskin cheap, there are various reasons why the Shakespeares and the Whateleys, or their nubile children, might become friendly. Sent on skin-buying errands to Temple Grafton, Will could have fallen for a comely daughter, sweet as May and shy as a fawn. He was eighteen and highly susceptible. Knowing something about girls, he would know that this was the real thing. Something, perhaps, quite different from what he felt about Mistress Hathaway of Shottery. But why, attempting to marry Anne Whateley, had he put himself in the position of having to marry the other Anne? I suggest that, to use the crude but convenient properties of the old women's-magazine morality-stories, he was exercised by love for the one and lust for the other. I find it convenient to imagine that he knew Anne Hathaway carnally, for the first time, in the spring of 1582

Whichever argument one chooses to accept, it is fact that Shakespeare, a minor at the time, married Anne Hathaway, who was twenty-six and already several months pregnant. Anne was the eldest daughter, and one of the seven children of Richard Hathaway, a twice-married farmer in Shottery. When Richard died in 1581, he requested his son, Bartholomew, move into the house we now know as Anne Hathaway's Cottage, and maintain the property for his mother, Richard's second wife and Anne's stepmother. Anne lived in the cottage with Bartholomew, her step-mother, and her other siblings. No doubt she was bombarded with a barrage of household tasks to fill her days at Hewland Farm, as it was then called. After her marriage to Shakespeare, Anne left Hewland Farm to live in John Shakespeare's house on Henley Street, as was the custom of the day. Preparations for the new bride were made, and for reasons unknown, her arrival greatly bothered John Shakespeare's current tenant in the house, William Burbage. A heated fight ensued, and John refused to release Burbage from his lease, so Burbage decided to take the matter to a London court. On July 24, 1582, lawyers representing both sides met and resolved the matter — John would release William Burbage from his lease.

The Shakespeares' first child was Susanna, christened on May 26th, 1583, and twins arrived in January, 1585. They were baptised on February 2 of that year and named after two very close friends of William — the baker Hamnet Sadler and his wife, Judith. The Sadlers became the godparents of the twins and, in 1598, they, in turn, named their own son William. Not much information is known about the life of Anne and her children after this date, except for the tragic fact that Hamnet Shakespeare died of an unknown cause on August 11, 1596, at the age of eleven. By this time Shakespeare had long since moved to London to realise his dreams on the English stage (a time in the Bard's life that will be covered in depth later on) and we do not know if he was present at Hamnet's funeral in Stratford. We can only imagine how deeply the loss of his only son touched the sensitive poet, but his sorrow is undeniably reflected in his later work, and, particularly, in a passage from *King John*, written between 1595 and 1597:

Young Arthur is my son, and he is lost:
I am not mad: I would to heaven I were!
For then, 'tis like I should forget myself:
O, if I could, what grief should I forget!
Preach some philosophy to make me mad,
And thou shalt be canonised, cardinal;
For being not mad but sensible of grief,
My reasonable part produces reason
How I may be deliver'd of these woes,
And teaches me to kill or hang myself:
If I were mad, I should forget my son,
Or madly think a babe of clouts were he:
I am not mad; too well, too well I feel
The different plague of each calamity....
I tore them from their bonds and cried aloud
'O that these hands could so redeem my son,
As they have given these hairs their liberty!'
But now I envy at their liberty,
And will again commit them to their bonds,
Because my poor child is a prisoner.
And, father cardinal, I have heard you say
That we shall see and know our friends in heaven:
If that be true, I shall see my boy again;

For since the birth of Cain, the first male child,
To him that did but yesterday suspire,
There was not such a gracious creature born.
But now will canker-sorrow eat my bud
And chase the native beauty from his cheek
And he will look as hollow as a ghost,
As dim and meagre as an ague's fit,
And so he'll die; and, rising so again,
When I shall meet him in the court of heaven
I shall not know him: therefore never, never
Must I behold my pretty Arthur more. (III.iv.45-91)

SHAKESPEARE'S FELLOW ACTORS

Richard Burbage (b.1567? d.1619)

Richard Burbage is considered to be the first great actor in the English theatre. He was the son of James Burbage, the theatrical entrepreneur who built "the Theatre" in Shoreditch on the outskirts of London, and the brother of another famous actor of the day, Cuthbert Burbage. Richard Burbage achieved success as performer by the age of 20 and during his career he appeared in plays by Jonson, Kyd, Beaumont and Fletcher, and John Webster. He also played many of the major Shakespearean characters, including Othello, Hamlet, Lear, and Richard III. "It is likely that *Richard III* was the most popular of all Shakespeare's plays with the Elizabethan public; it provided a superlative part for Burbage" (Rowse). Legend tells us that a woman fell in love with Burbage when she saw him play Richard III and begged him to come to her chambers that night under the name of King Richard. But Shakespeare overheard the proposition and, as a joke, left the theatre early to take Burbage's place. Shakespeare was 'at his game ere Burbage came. Then, message being brought that Richard III was at the door, Shakespeare caused return to be made that "William the Conqueror" was before Richard III" (Rowse). Early in his career Burbage probably would have been a member of both Lord Strange's Men and the Admiral's Men. Both companies performed at James Burbage's Theatre between 1590 and 1591. We do know that Burbage was a member of the Chamberlain's Men after 1594 and stayed with the group through its evolution into the King's Men in 1603. Although his last recorded performance was in 1610, he remained with the King's Men until his death in 1619.

In addition to acting, Richard Burbage was also an entrepreneur much like his father. When James Burbage died in 1597 he left the Theatre to Richard and his brother. Together they disassembled the Theatre and built the Globe in 1599. The Burbages kept half the shares in the new theatre and the rest were assigned equally to Shakespeare and other members of the Chamberlain's Men. James Burbage also left another theatre to Richard - the Blackfriars Theatre. Richard Burbage leased it to an acting company called the Children of the Chapel, but, after they could not make the payments, Burbage bought back the lease with his brother and four new partners from the King's Men - Shakespeare, Henry Condell, William Sly, and John Heminge. Richard Burbage was also a wonderful painter. Some believe that the anonymous oil painting of Burbage seen above is actually a self-portrait, and he has often been credited with painting the Chandos portrait of Shakespeare, seen on the right. Burbage's skills as an artist were often in demand. With Shakespeare as his partner, providing the commemorative words, Burbage designed an impresa, or personal badge, for the Earl of Rutland (1578-1632). The badge was to be worn on the Earl's shield at a tournament on March 24, 1613 to honour James I. When Shakespeare died in 1616, he left his dear friend Burbage money to buy a mourning-ring in his memory. Burbage died on March 9, 1619, and "the true sound of Shakespeare's lines, as he had conceived them [and] Burbage had interpreted them, was silenced forever" (Holmes).

William Kempe

William Kempe was one of the most beloved clowns in the Elizabethan theatre. Records tell us that Kempe was an actor with Leicester's Men on a tour of the Netherlands and Denmark in 1585-86. By 1593 Kempe was a member of Strange's Men, and theatre-goers and fellow actors were beginning to recognise his comedic talent. Thomas Nashe declared him the successor to the great Elizabethan performer, Richard Tarlton. Kempe joined the Chamberlain's Men in 1594 and acted in many of Shakespeare's plays. He was the original portrayer of Dogberry in *Much Ado About Nothing*, Peter in *Romeo and Juliet*, and possibly Falstaff. He also likely played Lancelot Gobbo in *The Merchant of Venice* and Bottom in *A Midsummer Night's Dream*. However it appears that Kempe suddenly left the Chamberlain's Men in 1599. The reason for his departure is not documented, although many believe that he was asked to leave due to his chronic improvising, and that Shakespeare made reference to this in *Hamlet*:

And let those that play
your clowns speak no more than is
set down for them;
for there be of them that will themselves laugh, to
set on some quantity of barren spectators to laugh too.

Once Kempe left the troupe Shakespeare's comic characters changed dramatically, indicating that earlier parts were written to fit Kempe's unique style. Examining Shakespeare's changes provides us with even more information about Kempe's stage presence. "He was a big man who specialised in Plebian clowns who spoke in earthly language...Kempe's characters have a tendency to confuse and mispronounce their words,. and contemporary references to his dancing and ability to "make a scurvy face" suggest a physical brand of humour." (Boyce) Now finished with Shakespeare's troupe and looking for another way to entertain the people of London, Kempe planned a wild publicity stunt. In 1600 he danced a morris dance from London to Norwich, almost 100 miles north. He wrote his own account of the event called *Kempe's Nine Days Wonder*, and the picture above is from the cover of the original copy. Kempe returned to acting in 1601 when he left England to tour Europe. When he arrived home in 1602 he joined Worcester's Men, but he disappears from the records shortly after. Some scholars conclude that he died from the 1603 plague in London - the year of one of the largest outbreaks of the disease during Shakespeare's life.

Chapter 3

Works of Shakespeare

Comedy

- All's Well That Ends Well
- As You Like It
- The Comedy of Errors
- Cymbeline
- Love's Labours Lost
- Measure for Measure
- The Merry Wives of Windsor
- The Merchant of Venice
- A Midsummer Night's Dream
- Much Ado About Nothing
- Pericles, Prince of Tyre
- Taming of the Shrew
- The Tempest
- Troilus and Cressida
- Twelfth Night
- Two Gentlemen of Verona
- Winter's Tale

History

- Henry IV, part 1
- Henry IV, part 2

- Henry V
- Henry VI, part 1
- Henry VI, part 2
- Henry VI, part 3
- Henry VIII
- King John
- Richard II
- Richard III

Tragedy

- Antony and Cleopatra
- Coriolanus
- Hamlet
- Julius Caesar
- King Lear
- Macbeth
- Othello
- Romeo and Juliet
- Timon of Athens
- Titus Andronicus

Poetry

- The Sonnets
- A Lover's Complaint
- The Rape of Lucrece
- Venus and Adonis
- Funeral

Chapter 4

Shakespeare's Globe Theatre

The Globe Theatre also known as the Shakespeare Globe Theatre was not only one of most famous playhouse's of all time, but the play house where Shakespeare performed many of his greatest plays. Built from oak, deal, and stolen playhouse frames, the 3 storey, 3000 capacity Globe Theatre, co-owned by William Shakespeare has become almost as famous as the playwright himself.

History: Shakespeare Needs a New Playhouse to Compete

The 1598 decision to build the famous playhouse came about as the answer to many of *The Lord Chamberlain's Men's* problems. With the end of a lease on the Blackfriars Theatre in 1597, *The Lord Chamberlain's Men* (Shakespeare, J & R Burbage, G Byran, John Hemminges, Augustine Phillips, Thomas Pope and Will Sly) had no where else to readily perform their plays.

This acting troupe needed a new playhouse and fast as their rivals, *The Admiral's Men* already had the the Rose Playhouse to perform their plays.

Clearly the Lord Chamberlain's Men would need a playhouse to compete, but there was one little problem; a lack of money.

Paying for the Playhouse: Shareholders become the Key

Though James and Richard Burbage of The Lord Chamberlain's Men had money, there still wasn't enough.

Instead they came up with a novel idea; they would each own 25 % of the new playhouse whilst the rest of The Lord Chamberlain's men would each chip in the remaining 50%. This, the Chamberlain's men did, Shakespeare and the other four members of the acting troupe each owning a 12.5 % share when Will Kemp another member of the troupe, backed out.

Sure enough the playhouse was completed, opening in 1599. Not only could the circular playhouse hold up to 3000 patrons but it turned out to be a good earner, earning Shakespeare and his troupe both money from hiring out the playhouse and from ticket sales for their own performances there.

Theft builds the Playhouse

Construction of the famous playhouse, set near the Thames in a place called Bankside in Southwark, began in early 1599. Said to be built by Cuthbert Burbage, brother of the famous Shakespearean actor Robert Burbage and son of James Burbage.

Interestingly the famous playhouse was not the Burbage son's first choice for a playhouse since they already had one in "The Theatre", the first of its kind in London and an inheritance from his father. Unfortunately for Shakespeare and the rest of The Lord Chamberlain's Men, the lease of the land it was built on expired in 1597.

Theoretically this playhouse should have reverted to the landlord Giles Allen as well. Instead Burbage tore it down and then discretely removed several 12 inch oak beams, transporting them to Bankside where they formed the structural frame for a 100 foot circular polygon, the heart of the new playhouse's structure.

Location, location, location

Though located near the river Thames, Shakespeare's playhouse was not in fact in central London but rather an outlying district called Southwark. Southwark had a "colourful" reputation of being not too different from what we would call a *"bad"* district today, certainly not the place to find respectable gentry.

Yet the famous playhouse by attracting commoners and gentry alike, brought people of all classes together in a region renowned for bear-baiting and other less than respectable activities.

Nonetheless, elements of England's strict class divisions remained; commoners were in the courtyard by comparison with England's gentry and nobility which were seated in the galleries or the balconies.

That playhouses could even exist at all was in part due to its Southwark location; it was outside the jurisdiction of a disapproving central London bureaucracy...

Advertising

To announce the arrival of the new playhouse, the Lord Chamberlain's Men took the bold move of flying a flag with Hercules carrying a Globe on his shoulders to announce the imminent performance of Shakespeare's play Julius Caesar.

The Playhouse's motto and crest.

True to it's name, above the main entrance was inscribed the words *"Totus mundus agit histrionem"* (the whole world is a playhouse), a phrase echoed in *As You Like It ("All the world's a stage")*. A crest displaying Hercules bearing the globe on his shoulders finished the effect...

General Appearance

Built to the engineering standards of 1599, the famous playhouse was a large circular structure, three stories high. A small straw hatched roof only partially covered the circular structure, giving it an appearance very much like a modern day football stadium where the centre is uncovered.

In the centre, pushed up against one interior side, extended the 5 feet high main stage. At the back of this stage facing the interior walls were two doors and a main entrance consisting of a central curtain. Behind this were changing rooms for the actors. To get back on stage, they would emerge from the arras or the two sidedoors at stage level. Above this stage was a balcony, flanked by two further balconies serving as playhouse boxes.

On the third level was a small house like structure supported by columns from the stage where announcements were made and the playhouse's flag would often fly, advertising plays currently being performed.

Again like a stadium, three rows of seating forming circular bands wrapped around the interior. These galleries at two pennies, cost more, but offered the comfort of seating. Those in the central uncovered courtyard had to stand through what could be a three hour performance, rain or shine.

"All the World's a Stage"

Set in the middle of the playhouse, the playhouse's 44 wide by 26 foot long stage stood five foot off the ground, low enough to command a good view to courtyard watchers yet high enough to discourage the occasional stage jumper.

Two doors allowed actors backstage to enter, this being closed in by a central arras or hanging curtain. Above this was a balcony famously used in *Romeo and Juliet* when Romeo hears Juliet cry *"Romeo, Romeo wherefore art thou Romeo"*. Similarly, the arras would have been pulled away in *The Tempest* to reveal the touchingly innocent scene of Miranda playing chess with Ferdinand and was also used for Hamlet's stabbing of Polionius in *Hamlet*.

Balconies to be Seen in

The balcony above the stage was not the only balcony in the playhouse. As mentioned, the central balcony was flanked by two balconies for the wealthy to be seen in just as celebrities today pick boxes and seats at sports games were they are likely to be noticed by today's media. Even vanity existed in the 1500's.

Cost of Entry

Open to all for the modest fee of just one-penny (roughly 10 % of a worker's daily wage), you could stand in the yard at the centre of the playhouse. Without an overhead roof, such a view was exposed, but with the stage set at eye level some 5 feet off the ground, you got the closest view in the house. For a little more (roughly two pennies), you could pay to sit in one of the playhouse's three circular galleries; the gentry with time on their hands and comfort on the minds frequently paying more for the comfort and status, the gallery seats conferred.

Watching a Play

Unlike today's spectacles, a Shakespearean playhouse-goer really had to use their imagination; there were no backdrops, no lighting to speak of, horrific acoustics, and few if any props. As such watching a play would involve watching the actors exaggerating their movements for patrons in the galleries and shouting their lines to be heard by all.

Much of the illusion of a play had to occur in the viewer's own imagination, the only notable exceptions, being the colourful use of costumes, heralds, banners, the odd cannon, and the dramatic use of the balcony's and arras. Because there was no artificial lighting, plays typically occurred in the early afternoon, lasting from 2 pm until roughly 4 or 5 pm.

Plays Performed

The first play we know of that was performed at Shakespeare's famous playhouse was Julius Caesar in 1599 when a Swiss tourist Thomas Platter recorded in his diary that on September the 21st " *we witnessed an excellent performance of the tragedy of the first Emperor Julius Caesar* '" said to be performed by some 15 actors.

Other plays known to have been performed by Shakespeare and rest of his acting troupe were Hamlet (1600-1601), Twelfth Night Or What You Will (1601), Richard II

(February 7th 1601) Troilus and Cressida (1601-1602), All's Well That Ends Well (circa 1602), Timon of Athens (c1604), King Lear (1605), Macbeth (1606), Pericles, Prince of Tyre (1607) possibly The Tempest in 1610, The Two Noble Kinsmen in 1611, Shakespeare's "lost" play Cardenio in 1612 and Henry VIII in 1613.

Burnt to the Ground and Rebuilt again

Tragedy struck the playhouse when amidst a performance of Henry VIII on June the 29th, 1613, a cannon fired during the play ignited the playhouse's thatched roof burning the playhouse to the ground. Rebuilt just one year later, the famous playhouse again opened its doors for business but on the opposite side of the Thames river in 1614, with the original's dangerous straw thatched roof now wisely replaced with tiles.

End of an Era

In 1642 as Puritanical forces made their presence felt in England, playhouses no longer were a place of laughter but one of evil sin. Predictably then, all of England's playhouses were promptly closed down to protect the good people of England. Just two years later in 1644, where Hamlet was once performed, the famous playhouse was taken down, its presence replaced by housing instead. One of the greatest eras in playhouse was at an end...

Today's Replica

Though the original playhouse is no longer with us, we can enjoy a very close approximation of it today in Southwark, the very same place the original was built in.

However the 1996 approximation is just that; first the replica's exits had to be enlarged to comply with today's rather more stringent fire regulations (few existed when the original burnt down!) and the new replica despite being built of the very same oak and deal timbers, is not in the same Maiden Lane (called Park Street today) location of the original, but is nearby.

The attention to detail has been painstaking; even the thatched roof made of Norfolk reeds has been faithfully recreated. Today with play's being performed there, only a little imagination is needed to recreate watching a play in Shakespeare's time...

Acting: Safe if you had the right connections...

Before the advent of Shakespearean and Elizabethan playhouse, there were no true playhouses or acting troupes in England.

Instead, traveling actors recreated religious plays held at market squares, inns or make shift stages. These actors traveled the country and were regarded as little more than layabouts or vagabonds. So when playhouse emerged in the late 1500s, acting was still considered a pretty vulgar profession to practice.

There were enemies of actors especially officials who could easily arrest actors for vagrancy. Only actors enjoying noble protection were safe, The Lord Chamberlain's Men were safe by virtue of first being sponsored by The Lord Chamberlain of Elizabeth I and later by King James' patent and patronage of Shakespeare's acting troupe.

Famous actors who performed at the Playhouse: Richard Burbage

Of The Lord Chamberlain's Men (Later named The King's Men to honour King James I), perhaps the acting troupe's most famous actor was not William Shakespeare who legend has it played King Hamlet's ghost, but was Richard Burbage.

Inheriting the smaller Blackfriar's playhouse from his father who built it, and the son of James Burbage who initially ran the Lord Chamberlain's Men, Richard Burbage was considered the greatest Elizabethan actor of them all, playing such challenging roles as Hamlet, King Lear and Othello.

His influence on Shakespeare is not certain but many have speculated that Shakespeare wrote the tragic figures of Othello,

King Lear and Hamlet with this subtle-performing actor in mind.

Other Actors in The Lord Chamberlain's Men

Despite the fame accompanying Shakespeare and Richard Burbage's association with the acting troupe, many others were famous in The Lord Chamberlain's Men.

Will Kemp who was a comic actor in their troupe, originally was one of the shareholder's in the famous playhouse. He is thought to have played amongst other characters, that of Falstaff in the King Henry IV plays, certainly Peter, a servant to Juliet's nurse in Romeo and Juliet and in all probability, Bottom, a weaver in *A Midsummer Night's* dream.

Instead of staying with The Lord Chamberlain's men, he left the other actors in 1599 to pick up his contribution to the new playhouse and instead Morris danced his way from London to Norwich.

Unhappy with this, he then danced across the Alps to take up acting at The Rose, one of the famous playhouse's competitors.

Arguably replacing Will Kemp in the more famous comic roles of Shakespeare's plays was Robert Armin. Most famous for his role as the deceptively wise Fool in *King Lear,* Robert Armin also distinguished himself as the insightful clown Feste in *Twelfth Night* and as Touchstone in *As You Like It.*

John Hemminges, known to us in history as one of the actors (the other was Henry Condell) who compiled The First Folio, from which all records of Shakespeare's plays are derived was with The Lord Chamberlain's Men from, 1594, later becoming its manager.

Augustine Phillips was known as a musician and jig writer; a merry jig or dance always followed the conclusion of a play.

Thomas Pope joined in 1594, becoming a co-owner of the famous playhouse and playing comic roles like Will Kemp before him, thought to include that of Falstaff in the King Henry IV plays before passing away in 1604.

Will Sly joined The Lord Chamberlain's men in 1594 along with Shakespeare at the same time. Along with becoming a co-owner in 1605, he also became a co-owner in the Blackfriar's playhouse in 1608.

The plot to kill Queen Elizabeth

Shakespeare and his famous playhouse, also distinguished themselves in controversy. In 1601, Sir Gilly Meyrick asked The Lord Chamberlain's Men to perform Richard II for two pounds. This was an old play and it was only the money that convinced the actors to perform it.

However the reason Meyrick wanted the play performed was because of its anti-monarchic message; King Richard II, a rightful king is removed from power for being a tyrant who breaks his own laws to be replaced by those who understood his subjects better.

Meyrick was obviously hoping that a well-attended performance the very day before the Essex rebellion began, would generate public sympathy for those attempting to kill Queen Elizabeth.

The Essex rebellion failed, The Earl of Essex and most of his supporters being killed. Shakespeare and the rest of the Chamberlain's Men were questioned for their part in this conspiracy, only having to play before the Queen as a consequence.

There is still some doubt as to whether Shakespeare could really not have known what he was doing. Perhaps Shakespeare may have been sympathetic to the conspirators? Little is known with complete certainty.

Chapter 5

Shakespeare as Actor and Playwright

We know very little about Shakespeare's life during two major spans of time, commonly referred to as the "lost years." The lost years fall into two periods: 1578-82 and 1585-92. The first period covers the time after Shakespeare left grammar school until his marriage to Anne Hathaway in November of 1582. The second period covers the seven years of Shakespeare's life in which he must have been perfecting his dramatic skills and collecting sources for the plots of his plays. "What could such a genius accomplish in this direction during six or eight years? The histories alone must have required unending hours of labour to gather facts for the plots and counter-plots of these stories. When we think of the time he must have spent in reading about the pre-Tudor dynasties, we are at a loss to estimate what a day's work meant to him. Perhaps he was one of those singular geniuses who absorbs books.

George Douglas Brown, when discussing Shakespeare, often used to say he knew how to 'pluck the guts' out of a tome" (Neilson). No one knows for certain how Shakespeare first started his career in the theatre, although several London players would visit Stratford regularly, and so, sometime between 1585 and 1592, it is probable that young Shakespeare could have been recruited by the Leicester's or Queen's men. Whether an acting troupe recruited Shakespeare in his hometown or he was forced on his own to travel to London to begin his career, he was nevertheless an established actor in the great city by the end of 1592. In this year came the first reference to Shakespeare in the world of the theatre. The dramatist Robert Greene declared in his death-bed autobiography that "There is an upstart crow, beautified with our feathers, that with his Tygers heart wrapt in a Players hide supposes he is as well able to bombast out a blank verse as the best of you; and, being an absolute Johannes Factotum, is in his own conceit the only Shake-scene in a country." After Green's death, his editor, Henry Chettle, publicly apologised to Shakespeare in the Preface to his *Kind-Heart's Dream*:

About three months since died M. Robert Greene, leaving many papers in sundry booksellers' hands, among other his Groatsworth of Wit, in which a letter written to divers play-makers is offensively by one or two of them taken, and because on the dead they cannot be avenged, they willfully forge in their conceits a living author....With neither of them that take offence was I acquainted, and with one of them I care not if I never be. The other, whom at that time I did not so much spare as since I wish I had, for that, as I have moderated the heat of living writers and might have used my own discretion (especially in such a case, the author being dead), that I did not I am as sorry as if the original fault had been my fault, because myself have seen his demeanor no less civil than he excellent in the quality he professes. Besides, the diver of worship have reported his uprightness of dealing, which argues his honesty, and his facetious grace in writing that approves his art.

Such an apology indicates that Shakespeare was already a respected player in London with influential friends and connections. Records also tell us that several of Shakespeare's plays were popular by this time, including *Henry VI*, *The Comedy of Errors*, and *Titus Andronicus*. The company that staged most of the early productions of these plays was Pembroke's Men, sponsored by the Earl of Pembroke, Henry Herbert. The troupe was very popular and performed regularly at the court of Queen Elizabeth. Most critics conclude that Shakespeare spent time as both a writer and an actor for Pembroke's Men before 1592. The turning point in Shakespeare's career came in 1593. The theatres had been closed since 1592 due to an outbreak of the plague and, although it is possible that Shakespeare toured the outlying areas of London with acting companies like Pembroke's Men or Lord Strange's Men, it seems more likely that he left the theatre entirely during this time to work on his non-dramatic poetry. The hard work paid off, for by the end of 1593, Shakespeare had caught the attention of the Earl of Southampton.

Southampton became Shakespeare's patron, and on April 18, 1593, *Venus and Adonis* was entered for publication. Shakespeare had made his formal debut as a poet. The dedication Shakespeare wrote to Southampton at the beginning of the poem is impassioned and telling, "phrased with courtly deference" (Rowse):

> To,
>
> The Right Honourable Henry Wriothesley,
> Earl of Southampton, and Baron of Tichfield.
>
> Right Honourable,
>
> I Know not how I shall offend in dedicating my unpolished lines to your lordship, nor how the world will censure me for choosing so strong a prop to support so weak a burden only, if your honour seem but pleased, I account myself highly praised, and vow to take advantage of all idle hours, till I have honoured you with some graver labour. But if the first heir of my invention prove deformed, I shall be sorry it had so noble a god-father, and never after ear so barren a land, for fear it yield me still so bad a harvest.
>
> I leave it to your honourable survey, and your honour to your heart's content; which I wish may always answer your own wish and the world's hopeful expectation.
>
> Your honour's in all duty,
>
> *William Shakespeare*

Although there is no concrete proof that Shakespeare had a long and close friendship with Southampton, most scholars agree that this was the case, based on Shakespeare's writings, particularly the early sonnets.

Shakespeare returned to the theatre in 1594, and became a leading member of the Lord Chamberlain's Men, formally known as Lord Strange's Men. The manuscript accounts of the treasurer of the royal chamber in the public records office tells us the following:

To William Kempe, William Shakespeare, and Richard Burbage, servants to the Lord Chamberlain, upon the council's warrent dated at Whitehall xv die Marcij 1594 for two several comedies or interludes showed by them before her Majesty in Christmas time last past, viz; upon St. Stephan's day and Innocent's day, xiiij li. vj s. viij d. and by way of her Majesty's reward...

This is proof that Shakespeare had performed with the Chamberlain's Men before Elizabeth I on several occasions. As payment for their performance the actors each received 10 pounds. During his time with the Chamberlain's Men Shakespeare wrote many plays, including *Romeo and Juliet, Richard II, King John,* and *Love's Labour's Lost.* As G.E. Bentley points out in *Shakespeare and the Theatre,* Shakespeare had by this time become immersed in his roles as actor and writer. He was "more completely and more continuously involved in theatres and acting companies than any other Elizabethan dramatist. [Shakespeare is] "the only one known who not only wrote plays for his company, acted in the plays, and shared the profits, but who was also one of the housekeepers who owned the building.

For seventeen years he was one of the owners of the Globe theatre and for eight years he was one of the housekeepers of the company's second theatre, the Blackfriars, as well" (Rowse). During the years Shakespeare performed with the Chamberlain's Men, before their purchase of the Globe in 1599, they played primarily at the well-established theatres like the Swan, the Curtain, and the Theatre. The troupe would also give regular performances before Elizabeth I and her court, and tour the surrounding areas of London. Some important events in Shakespeare's personal life also take place during this time period. The Shakespeares finally received a coat of arms 1596, and on August 11 of the same year, Shakespeare's son, Hamnet, died at the age of eleven. Shakespeare no doubt returned to Stratford for the burial, although we have no documented proof. In 1597, Shakespeare purchased the second largest house in Stratford: New Place. The house stood at the corner of Chapel Lane and Chapel Street, north of the Guild Chapel and right across from the very school he attended in his youth. He bought it from William Underhill for the low price of 60 pounds, and below is the actual deed (translated from the original Latin) transferring New Place from Underhill to Shakespeare on May 4, 1597:

Between William Shakespeare, complainant, and William Underhill, deforciant [wrongful occupier, supposed by the legal fiction on which the fine method of transfer was based to be keeping the complainant out of his rightful property], concerning one dwelling house, two barns, and two gardens with their appurtenances in Stratford-on-Avon, in regard to which a plea of agreement was broached in the same court: Namely, that the said William Underhill acknowledged the said tenements with their appurtenances to be the right of W. Shakespeare as being those which the same William Shakespeare has by gift of the said W. U., and remitted and waived claim to them from himself and his heirs to the said W.S. and his heirs forever....and agreement the same W.S. has given the foresaid W./U. sixty pounds sterling. (Brooke)

Many theorise that Shakespeare renewed his interest in Stratford only after the death of Hamnet and that, for the many years he was away in London, he neglected his family back home. However, it is just as likely that he made frequent yet unrecorded trips to Stratford while he was trying to find success in London.

Chapter 6

Shakespeare: A Poet or Playwright?

Great men are more distinguished by range and extent, than by originality. If we require the originality which consists in weaving, like a spider, their web from their own bowels; in finding clay, and making bricks, and building the house; no great men are original. Nor does valuable originality consist in unlikeness to other men. The hero is in the press of knights, and the thick of events; and, seeing what men want, and sharing their desire, he adds the needful length of sight and of arm, to come at the desired point. The greatest genius is the most indebted man. A poet is no rattle-brain, saying what comes uppermost, and, because he says every thing, saying, at last, something good; but a heart in unison with his time and country. There is nothing whimsical and fantastic in his production, but sweet and sad earnest, freighted with the weightiest convictions, and pointed with the most determined aim which any man or class knows of in his times.

The Genius of our life is jealous of individuals, and will not have any individual great, except through the general. There is no choice to genius. A great man does not wake up on some fine morning, and say, 'I am full of life, I will go to sea, and find an Antarctic continent: to-day I will square the circle: I will ransack botany, and find a new food for man: I have a new architecture in my mind: I foresee a new mechanic power:' no, but he finds himself in the river of the thoughts and events, forced onward by the ideas and necessities of his contemporaries. He stands where all the eyes of men look one way, and their hands all point in the direction in which he should go. The church has reared him amidst rites and pomps, and he carries out the advice which her music gave him, and builds a cathedral needed by her chants and processions. He finds a war raging: it educates him, by trumpet, in barracks, and he betters the instruction. He finds two counties groping to bring coal, or flour, or fish, from the place of production to the place of consumption, and he hits on a railroad. Every master has found his materials collected, and his power lay in his sympathy with his people, and in his love of the materials he wrought in. What an economy of power! and what a compensation for the shortness of life! All is done to his hand. The world has brought him thus far on his way. The human race has gone out before him, sunk the hills, filled the hollows, and bridged the rivers. Men, nations, poets, artisans, women, all have worked for him, and he enters into their labours. Choose any other thing, out of the line of tendency, out of the national feeling and history, and he would have all to do for himself: his powers would be expended in the first preparations. Great genial power, one would almost say, consists in not being original at all; in being altogether receptive; in letting the world do all, and suffering the spirit of the hour to pass unobstructed through the mind.

Shakspeare's youth fell in a time when the English people were importunate for dramatic entertainments. The court took offence easily at political allusions, and attempted to suppress them. The Puritans, a growing and energetic party, and the religious among the Anglican church, would suppress them. But the people wanted them. Inn-yards, houses without roofs, and extemporaneous enclosures at country fairs, were the ready theatres of strolling players. The people had tasted this new joy; and, as we could not hope to suppress newspapers now,—no, not by the strongest party,—neither then could king, prelate, or puritan, alone or united, suppress an organ, which was ballad, epic, newspaper, caucus, lecture, punch, and library, at the same time. Probably king, prelate, and puritan, all found their own account in it. It had become, by all causes, a national interest,—by no means conspicuous, so that some great scholar would have thought of treating it in an English history,—but not a whit less considerable, because it was cheap, and of no account, like a baker's-shop. The best proof of its vitality is the crowd of writers which suddenly broke into this field; Kyd, Marlow, Greene, Jonson, Chapman, Dekker, Webster, Heywood, Middleton, Peele, Ford, Massinger, Beaumont, and Fletcher.

The secure possession, by the stage, of the public mind, is of the first importance to the poet who works for it. He loses no time in idle experiments. Here is audience and expectation prepared. In the case of Shakspeare there is much more. At the time when he left Stratford, and went up to London, a great body of stage-plays, of all dates and writers, existed in manuscript, and were in turn produced on the boards. Here is the Tale of Troy, which the audience will bear hearing some part of every week; the Death of Julius Cæsar, and other stories out of Plutarch, which they never tire of; a shelf full of English history, from the chronicles of Brut and Arthur, down to the royal Henries, which men hear eagerly; and a string of doleful tragedies, merry Italian tales, and Spanish voyages, which all the London 'prentices know. All the mass has been treated, with more or less skill, by every playwright, and the prompter has the soiled and tattered manuscripts. It is now no longer possible to say who wrote them first. They have been the property of the Theatre so long, and so many rising geniuses have enlarged or altered them, inserting a speech, or a whole scene, or adding a song, that no man can any longer claim copyright on this work of numbers. Happily, no man wishes to. They are not yet desired in that way. We have few readers, many spectators and hearers. They had best lie where they are.

Shakspeare, in common with his comrades, esteemed the mass of old plays, waste stock, in which any experiment could be freely tried. Had the *prestige* which hedges about a modern tragedy existed, nothing could have been done. The rude warm blood of the living England circulated in the play, as in street-ballads, and gave body which he wanted to his airy and majestic fancy. The poet needs a ground in popular tradition on which he may work, and which, again, may restrain his art within the due temperance. It holds him to the people, supplies a foundation for his edifice; and, in furnishing so much work done to his hand, leaves him at leisure, and in full strength for the audacities of his imagination.

In short, the poet owes to his legend what sculpture owed to the temple. Sculpture in Egypt, and in Greece, grew up in subordination to architecture. It was the ornament of the temple wall: at first, a rude relief carved on pediments, then the relief became bolder, and a head or arm was projected from the wall, the groups being still arranged with reference to the building, which serves also as a frame to hold the figures; and when, at last, the greatest freedom of style and treatment was reached, the prevailing genius of architecture still enforced a certain calmness and continence in the statue. As soon as the statue was begun for itself, and with no reference to the temple or palace, the art began to decline: freak, extravagance, and exhibition, took the place of the old temperance. This balance-wheel, which the sculptor found in architecture, the perilous irritability of poetic talent found in the accumulated dramatic materials to which the people were already wonted, and which had a certain excellence which no single genius, however extraordinary, could hope to create.

In point of fact, it appears that Shakspeare did owe debts in all directions, and was able to use whatever he found; and the amount of indebtedness may be inferred from Malone's labourious computations in regard to the First, Second, and Third parts of Henry VI., in which, "out of 6043 lines, 1771 were written by some author preceding Shakspeare; 2373 by him, on the foundation laid by his predecessors; and 1899 were entirely his own." And the proceeding investigation hardly leaves a single drama of his absolute invention. Malone's sentence is an important piece of external history. In Henry VIII. I think I see plainly the cropping out of the original rock on which his own finer stratum was laid. The first play was written by a superior, thoughtful man, with a vicious ear. I can mark his lines, and know well their cadence. See Wolsey's soliloquy, and the following scene with Cromwell, where,—instead of the metre of Shakspeare, whose secret is, that the thought constructs the tune, so that reading for the sense will best bring out the rhythm,—here the lines are constructed on a given tune, and the verse has even a trace of pulpit eloquence. But the play contains, through all its length, unmistakable traits of Shakspeare's hand, and some passages, as the account of the coronation, are like autographs. What is odd, the compliment to Queen Elizabeth is in the bad rhythm.

Shakespeare knew that tradition supplies a better fable than any invention can. If he lost any credit of design, he augmented his resources; and, at that day, our petulant demand for originality was not so much pressed. There was no literature for the million. The universal reading, the cheap press, were unknown. A great poet, who appears in illiterate times, absorbs into his sphere all the light which is any where radiating. Every intellectual jewel, every flower of sentiment, it is his fine office to bring to his people; and he comes to value his memory equally with his invention. He is therefore little solicitous whence his thoughts have been derived; whether through translation, whether through tradition, whether by travel in distant countries, whether by inspiration; from whatever source, they are equally welcome to his uncritical audience. Nay, he borrows very near home. Other men say wise things as well as he; only they say a good many foolish things, and do not know when they have spoken wisely. He knows the sparkle of the true stone, and puts it in high place, wherever he finds it. Such is the happy position of Homer, perhaps; of Chaucer, of Saadi. They felt that all wit was their wit. And they are librarians and historiographers, as well as poets. Each romancer was heir and dispenser of all the hundred tales of the world,—

"Presenting Thebes' and Pelops' line
And the tale of Troy divine."

The influence of Chaucer is conspicuous in all our early literature; and, more recently, not only Pope and Dryden have been beholden to him, but, in the whole society of English writers, a large unacknowledged debt is easily traced. One is charmed with the opulence which feeds so many pensioners. But Chaucer is a huge borrower. Chaucer, it seems, drew continually, through Lydgate and Caxton, from Guido di Colonna, whose Latin romance of the Trojan war was in turn a compilation from Dares Phrygius, Ovid, and Statius. Then Petrarch, Boccaccio, and the Provençal poets are his benefactors: the Romaunt of the Rose is only judicious translation from William of Lorris and John of Meun: Troilus and Creseide, from Lollius of Urbino: The Cock and the Fox, from the *Lais* of Marie: The House of Fame, from the French or Italian: and poor Gower he uses as if he were only a brick-kiln or stone-quarry, out of which to build his house. He steals by this apology,—that what he takes has no worth where he finds it, and the greatest where he leaves it. It has come to be practically a sort of rule in literature, that a man, having once shown himself capable of original writing, is entitled thenceforth to steal from the writings of others at discretion. Thought is the property of him who can entertain it; and of him who can adequately place it. A certain awkwardness marks the use of borrowed thoughts; but, as soon as we have learned what to do with them, they become our own.

Thus, all originality is relative. Every thinker is retrospective. The learned member of the legislature, at Westminster, or at Washington, speaks and votes for thousands. Show us the constituency, and the now invisible channels by which the senator is made aware of their wishes, the crowd of practical and knowing men, who, by correspondence or conversation, are feeding him with evidence, anecdotes, and estimates, and it will bereave his fine attitude and resistance of something of their impressiveness. As Sir Robert Peel and Mr. Webster vote, so Locke and Rousseau think for thousands; and so there were fountains all around Homer, Menu, Saadi, or Milton, from which they drew; friends, lovers, books, traditions, proverbs,—all perished,—

which, if seen, would go to reduce the wonder. Did the bard speak with authority? Did he feel himself overmatched by any companion? The appeal is to the consciousness of the writer. Is there at last in his breast a Delphi whereof to ask concerning any thought or thing, whether it be verily so, yea or nay? and to have answer, and to rely on that? All the debts which such a man could contract to other wit, would never disturb his consciousness of originality: for the ministrations of books, and of other minds, are a whiff of smoke to that most private reality with which he has conversed.

It is easy to see that what is best written or done by genius, in the world, was no man's work, but came by wide social labour, when a thousand wrought like one, sharing the same impulse. Our English Bible is a wonderful specimen of the strength and music of the English language. But it was not made by one man, or at one time; but centuries and churches brought it to perfection. There never was a time when there was not some translation existing. The Liturgy, admired for its energy and pathos, is an anthology of the piety of ages and nations, a translation of the prayers and forms of the Catholic church,—these collected, too, in long periods, from the prayers and meditations of every saint and sacred writer, all over the world. Grotius makes the like remark in respect to the Lord's Prayer, that the single clauses of which it is composed were already in use, in the time of Christ, in the rabbinical forms. He picked out the grains of gold. The nervous language of the Common Law, the impressive forms of our courts, and the precision and substantial truth of the legal distinctions, are the contribution of all the sharp-sighted, strong-minded men who have lived in the countries where these laws govern. The translation of Plutarch gets its excellence by being translation on translation. There never was a time when there was none. All the truly idiomatic and national phrases are kept, and all others successively picked out, and thrown away. Something like the same process had gone on, long before, with the originals of these books. The world takes liberties with world-books. Vedas, Æsop's Fables, Pilpay, Arabian Nights, Cid, Iliad, Robin Hood, Scottish Minstrelsy, are not the work of single men. In the composition of such works, the time thinks, the market thinks, the mason, the carpenter, the merchant, the farmer, the fop, all think for us. Every book supplies its time with one good word; every municipal law, every trade, every folly of the day, and the generic catholic genius who is not afraid or ashamed to owe his originality to the originality of all, stands with the next age as the recorder and embodiment of his own.

We have to thank the researches of antiquaries, and the Shakspeare Society, for ascertaining the steps of the English drama, from the Mysteries celebrated in churches and by churchmen, and the final detachment from the church, and the completion of secular plays, from Ferrex and Porrex, and Gammer Gurton's Needle, down to the possession of the stage by the very pieces which Shakspeare altered, remodelled, and finally made his own. Elated with success, and piqued by the growing interest of the problem, they have left no book-stall unsearched, no chest in a garret unopened, no file of old yellow accounts to decompose in damp and worms, so keen was the hope to discover whether the boy Shakspeare poached or not, whether he held horses at the theatre door, whether he kept school, and why he left in his will only his second-best bed to Ann Hathaway, his wife.

There is somewhat touching in the madness with which the passing age mischooses the object on which all candles shine, and all eyes are turned; the care with which it registers every trifle touching Queen Elizabeth, and King James, and the Essexes, Leicesters, Burleighs, and Buckinghams; and lets pass without a single valuable note the founder of another dynasty, which alone will cause the Tudor dynasty to be remembered,—the man who carries the Saxon race in him by the inspiration which feeds him, and on whose thoughts the foremost people of the world are now for some ages to be nourished, and minds to receive this and not another bias. A popular player;—nobody suspected he was the poet of the human race; and the secret was kept as faithfully from poets and intellectual men, as from courtiers and frivolous people.

Bacon, who took the inventory of the human understanding for his times, never mentioned his name. Ben Jonson, though we have strained his few words of regard and panegyric, had no suspicion of the elastic fame whose first vibrations he was attempting. He no doubt thought the praise he has conceded to him generous, and esteemed himself, out of all question, the better poet of the two

If it need wit to know wit, according to the proverb, Shakspeare's time should be capable of recognizing it. Sir Henry Wotton was born four years after Shakspeare, and died twenty-three years after him; and I find, among his correspondents and acquaintances, the following persons: Theodore Beza, Isaac Casaubon, Sir Philip Sidney, Earl of Essex, Lord Bacon, Sir Walter Raleigh, John Milton, Sir Henry Vane, Isaac Walton, Dr. Donne, Abraham Cowley, Bellarmine, Charles Cotton, John Pym, John Hales, Kepler, Vieta, Albericus Gentilis, Paul Sarpi, Arminius; with all of whom exists some token of his having communicated, without enumerating many others, whom doubtless he saw,—Shakspeare, Spenser, Jonson, Beaumont, Massinger, two Herberts, Marlow, Chapman, and the rest. Since the constellation of great men who appeared in Greece in the time of Pericles, there was never any such society;—yet their genius failed them to find out the best head in the universe. Our poet's mask was impenetrable. You cannot see the mountain near. It took a century to make it suspected; and not until two centuries had passed, after his death, did any criticism which we think adequate begin to appear. It was not possible to write the history of Shakspeare till now; for he is the father of German literature: it was on the introduction of Shakspeare into German, by Lessing, and the translation of his works by Wieland and Schlegel, that the rapid burst of German literature was most intimately connected. It was not until the nineteenth century, whose speculative genius is a sort of living Hamlet, that the tragedy of Hamlet could find such wondering readers. Now, literature, philosophy, and thought, are Shakspearised. His mind is the horizon beyond which, at present, we do not see. Our ears are educated to music by his rhythm. Coleridge and Goethe are the only critics who have expressed our convictions with any adequate fidelity: but there is in all cultivated minds a silent appreciation of his superlative power and beauty, which, like Christianity, qualifies the period.

The Shakspeare Society have inquired in all directions, advertised the missing facts, offered money for any information that will lead to proof;—and with what result? Beside some important illustration of the history of the English stage, to which I have adverted, they have gleaned a few facts touching the property, and dealings in regard to property, of the poet. It appears that, from year to year, he owned a larger share in the Blackfriars' Theatre: its wardrobe and other appurtenances were his: that he bought an estate in his native village, with his earnings, as writer and shareholder; that he lived in the best house in Stratford; was intrusted by his neighbours with their commissions in London, as of borrowing money, and the like; that he was a veritable farmer. About the time when he was writing Macbeth, he sues Philip Rogers, in the borough-court of Stratford, for thirty-five shillings, ten pence, for corn delivered to him at different times; and, in all respects, appears as a good husband, with no reputation for eccentricity or excess. He was a good-natured sort of man, an actor and shareholder in the theatre, not in any striking manner distinguished from other actors and managers. I admit the importance of this information. It was well worth the pains that have been taken to procure it.

But whatever scraps of information concerning his condition these researches may have rescued, they can shed no light upon that infinite invention which is the concealed magnet of his attraction for us. We are very clumsy writers of history. We tell the chronicle of parentage, birth, birth-place, schooling, school-mates, earning of money, marriage, publication of books, celebrity, death; and when we have come to an end of this gossip, no ray of relation appears between it and the goddess-born; and it seems as if, had we dipped at random into the "Modern Plutarch," and read any other life there, it would have fitted the poems as well. It is the essence of poetry to spring, like the rainbow daughter of Wonder, from the invisible, to abolish the past, and refuse all history. Malone, Warburton, Dyce, and Collier, have wasted their oil. The famed theatres, Covent Garden, Drury Lane, the Park, and Tremont, have vainly assisted. Betterton, Garrick, Kemble, Kean, and Macready, dedicate their lives to this genius; him they crown, elucidate, obey, and express. The genius knows them not. The recitation begins; one golden word leaps out immortal from all this painted pedantry, and sweetly torments us with invitations to its own inaccessible homes. I remember, I went once to see the Hamlet of a famed performer, the pride of the English stage; and all I then heard, and all I now remember, of the tragedian, was that in which the tragedian had no part; simply, Hamlet's question to the ghost,

What may this mean,
That thou, dead corse, again in complete steel
Revisit'st thus the glimpses of the moon?"

That imagination which dilates the closet he writes in to the world's dimension, crowds it with agents in rank and order, as quickly reduces the big reality to be the glimpses of the moon. These tricks of his magic spoil for us the illusions of the green-room. Can any biography shed light on the localities into which the Midsummer Night's Dream admits me? Did Shakspeare confide to any notary or parish recorder, sacristan, or surrogate, in Stratford, the genesis of that delicate creation? The forest of Arden, the nimble air of Scone Castle, the moonlight of Portia's villa, "the antres vast and desarts idle," of Othello's captivity,—where is the third cousin, or grand-nephew, the chancellor's file of accounts, or private letter, that has kept one word of those transcendent secrets? In fine, in this drama, as in all great works of art,—in the Cyclopæan architecture of Egypt and India; in the Phidian sculpture; the Gothic ministers; the Italian painting; the Ballads of Spain and Scotland,—the Genius draws up the ladder after him, when the creative age goes up to heaven, and gives way to a new, who see the works, and ask in vain for a history.

Shakspeare is the only biographer of Shakspeare; and even he can tell nothing, except to the Shakspeare in us; that is, to our most apprehensive and sympathetic hour. He cannot step from off his tripod, and give us anecdotes of his inspirations. Read the antique documents extricated, analysed, and compared, by the assiduous Dyce and Collier; and now read one of those skiey sentences,—aerolites,—which seem to have fallen out of heaven, and which, not your experience, but the man within the breast, has accepted as words of fate; and tell me if they match; if the former account in any manner for the latter; or, which gives the most historical insight into the man.

Hence, though our external history is so meagre, yet, with Shakspeare for biographer, instead of Aubrey and Rowe, we have really the information which is material, that which describes character and fortune, that which, if we were about to meet the man and deal with him, would most import us to know. We have his recorded convictions on those questions which knock for answer at every heart,—on life and death, on love, on wealth and poverty, on the prizes of life, and the ways whereby we come at them; on the characters of men, and the influences, occult and open, which affect their fortunes; and on those mysterious and demoniacal powers which defy our science, and which yet interweave their malice and their gift in our brightest hours. Who ever read the volume of the Sonnets, without finding that the poet had there revealed, under masks that are no masks to the intelligent, the lore of friendship and of love; the confusion of sentiments in the most susceptible, and, at the same time, the most intellectual of men? What trait of his private mind has he hidden in his dramas? One can discern, in his ample pictures of the gentleman and the king, what forms and humanities pleased him; his delight in troops of friends, in large hospitality, in cheerful giving. Let Timon, let Warwick, let Antonio the merchant, answer for his great heart. So far from Shakespeare's being the least known, he is the one person, in all modern history, known to us. What point of morals, of manners, of economy, of philosophy, of religion, of taste, of the conduct of life, has he not settled? What mystery has he not signified his knowledge of? What office, or function, or district of man's work, has he not remembered? What king has he not taught state, as Talma taught Napoleon? What maiden has not found him finer than her delicacy? What lover has he not outloved? What sage has he not outseen? What gentleman has he not instructed in the rudeness of his behaviour?

Some able and appreciating critics think no criticism on Shakespeare valuable, that does not rest purely on the dramatic merit; that he is falsely judged as poet and philosopher. I think as highly as these critics of his dramatic merit, but still think it secondary. He was a full man, who liked to talk; a brain exhaling thoughts and images, which, seeking vent, found the drama next at hand. Had he been less, we should have had to consider how well he filled his place, how good a dramatist he was,—and he is the best in the world. But it turns out, that what he has to say is of that weight, as to withdraw some attention from the vehicle; and he is like some saint whose history is to be rendered into all languages, into verse and prose, into songs and pictures, and cut up into proverbs; so that the occasion which gave the saint's meaning the form of a conversation, or of a prayer, or of a code of laws, is immaterial, compared with the universality of its application. So it fares with the wise Shakespeare and his book of life. He wrote the airs for all our modern music: he wrote the text of modern life; the text of manners: he drew the man of England and Europe; the father of the man in America: he drew the man, and described the day, and what is done in it: he read the hearts of men and women, their probity, and their second thought, and wiles; the wiles of innocence, and the transitions by which virtues and vices slide into their contraries: he could divide the mother's part from the father's part in the face of the child, or draw the fine demarcations of freedom and of fate: he knew the laws of repression which make the police of nature: and all the sweets and all the terrors of human lot lay in his mind as truly but as softly as the landscape lies on the eye. And the importance of this wisdom of life sinks the form, as of Drama or Epic, out of notice. 'T is like making a question concerning the paper on which a king's message is written.

Shakespeare is as much out of the category of eminent authors, as he is out of the crowd. He is inconceivably wise; the others, conceivably. A good reader can, in a sort, nestle into Plato's brain, and think from thence; but not into Shakespeare's.

We are still out of doors. For executive faculty, for creation, Shakespeare is unique. No man can imagine it better. He was the farthest reach of subtlety compatible with an individual self,—the subtilest of authors, and only just within the possibility of authorship. With this wisdom of life, is the equal endowment of imaginative and of lyric power. He clothed the creatures of his legend with form and sentiments, as if they were people who had lived under his roof; and few real men have left such distinct characters as these fictions. And they spoke in language as sweet as it was fit. Yet his talents never seduced him into an ostentation, nor did he harp on one string. An omnipresent humanity coördinates all his faculties. Give a man of talents a story to tell, and his partiality will presently appear. He has certain observations, opinions, topics, which have some accidental prominence, and which he disposes all to exhibit. He crams this part, and starves that other part, consulting not the fitness of the thing, but his fitness and strength. But Shakspeare has no peculiarity, no importunate topic; but all is duly given; no veins, no curiosities: no cow-painter, no bird-fancier, no mannerist is he: he has no discoverable egotism: the great he tells greatly; the small, subordinately. He is wise without emphasis or assertion; he is strong, as nature is strong, who lifts the land into mountain slopes without effort, and by the same rule as she floats a bubble in the air, and likes as well to do the one as the other. This makes that equality of power in farce, tragedy, narrative, and love-songs; a merit so incessant, that each reader is incredulous of the perception of other readers.

This power of expression, or of transferring the inmost truth of things into music and verse, makes him the type of the poet, and has added a new problem to metaphysics. This is that which throws him into natural history, as a main production of the globe, and as announcing new eras and ameliorations. Things were mirrored in his poetry without loss or blur: he could paint the fine with precision, the great with compass; the tragic and the comic indifferently, and without any distortion or favour. He carried his powerful execution into minute details, to a hair point; finishes an eyelash or a dimple as firmly as he draws a mountain; and yet these, like nature's, will bear the scrutiny of the solar microscope.

In short, he is the chief example to prove that more or less of production, more or fewer pictures, is a thing indifferent. He had the power to make one picture. Daguerre learned how to let one flower etch its image on his plate of iodine; and then proceeds at leisure to etch a million. There are always objects; but there was never representation. Here is perfect representation, at last; and now let the world of figures sit for their portraits. No recipe can be given for the making of a Shakspeare; but the possibility of the translation of things into song is demonstrated.

His lyric power lies in the genius of the piece. The sonnets, though their excellence is lost in the splendor of the dramas, are as inimitable as they: and it is not a merit of lines, but a total merit of the piece; like the tone of voice of some incomparable person, so is this a speech of poetic beings, and any clause as unproducible now as a whole poem. Though the speeches in the plays, and single lines, have a beauty which tempts the ear to pause on them for their euphuism, yet the sentence is so loaded with meaning, and so linked with its foregoers and followers, that the logician is satisfied. His means are as admirable as his ends; every subordinate invention, by which he helps himself to connect some irreconcilable opposites, is a poem too. He is not reduced to dismount and walk, because his horses are running off with him in some distant direction: he always rides. The finest poetry was first experience: but the thought has suffered a transformation since it was an experience. Cultivated men often attain a good degree of skill in writing verses; but it is easy to read, through their poems, their personal history: any one acquainted with parties can name every figure: this is Andrew, and that is Rachel. The sense thus remains prosaic. It is a caterpillar with wings, and not yet a butterfly. In the poet's mind, the fact has gone quite over into the new element of thought, and has lost all that is exuvial. This generosity abides with Shakspeare. We say, from the truth and closeness of his pictures, that he knows the lesson by heart. Yet there is not a trace of egotism.

One more royal trait properly belongs to the poet. I mean his cheerfulness, without which no man can be a poet,—for beauty is his aim. He loves virtue, not for its obligation, but for its grace: he delights in the world, in man, in woman, for the lovely light that sparkles from them. Beauty, the spirit of joy and hilarity, he sheds over the universe. Epicurus relates, that poetry hath such charms that a lover might forsake his mistress to partake of them. And the true bards have been noted for their firm and cheerful temper. Homer lies in sunshine; Chaucer is glad and erect; and Saadi says, "It was rumored abroad that I was penitent; but what had I to do with repentance?" Not less sovereign and cheerful,—much more sovereign and cheerful, is the tone of Shakspeare. His name suggests joy and emancipation to the heart of men. If he should appear in any company of human souls, who would not march in his troop? He touches nothing that does not borrow health and longevity from his festal style. And now, how stands the account of man with this bard and benefactor, when in solitude, shutting our ears to the reverberations of his fame, we seek to strike the balance? Solitude has austere lessons; it can teach us to spare both heroes and poets; and it weighs Shakspeare also, and finds him to share the halfness and imperfection of humanity.

Shakspeare, Homer, Dante, Chaucer, saw the splendor of meaning that plays over the visible world; knew that a tree had another use than for apples, and corn another than for meal, and the ball of the earth, than for tillage and roads: that these things bore a second and finer harvest to the mind, being emblems of its thoughts, and conveying in all their natural history a certain mute commentary on human life. Shakspeare employed them as colours to compose his picture. He rested in their beauty; and never took the step which seemed inevitable to such genius, namely, to explore the virtue which resides in these symbols, and imparts this power:—what is that which they themselves say?

He converted the elements, which waited on his command, into entertainments. He was master of the revels to mankind. Is it not as if one should have, through majestic powers of science, the comets given into his hand, or the planets and their moons, and should draw them from their orbits to glare with the municipal fireworks on a holiday night, and advertise in all towns, "Very superior pyrotechny this evening!" Are the agents of nature, and the power to understand them, worth no more than a street serenade, or the breath of a cigar? One remembers again the trumpet-text in the Koran,—"The heavens and the earth, and all that is between them, think ye we have created them in jest?" As long as the question is of talent and mental power, the world of men has not his equal to show. But when the question is to life, and its materials, and its auxiliaries, how does he profit me? What does it signify? It is but a Twelfth Night, or Midsummer-Night's Dream, or a Winter Evening's Tale: what signifies another picture more or less? The Egyptian verdict of the Shakspeare Societies comes to mind, that he was a jovial actor and manager. I can not marry this fact to his verse. Other admirable men have led lives in some sort of keeping with their thought; but this man, in wide contrast. Had he been less, had he reached only the common measure of great authors, of Bacon, Milton, Tasso, Cervantes, we might leave the fact in the twilight of human fate: but, that this man of men, he who gave to the science of mind a new and larger subject than had ever existed, and planted the standard of humanity some furlongs forward into Chaos,—that he should not be wise for himself;—it must even go into the world's history, that the best poet led an obscure and profane life, using his genius for the public amusement.

Well, other men, priest and prophet, Israelite, German, and Swede, beheld the same objects: they also saw through them that which was contained. And to what purpose? The beauty straightway vanished; they read commandments, all-excluding mountainous duty; an obligation, a sadness, as of piled mountains, fell on them, and life became ghastly, joyless, a pilgrim's progress, a probation, beleaguered round with doleful histories of Adam's fall and curse, behind us; with doomsdays and purgatorial and penal fires before us; and the heart of the seer and the heart of the listener sank in them. It must be conceded that these are half-views of half-men. The world still wants its poet-priest, a reconciler, who shall not trifle with Shakspeare the player, nor shall grope in graves with Swedenborg the mourner; but who shall see, speak, and act, with equal inspiration. For knowledge will brighten the sunshine; right is more beautiful than private affection; and love is compatible with universal wisdom.

By Keith

Chapter 7

Shakespeare Plays and the Comedies

William Shakespeare's plays come in many forms. There are histories, tragedies, comedies and tragicomedies. Among the most popular are the comedies which are full of laughter, irony, satire and wordplay.

Many times the question is asked: what makes a play a comedy instead of a tragedy? Comedies treat subjects lightly, meaning that they don't treat seriously such things as love. Shakespeare's comedies often use puns, metaphors and insults to provoke 'thoughtful laughter'. The action is often strained by artificiality, especially elaborate and contrived endings. Disguises and mistaken identities are often very common.

The plot is very important in Shakespeare's comedies. It is often very convoluted, twisted and confusing, and extremely hard to follow. Other character- sticks of Shakespearean comedy are the themes of love and friendship, played within a courtly society. Songs - often sung by a jester or a fool, parallel the events of the plot. Foil and stock characters are often inserted into the storyline.

Love provides the main ingredient. If the lovers are unmarried when the play opens, they either have not met or there is some obstacle to their relationship. Examples of these obstacles are familiar to every reader of Shakespeare: the slanderous tongues which nearly wreck love in 'Much Ado About Nothing'; the father insistent upon his daughter marrying his choice, as in 'A Midsummer Nights Dream'; or the expulsion of the rightful Duke's daughter in 'As You Like It'.

Shakespeare uses many predictable patterns in his plays. The hero rarely appears in the opening lines; however, we hear about him from other characters. He often does not normally make an entrance for at least a few lines into the play, if not a whole scene. The hero is also virtuous and strong but always possesses a character flaw.

In the comedy itself, Shakespeare assumes that we know the basic plot and he jumps right into it with little or no explanation. Foreshadowing and foreboding are put in the play early and can be heard throughout the drama. All Shakespearean comedies have five acts. The climax of the play is always during the third act.

Shakespearean comedies also contain a wide variety of characters. Shakespeare often introduces a character and then discards him, never to be seen again during the play. Shakespeare's female leads are usually described as petite and often assume male disguises. Often, foul weather parallels the emotional state of the characters. The audience is often informed of events before the characters and when a future meeting is to take place it usually doesn't happen immediately. Character names are often clues to their roles and personalities, such as Malvolio from 'Twelfth Night' and Bottom in 'A Midsummer Nights Dream'.

Many themes are repeated throughout Shakespeare's comedies. One theme is the never-ending struggle between the the forces of good and evil. Another theme is that love has profound effects and that people often hide behind false faces.

The comedies themselves can be sub-categorised as tragicomedies, romantic comedies, comedies of justice and simple entertaining comedies with good wholesome fun.

A Midsummer Night's Dream' was written in 1596. It has become one of Shakespeare's most fond comedies. It makes fun of everything from love at first sight to realistic staging.

The play refers to "fair vestal throned by the west" which was once thought to have been a polite acknowledgement of the Queen's presence in the audience. The play was first printed in a quarto edition in 1600.

'Much Ado About Nothing' is a romantic comedy about a love relationship. It has a basic plot that's more orthodox than those of most of Shakespeare's plays. It's about two strong personalities who see each other as combatants rather than partners. The play exploits games of verbal punning and backchat between two reluctant lovers. 'Much Ado About Nothing' first appeared in a quarto 1599.

'Twelfth Night' is the most intricate of Shakespeare's great middle-period comedies. Written in 1601 it plays the familiar games of the time with boys playing girls who dress as boy pages. It is also filled with confusions of identity and memorable verbal put-downs. The play was not printed until the First Folio of 1623.

'The Winter's Tale' is a late tragicomedy written between 1609 -1610. It ranges through sixteen years in time, marked by the choric figure of Time himself and through a fantastic geographical range from Sicily to Bohemia. Shakespeare took this story, which shows the healing and restorative power of love, from an old romance. The play was printed originally in the First Folio of 1623.

'The Merry Wives of Windsor', written some time between 1597 and 1599, is the only comedy that Shakespeare set in his own time and country. For all the London scenes with Falstaff in the history plays, Shakespeare usually chose to set his comedies abroad. The use of local settings was still very new in the plays of this time. The play is an exciting piece of work, full of eccentric characters and slapstick comedy. The play first appeared in a memorial version in 1602 written down largely from memory. A better text appeared in the First Folio.

Chapter 8

Important Aspects of Elizabethan Drama

The Elizabethan Age in the world occurred in the sixteenth and seventeenth century in England. It is named for Queen Elizabeth, who is known mainly for her love of religion of the arts. The Elizabethan Age was most influential through its drama.

The Elizabethan Age in England showered the world with a burst of brilliant playwrights. Four of the most well known of early Elizabethan playwrights were John Lyly, Thomas Kyd, Robert Greene, and Christopher Marlowe. John Lyly's most famous work is "Endimion, Man in Moon." Thomas Kyd is the author of "Spanish Tragedy." Robert Greene is best known for "Friar Bacon Friar Bungay." Many people think that Christopher Marlowe was the greatest of early Elizabethan writers. His most well known play is "Doctor Faustus." This play is about a man named Faustus who sells his soul to the devil in exchange for power on earth. Christopher Marlowe was born shortly before William Shakespeare. He was supposed to be a shoemaker. The Archbishop of Canterbury offered him a scholarship to Cambridge University, but Christopher avoided becoming shoemaker to enter the theater. He started writing plays for an acting company called the Admiral's Men. His major literary works were tragedies, as lots of Elizabethan dramas were. Other than "Doctor Faustus", his other two greatest works were "Tamburlaine" and "Jew of Malta." Marlowe's major literary achievements are the use of refined blank verse, spiritual drama, dramatic action, and the Renaissance hero. He loved learning and hated ignorance. This was apparent in many of his literary works. Marlowe was a friend of Sir Walter Raleigh and a favourite of Queen Elizabeth, even though records show that Marlowe was not gentleman. Christopher Marlowe's roommate accused him of atheism and treason, which were crimes in that time. Records show that he was involved in two tavern brawls. In one of the brawls, a man lost his life. In the other brawl, Marlowe was stabbed in the eye. He died three days later. Conspiracy has been suspected about his death. Marlowe, Lyly, Kyd, Greene are known as the University Wits. They defined the London Theater.

William Shakespeare wrote in the middle of the Elizabethan Period, and he is the most famous writer in the era; maybe the greatest of all time. His plays have very good plots, characterization, and backgrounds. Other than tragedy, which was the most common drama of the time, Shakespeare wrote great comedies, tragicomedies, and histories. His characters come alive, and they are admired and even envied by people. His plots are full of action. "Hamlet" was the most popular of his tragedies. Shakespeare's most successful comedy was "A Midsummer Night's Dream." Perhaps his most famous tragicomedy was "The Tempest". "Richard III" and Henry V" are two of Shakespeare's histories that have been made into motion pictures. Shakespeare combined the best aspects of Elizabethan drama with classic drama. This enriched his imagination and humour. The age of Shakespeare was a great time in English history.

There are many important events that occurred during the Elizabethan Period. In approximately 1477, Caxton set up a printing press, and he printed the first books in England. Around 1500, "Everyman", a morality play, was written and performed. In 1533, John Heywood's "The Play of the Weather" was performed. A poetry collection called "Tottle's Miscellany" was published in 1557. This work included Wyatt and Surrey's sonnets. Besides drama, the sonnet is the epitome of literature in the Elizabethan period. In 1564, William

Shakespeare and Christopher Marlowe were born. "The Theatre", the first permanent structure for plays in England, was constructed in 1576. Christopher Marlowe directed his first play, "Tamburlaine", in 1587. In 1590, Shakespeare directed his first play, "The Comedy of Errors." Christopher Marlowe wrote "The Jew of Malta"a year later. He was killed in 1593. Shakespeare wrote "The Merchant of Venice" in 1597. In 1599, the Globe Theater was constructed. Shakespeare wrote "Macbeth" in 1605. He died in 1616.

Another very important aspect of Elizabethan Drama was the audiences. The audiences were always large and very excited at plays. The common people paid an equivalent to one penny to sit in the front of the theater. Unless it was raining, these people had the best seats in the theater. The audience would participate in the play by cheering, hissing, or even throwing rotten vegetables. The audience would know that plays were about to be performed by a flag that rose over the theater.

The theater played an important role in this era. Without theaters, there would be nowhere for the play to be performed. There were two types of theaters: indoor and outdoor. Outdoor theaters were public theaters. "The Theatre" is an example of an outdoor theater. Indoor theaters were private theaters.

Elizabethan Actors were all male. Females were not allowed to act in the theater. All female parts were played by men whose voices had not changed yet. Actors had to have good memories, strong voices, and the ability to fence. Actors also had to have the ability to sing and dance. The costumes that the actors wore were very elaborate, but not historic.

Many special effects were used in the theater. Death scenes were very gory and realistic. To show an eye falling out, a grape would fall to the floor. Animal organs were used to show scenes where organs fell out of actors' bodies.

The stage was the centre of the theater. It had several levels. The lowest level of the stage was used for a number of things. Devils, ghosts, graves, and ditched are a few of them.

The second level was the main stage. This is where the most important scenes were. The third level of the stage was a balcony. It was used for a number of things such as mountains or city walls. The fourth level of the stage was a series of pulleys where angels, birds, and thunderbolts could be sent down from the main stage. The highest level was a room where the musicians were.

There is one aspect of Elizabethan Drama that still remains a mystery. Vocabulary in the Elizabethan Era was very different than it is now. Modern historians are not sure about all of the word meanings. This is why some of the phrases used are hard to understand.

Elizabethan Drama is a very important addition to the literature world and to England. Drama is part of England's heritage, and helps make them who they are.

The most important aspects of Elizabethan Drama are is playwrights, events, audiences, theaters, actors, speech, special effects, and the stage. These things make it up, and help keep it alive. Elizabethan Drama is very important in literature.

Chapter 9

Historical Background

PASTORAL POETRY AND PASTORAL COMEDY

"Pastoral" (from *pastor,* Latin for "shepherd") refers to a literary work dealing with shepherds and rustic life. Pastoral poetry is highly conventionalised; it presents an idealised rather than realistic view of rustic life. Classical (Greek and Latin) pastoral works date back to the 3rd century B.C., when the Greek poet Theocritus wrote his *Idylls* about the rustic life of Sicily for the sophisticated citizens of the city of Alexandria. In the first century B.C., Virgil wrote Latin poems depicting himself and his equally sophisticated friends and acquaintances as shepherds living a simple, rural life. Shakespeare's knowledge of pastoral conventions was drawn both from his humanist education (which included Virgil and possibly Theocritus) and from his familiarity with the works of contemporaries who imitated the ancients by writing pastoral poetry in English.

Common topics of pastoral poetry include love and seduction; the value of poetry; death and mourning; the corruption of the city or court vs. the "purity" of idealised country life; politics (generally treated satirically: the "shepherds" critique society or easily identifiable political figures). A common pastoral poetic genre is the *eclogue* (a dialogue between two shepherds). This conversation may be between a shepherd and the shepherdess he loves (generally his attempt to seduce her); a "singing contest" to see which shepherd is the better poet (a third may act as judge); or sophisticated banter between two supposedly "rude swains" who discuss a lady, their flocks, or a current event; lament a dead friend (a *eulogy* or *elegy*); or praise a notable individual. Laudatory poems, laments upon a death, songs of courtship and the complaints of a lovesick shepherd also occur as pastoral monologues.

An important subgroup of the pastoral eclogue or monologue is the *elegy*, which expresses the poet's grief at the loss of a friend or an important person. Conventional features of pastoral elegies include: the invocation of the Muse; expression of the "shepherd"-poet's grief; praise of the dead "shepherd"; invective against death; effects of the death upon nature (disruptions in climate etc. as expressions of a personified Nature's grief and sympathy); and ultimately, the poet's acceptance of the inevitability of death and hope for immortality. Pastoral elegies may also include such elements as a procession of mourners; digressions on a topical issue (frequently satirical); flower symbolism; the use of a refrain; rhetorical questions. The pastoral elegy was still practiced by 19th-century Romantic and Victorian poets; see e.g. Shelley's *Adonais* and Arnold's *Thyrsis*.

Shakespeare's contemporaries revived and imitated the topics and forms of classical pastoral poetry. For example, Christopher Marlowe's "The Passionate Shepherd to His Love," Sir Walter Ralegh's "The Nymph's Reply to the Shepherd," and Thomas Campion's "I Care Not For These Ladies" are pastoral songs of courtship and seduction. Eclogue 4 of Edmund Spenser's *Shepheardes Calender* (1579) and Mary Herbert's "A Dialogue Between Two Shepherds" (1599) praise Queen Elizabeth, while John Milton's *Lycidas* (1637) is a pastoral elegy lamenting the loss of a classmate. Both Spenser's and Milton's pastoral poems include satirical elements: *Lycidas* denounces the corruption of the clergy, while the *Shepheardes Calender* attacks those responsible for the neglect of poetry (Eclogue).

Renaissance poets not only imitated these classical topics and forms, they also expanded the pastoral mode to include the romance and drama. Pastoral drama and romance lacked classical models, but were strongly influenced by Italian Renaissance models, e.g. Tasso's pastoral dramatic poem *Aminta* (1573) and Guarini's pastoral tragicomedy *Il Pastor Fido* (1590). Pastoral romances of the English Renaissance include Sidney's *Arcadia* (1590) and Lodge's *Rosalynde: Euphues Golden Legacie* — the work which supplied the story of *As You Like It*. Examples of English pastoral dramas include John Fletcher's *The Faithful Shepherdess* (Fletcher, 1579-1625, is the poet who collaborated with Shakespeare on *Henry VIII* and *The Two Noble Kinsmen*) and Ben Jonson's *The Sad Shepherd* (left unfinished at Jonson's death in 1637).

The affectation of rustic life in pastoral poetry is a purely artistic device; it creates a distancing effect which allows the poet to step back from and critique society. The artificiality of pastoral poetry is most explicit in the courtly language and dress of the "shepherds," which better fit the drawing rooms of polite society than the hills, swamps and sheepfolds of real rustic life. Thus, Shakespeare's pastoral comedy *As You Like It* contrasts the corruption of the court with the idealised Forest of Arden, in which the banished Duke Senior and his followers live a decidedly courtly existence. Note also that while Rosalind and Celia play at being shepherds, they never seem to spend any time taking care of sheep (no more than do Corin, Audrey, Silvius and Phebe). But while *As You Like It* is clearly pastoral in setting and themes, it transcends pastoral conventions, inviting the audience to a meditation on serious issues such as what constitutes "natural" behaviour, or the connection between language and truth. On one level, *As You Like It* is about the power of language: it explores the ways in which figurative language or poetic conventions can help or hinder communication; the "truth" (or lack of same) of figurative speech; and the ways in which language can be abused (deliberately used to mislead; unwittingly misinterpreted; twisted in the pursuit of "unnatural" ends).

THE CONVENTIONS OF SHAKESPEAREAN ROMANTIC COMEDY

Conventions assist us in understanding literary works belonging to a particular genre; they help to categorise them and illuminate their common features. Genres set up certain expectations because of their shared characteristics. For example, you know to expect specific features when reading or viewing a western (good guys and bad guys; shoot-outs or duels), a detective thriller (false clues that lead in the wrong direction; ingenious solution to a mystery), science fiction (humans and aliens; futuristic technology; special effects). One's judgment of a given work is affected in part by how it meets or fails to meet generic expectations. An artist may deliberately manipulate or play with conventions, parodying or transcending the limits of a literary genre: *Monty Python's Holy Grail* parodies Arthurian romances; *Blazing Saddles* parodies Westerns; the *Pyramus and Thisbe* play in *A Midsummer Night's Dream* parodies Shakespeare's own *Romeo and Juliet. The Purple Rose of Cairo* transcends sentimental romance by raising questions about the boundaries of art, reality and fantasy; *Hamlet* transcends previous Renaissance revenge tragedy.

The major conventions of Shakespearean Romantic Comedy are:

- The main action is about love.
- The would-be lovers must overcome obstacles and misunderstandings before being united in harmonious union. The ending frequently involves a parade of couples to the altar and a festive mood or actual celebration (expressed in dance, song, feast, etc.) *A Midsummer Night's Dream* has four such couples (not counting Pyramus and Thisbe!); *As You Like It* has four; *Twelfth Night* has three; etc.
- Frequently (but not always), it contains elements of the improbable, the fantastic, the supernatural, or the

miraculous, e.g. unbelievable coincidences, improbable scenes of recognition/lack of recognition, willful disregard of the social order (nobles marrying commoners, beggars changed to lords), instantaneous conversions (the wicked repent), enchanted or idealised settings, supernatural beings (witches, fairies, Gods and Goddesses). The happy ending may be brought about through supernatural or divine intervention (comparable to the *deus ex machina* in classical comedy, where a God appears to resolve the conflict) or may merely involve improbable turns of events.

- In the best of the mature comedies, there is frequently a philosophical aspect involving weightier issues and themes: personal identity; the importance of love in human existence; the power of language to help or hinder communication; the transforming power of poetry and art; the disjunction between appearance and reality; the power of dreams and illusions).

Chapter 10

Introduction to "As You Like It"

The Author and his Times

Like most of the major characters in As You Like It, William Shakespeare experienced life in both the country and the city. His birthplace- Stratford, on the Avon River- was a bustling country town. He arrived in London, the social, commercial, and intellectual centre of England, during the reign of Elizabeth I, at the height of the English Renaissance. All classes of Englishmen, including artisans, the new middle class, and the nobility, shared a keen desire to be entertained. The influx of wealth from the New World had given many of them money to spend. Since Shakespeare's plays were- and still are- crowd pleasers, he quickly became one of the most successful playwrights of his time.

It should be helpful to examine a few ways in which As You Like It reflects the interests of the audience for which it was written. For example, Elizabethan audiences took great pleasure in the type of complex wordplay practiced by Rosalind, Celia, and Touchstone. During the Renaissance, the English had begun to take their own language seriously for the first time. It had previously been considered too coarse for the expression of subtle ideas or fine shades of meaning. ("Serious" writing was still done in Latin.) Shakespeare probably shared his audience's enthusiasm for exploring the potential of their native tongue.

As You Like It draws upon an Elizabethan genre (type of literature) known as the pastoral romance. As escapist literature, the pastoral romance (a love story with a country setting) was extremely popular. Its conventions were as fixed and artificial as the formula plots of today's romance novels. These love stories were set in idealised country locales, where life was pure and innocent. The rustic settings were populated by shepherds and shepherdesses who thought only of love and spoke of their passion in elaborate (and sometimes awful) verse. Love at first sight was commonplace. The characters suffered the pangs of unrequited love. In the forest settings of these stories, you might encounter a lion, a magician, or a band of thieves. Elizabethans would have recognised the poetic rustics Silvius and Phebe from As You Like It as stock characters out of such a pastoral romance. They would have enjoyed seeing Rosalind save Orlando from becoming just another lovesick young man like Silvius.

Many noble Elizabethan households kept professional fools such as Touchstone for entertainment. His role was actually written for Robert Armin, who had been a professional fool before joining Shakespeare's acting company. Jesters occupied a special place in Elizabethan society. They could mix with both kings and servants. As long as they pleased their masters, they could say almost anything they wished. Often, Shakespeare's fools tell the truth when nobody else will. As you will see, Touchstone exposes pretension and foolishness wherever he finds them.

The romance and humour of As You Like It are played out against a backdrop of danger and political intrigue. Rosalind and Orlando both flee the city under threat of death. Much is made of the "envious court," where nobody can be trusted and where flatterers are always seeking to add to their own power. This darker side of life was also a part of Shakespeare's England. When Elizabeth became queen in 1558, she inherited both religious tensions and grave financial difficulties. Fortunately, she was a shrewd politician and skillfully played her noblemen against each other, so that no individual could gain enough power to threaten her.

A very real threat to Elizabeth was posed by Mary, Queen of Scots. Until Mary's execution in 1587, Elizabeth lived with the fear that the Roman Catholics might rally around Mary and mount a rebellion. In this play, Duke Frederick fears that Rosalind's graces will remind the people of her father and cause them to revolt.

So As You Like It does mirror the concerns of Shakespeare's audience. But what about the author, what of Shakespeare the man? Very little is actually known about him. Neither he nor anybody else of his era ever recorded the story of his life. A few facts are known. He was born in Stratford, a small English country town on the Avon River, and baptised on April 26, 1564. Since infants were generally baptised at three days, his birth date may have been April 23. His father was John Shakespeare, a prosperous Stratford businessman and town council member. William's mother, Mary, was the daughter of a well-to-do landowner. William was the eldest of their six children. Shakespeare almost certainly attended the local grammar school. There, his studies would have included Latin, rhetoric (grammar, composition), and literature.

In November 1582 he married Anne Hathaway, eight years his senior. Anne's age, combined with the fact that their first child was born only six months after the wedding, has led some scholars to believe that the marriage was one of necessity. That may not be the case, however, because at that time it was socially acceptable for an engaged couple to sleep together. William and Anne had two girls, Susanna and Judith, and one son, Hamnet, who died young.

Nobody knows what work Shakespeare did while in Stratford. He may have been a schoolteacher or a private tutor in a wealthy household. Like Orlando in As You Like It, he had to leave his birthplace to find his future. Unlike Orlando, who fled to the country, William headed for the big city, London. (Legend has it that he had to leave Stratford after being caught hunting illegally on a large estate, but no records exist to verify that story.) In London he became first an actor and later a playwright. Along with success, he found envy.

The first mention of Shakespeare in London is in a pamphlet by a rival playwright, Robert Greene. In "A Groatsworth of Wit" (groat: an old English coin worth four pennies), Greene warned fellow university-educated playwrights of an upstart actor (Shakespeare) who had the gall to write plays. Nevertheless, Shakespeare became the most successful playwright of his day. He was an actor (of small parts), a playwright, and a partner in the Lord Chamberlain's Men, a theater company favoured by Queen Elizabeth. Her successor, James I, elevated the company to the rank of King's Men in 1603.

Although plays were a popular form of entertainment, they weren't highly regarded as literature. To secure his artistic reputation, Shakespeare wrote poems. Between 1592 and 1601, he penned three long narrative poems- Venus and Adonis, The Rape of Lucrece, and The Phoenix and the Turtle- as well as a famous series of sonnets.

As You Like It premiered in 1599 or 1600, about the same time that Shakespeare's company moved into the Globe Theatre, across the Thames River from the city of London. Shakespeare's reputation had been firmly established by nineteen previous plays. Among the eighteen to follow would be his four great tragedies- Hamlet, Othello, King Lear, and Macbeth. By 1612, Shakespeare had returned to live in Stratford, where he owned a fine house called New Place. He died there, presumably on his birthday, April 23, 1616.

As You Like It was rarely performed in the first century after Shakespeare's death. In 1723 an enterprising London producer combined the play with Shakespeare's Much Ado About Nothing and A Midsummer Night's Dream to create a collage called Love in a Forest. But by the nineteenth century, As You Like It had become one of Shakespeare's most frequently performed works. The Romantic spirit of that time probably helped the play to find new favour with audiences. In addition, many leading ladies wanted to play the showcase rôle of Rosalind. As You Like It is still popular today. Audiences enjoy its blend of humour and romance, and fall in love with Rosalind just as Orlando does.

Chapter 11

Context of "As You Like It"

The Most Influential Writer in all of English literature, William Shakespeare was born in 1564 to a -successful middle-class glover in Stratford-upon-Avon, England. Shakespeare attended grammar school, but his formal education proceeded no further. In 1582 he married an older woman, Anne Hathaway, and had three children with her. Around 1590, he left his family behind and traveled to London to work as an actor and playwright. Public and critical acclaim quickly followed, and Shakespeare eventually became the most popular playwright in England and part-owner of the Globe Theater. His career bridged the reigns of Elizabeth I (ruled 1558–1603) and James I (ruled 1603–1625), and he was a favourite of both monarchs. Indeed, James granted Shakespeare's company the greatest possible compliment by bestowing upon its members the title of King's Men. Wealthy and renowned, Shakespeare retired to Stratford and died in 1616 at the age of fifty-two. At the time of Shakespeare's death, literary luminaries such as Ben Jonson hailed his works as timeless.

Shakespeare's works were collected and printed in various editions in the century following his death, and by the early eighteenth century, his reputation as the greatest poet ever to write in English was well established. The unprecedented admiration garnered by his works led to a fierce curiosity about Shakespeare's life, but the dearth of biographical information has left many details of Shakespeare's personal history shrouded in mystery. Some people have concluded from this fact and from Shakespeare's modest education that Shakespeare's plays were actually written by someone else—Francis Bacon and the Earl of Oxford are the two most popular candidates—but the support for this claim is overwhelmingly circumstantial, and the theory is not taken seriously by many scholars.

In the absence of credible evidence to the contrary, Shakespeare must be viewed as the author of the thirty-seven plays and 154 sonnets that bear his name. The legacy of this body of work is immense. A number of Shakespeare's plays seem to have transcended even the category of brilliance, becoming so influential as to affect profoundly the course of Western literature and culture ever after.

As You Like It was most likely written around 1598–1600, during the last years of Elizabeth's reign. The play belongs to the literary tradition known as *pastoral:* which has its roots in the literature of ancient Greece, came into its own in Roman antiquity with Virgil's *Eclogues,* and continued as a vital literary mode through Shakespeare's time and long after. Typically, a pastoral story involves exiles from urban or court life who flee to the refuge of the countryside, where they often disguise themselves as shepherds in order to converse with other shepherds on a range of established topics, from the relative merits of life at court versus life in the country to the relationship between nature and art. The most fundamental concern of the pastoral mode is comparing the worth of the natural world, represented by relatively untouched countryside, to the world built by humans, which contains the joys of art and the city as well as the injustices of rigid social hierarchies. Pastoral literature, then, has great potential to serve as a forum for social criticism and can even inspire social reform.

In general, Shakespeare's *As You Like It* develops many of the traditional features and concerns of the pastoral genre. This comedy examines the cruelties and corruption of court life and gleefully pokes holes in one of humankind's greatest artifices: the conventions of romantic love. The play's investment in pastoral traditions leads to an indulgence in rather simple rivalries: court versus country, realism versus romance, reason versus mindlessness, nature versus fortune, young versus old, and those who are born into nobility versus those who acquire their social standing. But rather than settle these scores by coming down on one side or the other, *As You Like It* offers up a world of myriad choices and endless possibilities. In the world of this play, no one thing need cancel out another. In this way, the play manages to offer both social critique and social affirmation. It is a play that at all times stresses the complexity of things, the simultaneous pleasures and pains of being human.

Chapter 12

Plot of "As You Like It"

As You Like It is a complicated drama, for Shakespeare simultaneously and masterfully develops several plots. Two of them, the Oliver/Orlando conflict and the Duke Senior/Duke Frederick conflict, centre on the theme of hatred. The other plots are developed around the theme of love, including the Orlando/Rosalind relationship, the Touchstone/Audrey relationship, the Oliver/Celia relationship, and the Phebe/Silvius relationship.

In spite of the varied plots, Shakespeare adheres to the unities of time, place, and character. Although there is much action in the play, with several characters going into exile and several couples falling in love, the play actually takes place in a tight time frame, spanning only a few days. Likewise, there are only two settings in the entire play, which are total contrasts to one another. The court of the duke is characterised by formality, deception, and hostility; the Forest of Arden is characterised by beauty, freedom, and naturalness. Finally, even though there are a number of characters in the play, Shakespeare focuses the attention of his audience on the two main characters, Orlando and Rosalind. The other key characters appear in a relationship with one of them. For example, Oliver is Orlando's brother, Celia is Rosalind's cousin and friend, Duke Senior is Rosalind's father, Duke Frederick is Rosalind's uncle and Celia's father, Touchstone is the chaperone of Rosalind and Celia to the forest, and Adam is Orlando's faithful servant.

To further unify the plot, it is developed along classical lines. Act I provides an introduction to the key characters and the conflict of hatred. It clearly projects the hostility between Duke Senior and Duke Frederick and between Orlando and Oliver. It also introduces the theme of love, for Orlando and Rosalind have fallen in love with one another. The real rising action of the play begins at the end of Act I, when Duke Frederick banishes Rosalind from court, and she and Celia head towards the Forest of Arden, when Duke Senior is already in exile.

Acts II, III, and IV develop the complications of the plot through the rising action. Orlando is forced to flee into the forest, for Oliver is threatening to have him killed. Touchstone meets Audrey and wants to marry her. Rosalind, dressed in disguise as a young man, meets Orlando in the forest and tricks him into a love cure by which he will woo Ganymede as a practice to woo Rosalind. Oliver falls in love with Celia, disguised as Aliena, and makes plans to marry her. Phebe falls in love with Ganymede, unaware that he is really a girl in disguise. Rosalind comes up with a plan to solve all the problems in the love affairs. She asks everyone to meet in a clearing in the forest.

In the fifth and final action, the climax is reached. Rosalind and Celia shed their disguises, freeing them to marry Orlando and Oliver. During the grand ceremony, Touchstone and Audrey finally tie the knot, and even Phebe and Silvius are wed. The falling action occurs when it is learned that Duke Frederick has undergone a conversion and will restore the dukedom to Duke Senior, freeing the way for all the exiles in the forest to return to their normal life in court. The denouement, or conclusion, is given in the epilogue, when Rosalind addresses the audience, asking them for applause for this successful romantic comedy, where all the protagonists overcome their antagonists to meet with a happy end.

Chapter 13

Characters Sketch

Major Characters

Orlando de Boys

Orlando, Oliver's younger brother and Sir Rowland de Boys youngest son, is one of the protagonists of the play. He is an attractive and noble young man who is "enchantingly beloved" by everyone except Oliver, who is jealous of his brother. Because of Oliver's jealousy, Orlando has not been given his rightful inheritance or experienced a real education. In spite of the deprivations, he is "gentle, never school'd and yet learned." Throughout the play he proves himself to be modest, kind, and unselfish. Additionally, he is brave and strong, as proven by his overpowering the lioness and winning the wrestling match with Charles.

Because he does not want to share his wealth with Orlando, Oliver attempts to have his younger brother killed. In order to save himself, Orlando escapes to the Forest of Arden; however, he is later willing to risk his own life to save Oliver when he protects him from the lioness. In a similar manner, Orlando watches over and cares for Adam, his old faithful servant. When Adam is tired and can walk no more, the master carries him. Orlando also goes to find the servant food to eat.

Shakespeare mainly presents Orlando as a young man in love. He is "overthrown" emotionally by Rosalind the first time he meets her - at the wrestling match with Charles. When she presents him with a necklace, a token of her own affection for him, he is hopelessly smitten. While he is in the Forest of Arden, he yearns to see her again. To express his love, he writes verses about Rosalind, hangs them in the trees, and carves her name into the bark. He is so love-sick that he falls pray to Ganymede's offer of a love cure. Rosalind, in disguise, pretends to be the real Rosalind, and Orlando pretends to woo her. Both the audience and Rosalind enjoy knowing that an unaware Orlando is really courting the woman he loves. In the end, Rosalind presents herself without disguise, and Orlando marries her on the same day. In Orlando, Shakespeare has created an ideal young knight, endowed with all the virtues; he is really the hero of the play.

Rosalind

Rosalind, the daughter of Duke Senior, is a noble young lady of charm and vitality. Although she misses her father, who is in exile during the play, she has remained at court to be the companion to Celia, her cousin and best friend. In the beginning of the play, she seems somewhat sad, and Celia encourages her to be more merry. Later in the play, her wit and liveliness come forth.

Before she ever meets Orlando, Rosalind has talked to Celia about love. She says she wants to fall in love, even if in sport. However, when she sees Orlando at the wresting match, she falls deeply in love. When she is banished from the dukedom by Duke Frederick she is saddened to think about leaving Orlando behind; however, she takes Celia with her to the forest. In order to be safer, they disguise themselves. Rosalind, the taller of the two girls, dresses as a young man named Ganymede. Her disguise causes several complications in the play.

Rosalind, natural by nature, enjoys her life in the forest; her days are filled with sunshine and laughter. When she sees the love verses hanging in the trees and learns that Orlando has written them about her, she is delighted that he cares; but she is also concerned about the fact that she is disguised as a young man. The quick-witted Rosalind comes up with a plan to be wooed by Orlando, even though she is in disguise. She promises to cure Orlando's love-sickness; he must pretend that Ganymede is really Rosalind so he can practice winning her love. He agrees to the plan, fully unaware that he is really wooing his own true love.

With the same kind of cleverness and manipulation, Rosalind also presents herself to Orlando at the appropriate time. She also masterminds her marriage, as well as the marriage of Phebe and Silvius, proving she is a totally clever young lady. Endowed with beauty, charm, wit, and deep emotion, Rosalind certainly emerges as the heroine of the play.

Celia

Celia, the daughter of Duke Frederick and cousin of Rosalind, is the other major female character in the play. Like Rosalind, she is a likable, fine, charming, and witty, but she pales in comparison to her cousin; however, there is not an ounce of jealousy in her. She truly cares for Rosalind. In fact, she goes into exile with her, standing up to her villainous father. During her exile in the forest, Celia disguises herself as a poor young girl named Aliena.

Like Rosalind's love for Orlando, Celia's love for the reformed Oliver is spontaneous. Since she is disguised as a female, Oliver is free to pursue her, and "Aliena" submits. Much to Rosalind's surprise, she accepts Oliver's offer for marriage. Orlando cannot believe that "on so little acquaintance" the two of them will be wed and that Oliver will remain in the forest to live with Aliena forever.

When Celia takes off her disguise at the gathering in the forest, Oliver is delighted to learn that the woman he loves is not really a poor forest girl. He is now even more eager to marry her. The two of them wed at the same time that Rosalind marries Orlando and Touchstone marries Audrey.

Although Celia's role is secondary to Rosalind's role throughout the play, she clearly emerges as a charming, witty, intelligent, devoted, and delightful young lady and companion to Rosalind. Duke Senior

Duke Senior is Rosalind's father and one of the protagonists of the play. He is living in exile in the Forest of Arden because he was banished by his younger brother, Duke Frederick, who also stole his dukedom. Although he misses his daughter, he enjoys the freedom of the forest and sees himself as a Robin Hood with a merry band of lords surrounding him. Although he lives a more natural life in Arden, the duke is a product of his courtly upbringing. When Orlando comes, with sword drawn, demanding food for his servant, Duke Senior lectures him about common courtesy. He also shows that he is a generous man, for he willing shares his meal; he tells Orlando to bring Adam to dinner to eat his fill.

At the end of the play, everything turns out well for Duke Senior. He is delighted to be reunited with Rosalind and gives his blessings on her marriage to Orlando. He is also delighted to learn that his brother, Duke Frederick, has had a moral conversion and that he will be given back his dukedom. Although he has enjoyed his exile in the forest, he looks forward to returning to court.

Duke Frederick

Duke Frederick, the younger brother of Duke Senior, is a villainous man and one of the antagonists of the play. By usurping the ducal rights of his elder brother, he becomes a symbol of disorder, hatred, and hostility. He is also mainly responsible for driving the main characters into the forest of Arden, for he banishes both Duke Senior and Rosalind there. Towards the end of the play a sudden conversion takes place in him because of his encounter with a religious man. Although the sudden conversion seems a bit trite, it allows Shakespeare to create a happy ending for all the key characters, including Duke Frederick and Duke Senior.

Oliver

Oliver, the jealous older brother of Orlando, is another antagonist of the play. He deprives Orlando of the inheritance from his father and denies him the education that would make him a gentleman. In fact, he is so greedy and so jealous that he even tries to have Orlando killed. He instructs Charles to break his neck during the wrestling match. Oliver's attitude towards his brother changes when Orlando risks his own life to save Oliver from the lioness. Oliver begs for forgiveness, and the kind Orlando obliges. Oliver is further softened when he falls in love with Aliena. Wanting to marry her and stay in the forest, he promises to give his property and fortune to Orlando. At the end of the play, the two brothers are again united in familial love.

Touchstone

Although Touchstone is the court fool, he plays a very important part in the play. When asked by the girls, he eagerly accompanies Rosalind and Celia into exile. Amidst the freedom of the Forest of Arden, he is able to constantly display his wit, bringing a great deal of humour into the play. Although he originally gripes about his deprivations in the forest and longs to return to court, he changes his mind when he meets Audrey. Driven by sexual fantasies, Touchstone feels he is in love and decides he should marry Audrey. He tells her, "We must be married or we must live in bawdy." Touchstone justifies his choice of a wife to Duke Senior by saying, "An ill-favoured thing, Sir, but mine own." By the end of the play, Touchstone has truly emerged as the classic fool.

Analysis of Major Characters

Rosalind

Rosalind dominates *As You Like It*. So fully realised is she in the complexity of her emotions, the subtlety of her thought, and the fullness of her character that no one else in the play matches up to her. Orlando is handsome, strong, and an affectionate, if unskilled, poet, yet still we feel that Rosalind settles for someone slightly less magnificent when she chooses him as her mate. Similarly, the observations of Touchstone and

Jaques, who might shine more brightly in another play, seem rather dull whenever Rosalind takes the stage.

The endless appeal of watching Rosalind has much to do with her success as a knowledgeable and charming critic of herself and others. But unlike Jaques, who refuses to participate wholly in life but has much to say about the foolishness of those who surround him, Rosalind gives herself over fully to circumstance. She chastises Silvius for his irrational devotion to Phoebe, and she challenges Orlando's thoughtless equation of Rosalind with a Platonic ideal, but still she comes undone by her lover's inconsequential tardiness and faints at the sight of his blood. That Rosalind can play both sides of any field makes her identifiable to nearly everyone, and so, irresistible.

Rosalind is a particular favourite among feminist critics, who admire her ability to subvert the limitations that society imposes on her as a woman. With boldness and imagination, she disguises herself as a young man for the majority of the play in order to woo the man she loves and instruct him in how to be a more accomplished, attentive lover—a tutorship that would not be welcome from a woman. There is endless comic appeal in Rosalind's lampooning of the conventions of both male and female behaviour, but an Elizabethan audience might have felt a certain amount of anxiety regarding her behaviour. After all, the structure of a male-dominated society depends upon both men and women acting in their assigned roles. Thus, in the end, Rosalind dispenses with the charade of her own character. Her emergence as an actor in the Epilogue assures that theatergoers, like the Ardenne foresters, are about to exit a somewhat enchanted realm and return to the familiar world they left behind. But because they leave having learned the same lessons from Rosalind, they do so with the same potential to make that world a less punishing place.

Orlando

According to his brother, Oliver, Orlando is of noble character, unschooled yet somehow learned, full of noble purposes, and loved by people of all ranks as if he had enchanted them (I.i.141–144). Although this description comes from the one character who hates Orlando and wishes him harm, it is an apt and generous picture of the hero of *As You Like It.* Orlando has a brave and generous spirit, though he does not possess Rosalind's wit and insight. As his love tutorial shows, he relies on commonplace clichés in matters of love, declaring that without the fair Rosalind, he would die. He does have a decent wit, however, as he demonstrates when he argues with Jaques, suggesting that Jaques should seek out a fool who wanders about the forest: "He is drowned in the brook. Look but in, and you shall see him," meaning that Jaques will see a fool in his own reflection (III.ii.262–263). But next to Rosalind, Orlando's imagination burns a bit less bright. This upstaging is no fault of Orlando's, given the fullness of Rosalind's character; Shakespeare clearly intends his audience to delight in the match. Time and again, Orlando performs tasks that reveal his nobility and demonstrate why he is so well-loved: he travels with the ancient Adam and makes a fool out of himself to secure the old man food; he risks his life to save the brother who has plotted against him; he cannot help but violate the many trees of Ardenne with testaments of his love for Rosalind. In the beginning of the play, he laments that his brother has denied him the schooling deserved by a gentleman, but by the end, he has proven himself a gentleman without the formality of that education.

Jaques

Jaques delights in being sad—a disparate role in a play that so delights in happiness. Jaques believes that his melancholy makes him the perfect candidate to be Duke Senior's fool. Such a position, he claims, will "Give me leave / To speak my mind," and the criticism that flows forth will "Cleanse the foul body of th'infected world" (II.vii.58–60). Duke Senior is rightly cautious about installing Jaques as the fool, fearing that Jaques would do little more than excoriate the sins that Jaques himself has committed. Indeed, Jaques lacks the keenness of insight of Shakespeare's most accomplished jesters: he is not as penetrating as *Twelfth Night*'s Feste or *King Lear*'s fool. In fact, he is more like an aspiring fool than a professional one. When Jaques philosophises on the seven stages of human life, for instance, his musings strike us as banal. His "All the world's a stage" speech is famous today, but the play itself casts doubt on the ideas expressed in this speech (II.vii.138). No sooner does Jaques insist that man spends the final stages of his life in "mere oblivion, / Sans teeth, sans eyes, sans taste, sans everything" than Orlando's aged servant, Adam, enters, bearing with him his loyalty, his incomparable service, and his undiminished integrity (II.vii.164–165).

Jaques's own faculties as a critic of the goings-on around him are considerably diminished in comparison to Rosalind, who understands so much more and conveys her understanding with superior grace and charm. Rosalind criticizes in order to transform the world—to make Orlando a more reasonable husband and Phoebe a less disdainful lover—whereas Jaques is content to stew in his own melancholy. It is appropriate that Jaques decides not to return to court. While the other characters merrily revel, Jaques determines that he will follow the reformed Duke Frederick into the monastery, where he believes the converts have much to teach him. Jaques's refusal to resume life in the dukedom not only confirms our impression of his character, but also resonates with larger issues in the play. Here, the play makes good on the promise of its title: everyone gets just what he or she wants. It also betrays a small but inevitable crack in the community that dances through the forest. In a world as complex and full of so many competing forces as the one portrayed in *As You Like It,* the absolute best one can hope for is consensus, but never complete unanimity.

Chapter 14

Chapter Wise Summary

Act I, Scene 1

Summary

The opening scene of the play is set in the orchard of Oliver. He is the eldest of the three sons of the late Sir Rowland De Boys; his brothers are Jaques and Orlando. As the play opens, Orlando is complaining to Adam, his old faithful servant, about the unfair treatment meted out to him by his oldest brother, Oliver. Orlando says that his late father left a thousand crowns to be used for his education. Although Oliver pays for the education of the middle brother, Jaques, he has refused to pay for Orlando's education. Instead, he keeps him "rustically at home" in a near poor condition.

When Oliver enters, Orlando accosts him, almost violently. He demands that he be educated like a gentleman or else be given the inheritance left by Sir Rowland. Oliver grudgingly promises to give him the money. He then rudely orders Orlando and Adam out of his sight. Alone, Oliver contemplates getting rid of Orlando without giving him his inheritance.

Dennis, Oliver's servant, enters and informs his master that Charles, Duke Frederick's wrestler, has arrived. When Charles is shown in, he and Oliver discuss the affairs of the court. It is learned that Duke Senior has been banished by Duke Frederick, his younger brother. Supposedly, Duke Senior and some of his lords are living in the Forest of Arden, where they behave like Robin Hood and his band of merry men. Duke Senior's daughter, Rosalind, has not been allowed to accompany her father to the forest, because Duke Frederick's daughter, Celia, is fond of Rosalind's company.

The conversation shifts to the wrestling match that is to take place the next day. Charles tells Oliver that it is rumored that Orlando will wrestle with him. Charles is worried that Orlando will be injured and tells Oliver that he should try to dissuade Orlando from participating in the match. The wicked Oliver paints a horrible and untrue picture of his youngest brother and urges Charles to break Orlando's neck. Charles agrees to do his best.

The scene ends with a short soliloquy by Oliver in which he expresses the real reason for his hatred of Orlando. He is terribly jealous of Orlando's many noble qualities and fears that the people love his younger brother more than himself.

Notes

Shakespeare's masterful first scene serves as an introduction to the plot and the major characters of the play. It is quickly established in their argument with each other that there is a deep conflict between Orlando, the noble youngest son of Sir Rowland, and Oliver, the greedy and wicked oldest son. Oliver has refused to give his youngest brother his fair share of the inheritance, which was intended for Orlando's education. When Orlando demands the money or an education, Oliver thinks about doing away with his brother, for he does not want to part with the money and is also very jealous of Orlando. When he learns that Orlando is planning to wrestle with Charles, the Duke's chosen fighter, he urges Charles to break Orlando's neck or kill him. The dull-witted Charles agrees to do his best. It is also learned, through conversation, that there is a deep and similar conflict between Duke Frederick and his older brother, Duke Senior. Frederick, greedy and power hungry, has banished his brother and stolen his dukedom.

It is obvious that Shakespeare totally disapproves of the banishment of Duke Senior by his younger brother and of the mistreatment of Orlando by Oliver. Through these brotherly rivalries, Shakespeare is pointing out that hatred and hostility have erroneously taken the place of love, which should unite a family. As a result, life in this play has been thrown into disorder. Ironically, the disarray occurs in the court, which should be well ordered and unified. In contrast, the natural world of the Forest of Arden, characterised by freedom and a lack of rules, appears unified and filled with love. The banished duke enjoys life there, surrounded by admirers. Shakespeare even compares him to Robin Hood and his band of merry men. It is clear that the dramatist prefers the simplicity of country life over the sophisticated and unnatural life found in the court.

In sharp contrast to the relationship of the two sets of brothers in this first scene is the intimacy between two cousins, Rosalind and Celia. Although neither girl is seen on stage during this opening scene, it is revealed that "never two ladies loved as they do." As a result, Rosalind has stayed in court, even though her father, Duke Senior, has been banished, for Celia could not live without her.

Act I, Scene 2

Summary

This scene is set on the lawn outside Duke Frederick's palace, where Rosalind and Celia are conversing with one another. Celia is attempting to cheer up Rosalind, who is saddened by her father's banishment. She assures Rosalind that when she inherits the dukedom from her father, Duke Frederick, she will restore to Rosalind everything that has been wrongly taken away. Moved by Celia's love, Rosalind promises to be more cheerful. She then changes the subject and talks first of falling in love, even just for sport. After switching the conversation again to blind fortune, the girls are interrupted by the arrival of Touchstone, the court fool. After informing Celia that her father has sent for her, he enters into a witty conversation with the girl. They are then interrupted by Le Beau, one of Duke Frederick's courtiers. He tells the ladies that they have missed several good wrestling matches. Charles has already defeated three opponents, leaving them with broken ribs. The last match is about to take place on the lawn nearby; it will be between Charles and Orlando.

Duke Frederick enters with his lords to watch the last wrestling match. When Charles and Orlando take their places, the Duke feels that the odds are unfairly against Orlando. He asks the ladies to persuade him to withdraw from the match. Rosalind and Celia try to talk Orlando out of fighting, telling him that he is too young and no match for Charles. Orlando, however, insists on wrestling, for he does not care if he gets hurt. He tells Rosalind and Celia, "In the world I fill up a place, which may be better supplied when I have made it empty."

To everyone's amazement, Orlando defeats Charles. Duke Frederick congratulates the young man, but when he finds out that Orlando is the son of Sir Rowland de Boys, his mood changes. Since Sir Rowland was his enemy, he has no use for Orlando and departs. Celia is ashamed of the way in which her father has behaved; she tries to make up for his rudeness by encouraging Orlando.

Rosalind is happy to learn about Orlando's parentage, for her own father, Duke Senior, loved Sir Rowland. She also seems to be smitten by the young man. She warmly congratulates Orlando, presents him with a necklace, and comments that he has overthrown more than his enemy. Obviously, it is a case of love at first sight. After they converse, Rosalind departs and Orlando admits that he is hopelessly in love with her.

Le Beau comes to advise Orlando to flee from the court for the capricious Duke is ill-disposed towards him. Orlando also learns from Le Beau that the Duke's malice against Rosalind may break forth at any moment, for he is displeased with the way people praise her for her virtues.

Notes

The second scene brings the cousins, Celia and Rosalind, on the stage. The dialogue between the two confirms that they are charming and bound in close affection. Although neither young lady receives a central focus in the scene, before long it will be obvious that Rosalind is much more important to the play. In fact, before the delightful Rosalind, the figure of Celia pales almost into insignificance. Celia, however, is entertaining. When Touchstone, the court fool, enters, the two of them enter into a lively conversation. It is obvious that both of them are full of wit.

Celia is also a realist. She has no illusions about the wickedness of her father, Duke Frederick. As a result, it is easy for her to decide to leave with Rosalind for the forest when she is banished. Their devotion to each other emphasizes the importance of family love. Additionally, romantic love is introduced when Rosalind talks about falling in love for sport.

Ironically, the wrestling match further develops the theme of love. When Orlando defeats Charles in front of Rosalind, she is smitten by the charming young man. With a play on words, Rosalind tells Orlando that he has "overthrown" more than Charles. In romantic comedies, it is often the woman who initiates a love affair, as does Rosalind in this scene. It is also ironic that Rosalind has recently spoken about falling in love as a sport, but now she has fallen in love in earnest. Orlando is equally enamored with her; he admits to himself that he is also overthrown by Rosalind. It is love at first sight for both of them.

The theme of hatred is also further developed in the scene. At first Duke Frederick is charmed by Orlando; however, his attitude towards him changes when he finds out that he is the son of the deceased Sir Rowland, a man that he hated. It is also learned that the duke is jealous of Rosalind's noble qualities and popularity. As a result, he is planning on banishing her.

Shakespeare's masterful abilities as a playwright become obvious in this scene. He carefully balances the theme of love with the theme of hatred. He also masterfully develops the plot, drawing the key characters into the action at the appropriate time. He places Rosalind and Celia outside on the lawn so they will be nearby when the wrestling match between Charles and Orlando begins. As soon as the crowd gathers at the match, the two ladies are in a position to be drawn towards it.

Shakespeare also shows his mastery of handling important information through conversation. It is reported that Charles has already had three wrestling matches. Since it would be tedious to show all of them on stage, the outcome of the matches is merely relayed by LeBeau. It is further learned that Charles has injured each of his opponents. Such news is intended to build suspense in the audience, who is made to wonder if he might indeed injure Orlando - or even kill him as Oliver has requested. The scene brings into sharp focus the capricious and ruthless nature of Duke Frederick. He is displeased with Rosalind because people praise her for her virtues. This is strikingly similar to the reason for which Orlando is hated by his brother. Oliver hates him for his noble qualities and for the way in which he is loved by all, just as Frederick resents Rosalind.

It is important to notice Orlando's mental frame of mind in this scene. Upset with his brother and his plight, he tells Rosalind and Celia that he is merely taking up space on earth and hints that the world would be better without him. Once he falls in love with Rosalind, however, his mood will be drastically altered, again proving the importance and value of love.

Act I, Scene 3

Summary

In one of the rooms in the duke's palace, Rosalind and Celia are seen in conversation. Celia is surprised at the immediacy and intensity of her cousin's passion for Orlando. She advises her to slow down and take charge of herself. Their conversation is interrupted by Duke Frederick, who enters to tell Rosalind that she must leave the court. Rosalind demands to know the reason. He calls her a traitor, to which Rosalind responds that his mistrust of her does not make her a traitor. Additionally, Celia vigourously defends her cousin to her father, but it is to no avail. The duke is determined to be rid of Rosalind and tells her that she must be prepared to die if she stays at court.

Celia, ever faithful to Rosalind, insists on going with her to the Forest of Arden. Since it is not wise for two young beautiful girls to travel alone through the forest, they decide to disguise themselves. Since Rosalind is taller than the average woman, she will disguise herself as a man and call herself Ganymede. Celia will wear the clothes of a country maid and call herself Aliena. Rosalind suggests that they ask Touchstone to accompany them. Celia agrees and says that she is certain that Touchstone will oblige them if he is asked.

Notes

The scene brings out the intensity of Rosalind's love for Orlando. She tells Celia that she is helplessly smitten by him, even though she has only just met him. Part of the reason she is attracted to him is because her own father, Duke Senior, loved his deceased father, Sir Rowland. Celia advises her to slow down and be less emotional.

There is a fine example of dramatic irony in the scene, for the audience already knows from Le Beau's report that Duke Frederick is ill-disposed towards Rosalind. As a result, the audience is not terribly surprised when the duke interrupts the ladies and tells Rosalind that she must leave the court immediately. Celia insists upon going to the Forest of Arden with her, and from this point forward in the play, the forest will be the setting for all the action. Shakespeare will show it to be a much more free and pleasant place than the court.

Celia and Rosalind prove that they are not unthinking scatterbrains in this scene. First, Rosalind challenges the duke's banishment, questioning about his reasons. When he claims she is a traitor, Rosalind is not afraid to stand up to him. In making their travel plans, both Rosalind and Celia prove their rationality. Because they know it could be dangerous to travel alone as two beautiful young women, they decide to disguise themselves; Rosalind will dress as a young man, and Celia as a country maid. Their disguises will complicate the plot later in the play.

The decision of the girls to take Touchstone with them is significant. First, it again proves their rationality, for they trust him as a chaperone. More importantly, it keeps the fool in the middle of the action to comment on the affairs of men and the state of society. It also puts him in a place to fall in love with Audrey and to exercise his wit. Shakespeare's decision to have Rosalind take on the name of Ganymede is also significant. Ganymede is a mythic Greek youth whose boyish good looks made him a favourite of the Greek gods. In the Renaissance, Ganymede is used in poetry and drama as a symbol of same-sex love. Later in the play, other young men will be attracted to Ganymede.

Act II, Scene 1

Summary

In this scene, the action of the play moves into the pastoral setting of the Forest of Arden. In the beginning, Duke Senior, seen in the company of Amiens and some other lords, reveals that he is leading a life of simplicity and contentment. He addresses the lords as his "co-mates and brothers in exile" and tells them that their present condition is sweeter than the pomp of the court. Amiens admires the duke's capacity to see the bright side of an adverse situation.

When the duke suggests that they go hunting, one of the lords tries to dissuade him. He says that the melancholy Jaques, another of the lords, feels that Duke Senior is a greater usurper than his brother, Duke Frederick. While Frederick has usurped the dukedom, Duke Senior has usurped the natural habitat of animals, like the deer. The lord tells how Jaques has seen a wounded deer, which seemed to be weeping by a brook. Then a herd of deer passes by the wounded one without stopping in concern. Jaques compares the herd of deer to a group of fat, wealthy citizens who would also pass by, failing to take notice of the poor and broken.

After listening to the report on Jaques' philosophy, Duke Senior asks that he be taken to where Jaques is located. He always enjoys the lord when he is in his melancholy mood, for his talk is always engaging.

Notes

Although this scene contains no real action, it serves as a transition from the court setting to the Forest of Arden. Duke Senior is leading a life of contentment in the forest; he is delighted to be away from the envy, flattery, and falsehood of the court. He says that in the forest, he finds "books in the running brooks, sermons in the stones, and good in everything." Through the duke, Shakespeare begins to show how the forest charms people into a better, more carefree life. All of the characters who come to Arden from the city will meet with happier of times.

Jaques is also introduced in this scene, although he does not appear on stage. One of the lords tells how Jaques has seen a wounded deer, standing by the brook and seeming to weep. The upset Jaques believes that Duke Senior, with help from his lords, has usurped the natural environment of the forest animals, like the deer. Jaques is also distraught by the fact that a herd of deer passes by the wounded one without stopping to help; he compares the herd to wealthy men, who would never stop to help a poor or broken human being. It is obvious that Jaques is a sentimental moralizer, who seems out of place in the Forest of Arden; ironically, Duke Senior enjoys arguing with the melancholy man and asks to be taken to Jaques.

Act II, Scene 2

Summary

This short scene takes the audience back to the Palace of Duke Frederick. The duke is angry, for he has learned that Celia and Touchstone are missing. He fears that they have left with Rosalind. One of the lords enters to report that the gentlewoman who had attended Rosalind and Celia overhead their praises of Orlando and believes that he has joined the women. This information increases the duke's anger. He orders that Orlando be quickly found and brought to the court. If he is not found, Oliver, Orlando's brother, should be brought. Then the duke will make Oliver find Orlando. The Duke also orders speedy action to bring back Celia.

Notes

This scene is very brief, but it is tense and powerful. The duke's anger and tyranny is a sharp contrast to the happy, carefree mood of the previous scene, set in the Forest of Arden. It also serves to advance the plot, for the audience learns that Oliver will be sent into the forest to look for his missing brother, Orlando.

Act II, Scene 3

Summary

This scene, like the first one of the play, opens with Orlando in Oliver's orchard. Adam, the loyal servant, rushes towards him and begs his master to leave the house. He reports that Oliver is so full of jealousy that he wants to kill Orlando. Adam mourns that Orlando's virtues and graces, coupled with his victory at the wrestling match, have become his enemies, leading him to death.

Orlando is stunned at the news. He tells Adam that he has no place to go and no money to support himself since he refuses to beg or rob. Adam then spontaneously and generously offers Orlando the five hundred crowns he has saved from his salary. After handing over his life's savings that were to support him when he is too old to work, Adam volunteers to follow Orlando. He claims that he is still strong, even though he is old. Orlando is deeply moved by this generous gesture of Adam. Together the two of them leave the orchard; although they do not state that they are headed for the Forest of Arden, the audience assumes this is where they will go.

Notes

The scene brings out the evil and jealous intentions of Oliver and contrasts them to the goodness and virtue of Orlando and Adam. Although Adam is a lowly servant, he proves that he is much more noble than anyone in Frederick's court, including the duke. He is willing to give his life's savings to his master, while Oliver wants to kill Orlando out of sibling jealousy.

Act II, Scene 4

Summary

The disguised Rosalind and Celia, accompanied by Touchstone, have arrived in the Forest of Arden. All three of them are tired, but the girls feel energised by the pastoral setting. In contrast, Touchstone says that he feels more a fool in the forest and would like to be back at court.

The girls spy two shepherds, Corin and Silvius, and learn that Silvius is in love with Phebe, who scorns him. When Silvius complains that Corin cannot understand the intensity of his love, Corin reminds him that he had also been in love when he was young; now, however, he has no used for romantic fantasies. Rosalind sympathises with the agony experienced by Silvius, for she herself is agonised by her love for Orlando. After humourously telling how he has also been in love, Touchstone says that being in love is folly.

Rosalind tells Corin that she and Celia are in need of food and lodging. He explains that the cottage of his master is now for sale, along with the pastures. Rosalind suggests that Corin should bargain with the master, and she will pay for the cottage with the gold they have brought with them. Corin agrees to help.

Notes

In this scene, Rosalind comes to the forefront and takes charge. She states that she feels energised by the pastoral setting and by her man's clothing. She comforts and encourages Celia and makes arrangements with Corin to purchase a cottage for she and Celia to stay in.

Corin and Silvius, two shepherds, are stock figures out of a pastoral romance, but Shakespeare uses them to advance his theme of love. When Silvius talks of love, Coring, the old shepherd, reminds the young man that he too had been in love when he was younger, which emphasises the universality of love. At present, Silvius is madly in love with Phebe, but she scorns him. Rosalind quickly identifies with the young shepherd, for she also feels frustrated in her love for Orlando. Only Touchstone, the fool, dares to laugh at love, just as he derides forest life.

This scene also addresses the fact that people must be realistic, even in the romantic setting of the Forest of Arden. Rosalind understands that she and Celia need to find shelter and food. It is her motivation for engaging the shepherds in conversation. She is relieved to learn that Corin's master has his cottage up for sale. She easily persuades the old shepherd to purchase it for them, with gold that the girls have brought along. She also offers Corin a job that will pay him more than he is currently making.

Act II, Scene 5

Summary

Jaques, Amiens, and several lords are seated in the forest, near the cave of Duke Senior. Amiens is singing a song, which begins with "under the greenwood trees." He warns Jaques that the song will make him more melancholy. Jaques, however, is pleased that he will be able to "suck melancholy out of a song as a weasel sucks eggs." Jaques also reveals that he has been avoiding Duke Senior, for he feels the duke is too argumentative, an ironic statement coming from the man who thrives on argument. When the singing is over and Jaques lays down to rest, Amiens departs to go and bring the duke. The others begin to prepare a meal, which will be eaten by the duke and the lords.

Notes

This is another pleasant, pastoral scene set in the Forest of Arden. Amiens and several lords sit under the trees and sing. The words of the song emphasize the loveliness and cleanliness of the country in comparison to the city, which is filled with corruption; the song further underscores a theme that Shakespeare has already introduced and emphasized. The singing also makes the play seem more like a masque, which emphasizes a pastoral setting, quickly changing scenes, and the importance of music and/or dance.

In addition, the scene gives more information about the character of Jaques. He is an argumentative man, who never sees good in anything or anybody. He also believes that he is very intelligent and that his arguments are important and enlightening. The audience is led to judge him for what he is: a melancholic moralizer with misplaced self-importance. It also becomes obvious that Jaques' melancholy has been intentionally assumed and developed by him, rather than being caused by some trauma in his life. When he adds a verse to Amiens's romantic tune, it is appropriately filled with realism and scorn about country life. Ironically, at the end of the play, Jaques will remain in the forest, while the others return to court.

Act II, Scene 6

Summary

As expected, Orlando and Adam arrive in the Forest of Arden. Adam, weak with hunger, has nearly fainted. As a result, the master carries him and props him up against a tree. Orlando urges Adam not to die before he returns. He then departs to search for food.

Notess

This scene again introduces a realistic element to the romantic setting in the forest. Adam is weak with hunger, and Orlando fears he is close to death. After making the old man as comfortable as possible, Orlando departs to search for food. The scene also emphasizes the closeness between Adam and Orlando. When the old man grows weak, Orlando carries him, even though he is the master. He seems pleased to be able to return the kindness that Adam has shown to him. Orlando truly shows that he is a noble, but gentle, young man.

Act II, Scene 7

Summary

Once again the scene is set near the cave of Duke Senior, where a meal of fruit and wine has been set under the trees. The duke is waiting for Jaques, who soon arrives in an excited state. He has met a fool in the forest and has found him to be entertaining. He admits that he always admires and envies a fool for his freedom to articulate what he wishes and to criticize whomsoever he pleases.

Suddenly, Orlando rushes onto the scene with a drawn sword. He is in search of food for Adam and is ready to fight for it. He demands that no one eat what is before them until he receives provisions. The duke tells him that desperation has driven Orlando to ill-manners and reminds him that gentleness is always more persuasive. Then he kindly asks Orlando to dine with them.

Orlando apologises for his behaviour and tells the Duke that his faithful servant must be served before he can eat. When the duke tells Orlando to bring the servant, Orlando departs. While they wait for Orlando's return, Jaques describes the seven ages of man, from infancy to old age. He states that all the world is a stage, and all men and women play the seven ages of life upon it.

Orlando returns, carrying Adam in his arms. The servant, after thanking the duke for his hospitality, is eager to eat. As everyone dines, Amiens sings, "Blow, blow thou winter wind." The duke converses with Orlando and is happy to learn that he is the son of Sir Rowland. He offers for Orlando and Adam to join his merry band of followers.

Notes

By this point in the play, all the key characters are in the Forest of Arden, including Orlando, Rosalind, Celia, Touchstone, and Duke Senior. Now Shakespeare must gradually bring them all together from their scattered locations. This scene marks the beginning of the convergence. Jaques' enjoyable meeting with the fool (obviously Touchstone) puts the duke's party in touch with Rosalind's party. It is not surprising that Jaques found Touchstone amusing, for he is not deep enough himself to realise the fool was making fun of him.

Orlando's desperate search for food to revive Adam also joins him with the duke's party. When he enters with drawn sword and demands provisions, the duke chides Orlando for his lack of manners. Orlando apologises and states that his distress over Adam has caused his rudeness.

The famous lines related to the seven ages of man occur in this scene. Almost every student of literature has learned, "All the world's a stage! And all the men and women merely players;" it is one of Shakespeare's most famous quotes. The explanations of the stages, spoken by Jaques, are basically filler, intended to occupy the time when the Duke is waiting for Orlando to return with Adam. The words of Jaques' speech, however, are imaginative and filled with imagery. He describes the "mewling and puking" infant, the whining schoolboy who does not want to go to class, the lover "sighing like a furnace," the soldier "full of strange oaths...and quick in quarrel," the justice with his "round belly...and eyes severe," the dotard "turning again toward childish," and the senile, sick elder "sans teeth, sans eyes, sans taste, sans everything."

When Orlando returns with Adam, it is ironic that the servant is more well-mannered than his master. Although he is starving, Adam takes the time to greet and thank the duke for his hospitality before he begins to eat. During the meal, Amiens entertains with song. Although the words, "Blow, blow thou winter wind," portray the harsher side of nature, the music adds to the carefree nature of the forest, where friends are gathered to enjoy a casual meal.

Act III, Scene 1

Summary

This scene returns to a room in the Duke Frederick's Palace. The duke has summoned Oliver to interrogate him about the whereabouts of Orlando. He refuses to believe Oliver when he says he has not seen his brother and demands that he produce Orlando dead or alive within a year; during his absence, the duke will hold Oliver's property. However, if Oliver does not succeed in finding his brother, he need not come back to live in the dukedom.

When Oliver explains to the duke that he has never loved his brother and has attempted to have him killed, the duke reacts violently. He calls Oliver a villain, throws him out, and orders the confiscation of his property.

Notes

In this scene, Oliver gets his just reward for the treatment he has meted out to his brother. Even though Duke Frederick is upset with Orlando and wants to punish him, he is shocked to learn how Oliver has behaved towards his brother. When the duke finds out that Oliver has attempted to have Orlando killed, he banishes Oliver from the dukedom and confiscates his land. Now that he is homeless, the audience assumes that Oliver will head toward the Forest of Arden, like the others.

Duke Frederick's criticism of Oliver is totally ironic. When he calls Oliver a villain who has not bothered to love his brother, he is really describing himself, for he has seized the dukedom from Duke Senior, his older brother, and banished him to the forest.

Act III, Scene 2

Summary

This long scene is again set in the Forest of Arden and shows all the major characters. It opens with the love-sick Orlando. He has been writing verses about Rosalind, which he hangs in the trees. He also carves her name into the bark.

Corin and Touchstone are seen walking through the forest while they discuss the advantages and disadvantages of court life vs. country life. The fool makes long speeches in which he constantly contradicts himself. Corin, an uneducated man of the forest, is almost as foolish as Touchstone. He states that his greatest pride is to see his "ewes graze" and his "lambs suck." Touchstone argues that it is sinful to make a living by the copulation of cattle. The two men are interrupted by Rosalind, disguised as Ganymede. She plucks and reads one of the verses that Orlando has hung in a tree. Touchstone mocks the mediocre quality of the verses, saying that the tree has yielded bad fruit. As Touchstone departs with Corin, Celia joins Rosalind.

Celia comments on the fact that Rosalind's name is found in all the verses hanging in the trees. Rosalind begs her friend to reveal the identity of the author of these verses. After a good bit of teasing, Celia reveals that Orlando has written the poetry. Swooning over Orlando, Rosalind immediately regrets her man's attire and wants to know where she can find the man of her dreams. Celia tells Rosalind that she has seen Orlando lying under a tree like a dropped acorn or a wounded knight.

As Celia and Rosalind are talking, Orlando and Jaques come through the trees. The girls hide themselves from view, but stay close enough to overhear the conversation between the two men. Jaques insults Orlando, telling him not to spoil trees with his verses. Orlando retorts by telling Jaques not to mar his verses by reading them badly. Jaques comments that he does not like the name Rosalind. Orlando snaps back that there was no plan to please the fool when she was christened. Jaques further insults Orlando by saying he was looking for a fool when he found him. Orlando tells the fool he needs to look into the brook to find a fool, for there he will see his own reflection. After their verbal volley, Jaques seems happy to part company with Orlando.

Rosalind, still disguised as Ganymede, comes out of hiding after Jaques leaves and enters into conversation with Orlando. Of course, he cannot recognise her. When she inquires what time it is, he says that there are no clocks in the forest. Rosalind responds with a challenge: "Then there is no true lover in the forest," for if there was one he would want to sigh every minute with the movement of the clock. Rosalind then comments on time in general; she says that time trots with a young man, ambles with an ill-learned priest and a rich man, gallops with a thief, and stays with lawyers in the vacation. Rosalind then changes the subject. She tells how there is a man who haunts the forest abusing trees by carving the name of Rosalind into the bark. She says if she meets him, she plans to cure him of his love malady, for she has cured others of love sickness

When Orlando admits that he is the guilty party, Rosalind pretends not to believe it. She says that her uncle has taught her to identify a love-sick man, by his lean cheeks, somber eyes, neglected beard, ungaitered hose, unbuttoned sleeves, and untied shoes. She comments that Orlando has none of these characteristics. She accuses him of perhaps only loving himself.

Rosalind, still disguised as Ganymede, explains how she has cured other men of their love sickness. As a young boy, she would play the role of the mistress to the love sick man. Then Ganymede, behaving like an unpredictable woman, would rapidly change from grieving, to acting proud, to crying, to smiling. Such play acting usually cured the men of their emotions.

Orlando says that he does not want to be cured of his love, but Ganymede still tempts him. She asks Orlando to pretend that she is Rosalind; then he can practice pursuing and wooing her. Orlando agrees to try the scheme, still fully unaware that Ganymede is really Rosalind.

Notes

In this scene, the major characters are brought together; Rosalind, Celia, Orlando, Jaques, and Touchstone all interact. The theme of country vs. city life is also developed as Corin and Touchstone discuss the advantages and disadvantages of both sides. More importantly, the theme of love is advanced by Orlando and his poems, as well as his defence of love to Jaques. It is also advanced by Rosalind's teasing Orlando, while she is in disguise, about his love sickness.

Orlando's argument with Jaques is filled with wit and humour; it is a complete contrast to the romantic, emotional extremes of his poetry. In his verse, Orlando describes Rosalind as a semi-divine being, the embodiment of perfection. He states that she has the beauty of Helen of Troy, the dignified bearing of Cleopatra, the symmetry of form of Atlanta, and the virtue and honour of Lucretia. Jaques claims that the verses are spoiling the trees.

When Rosalind finds the poems and learns from Celia that they were written by Orlando, the man of her dreams, she is delighted. She is also concerned about the fact that she is disguised as a young man. With quick thought and action, she takes advantage of the situation by asking Orlando questions about his love and enjoying the thrill of hearing herself glorified. Moreover, she cleverly challenges him to imagine that Ganymede is Rosalind in order to practice wooing her. The purpose, obviously, is to please herself, but he is made to believe that it will be a cure for his love sickness. The love cure offered by Rosalind to Orlando is a form of make-believe, which is totally appropriate. Life in the Forest of Arden seems too good to be true, almost like make-believe.

Act III, Scene 3

Summary

This scene is set in another part of the forest, where Touchstone and Audrey are found together. They make an odd pair: the court fool and the dull, country wench. Although Touchstone finds her simple and naïve, he wants to marry her and is trying to persuade her to become his wife. He tells Audrey of his emotions for her, using exalted expressions, which she cannot possibly understand. When Touchstone wishes out loud that the gods had made her poetic, Audrey says that she does not know what poetic means. Touchstone, in his typical style, answers that the truest poetry is the most false one; the words have lots of meaning.

In the end, Audrey agrees to the marriage, and the couple sets out to find Vicar Martext, from the neighbouring village, who has agreed to perform the ceremony. Jaques, who has been following the couple, overhears their conversation. In an aside, he comments that Touchstone is a "material fool," even though he has succeeded in convincing Audrey to become his wife. When the Vicar arrives, Jacque agrees to give the bride away in order to make the marriage legal, but he admonishes Touchstone for getting married under a bush like a beggar instead of in a church. Touchstone retorts that it is best if he is not married well; then if the marriage does not work out, he can use it as an excuse to leave his wife. Jaques tells Touchstone he should wait to get married in order to make sure it is what he wants. Finally Touchstone agrees, and the wedding is postponed.

Notes

This humourous scene presents the unromantic side of love. Touchstone has neither love nor admiration for Audrey, a dull- witted country girl who does not know the meaning of poetic; but Touchstone wants to marry her quickly out of lust. He says, "We must be married, or we must live in bawdry." Before she becomes his wife, however, he thinks of eventually leaving her. When Jaques criticizes him for getting married outside under a bush, like a beggar, Touchstone says he can use that as an excuse for later deserting Audrey. The scene is intended to be humourous; it is also a sharp contrast to the permanent and romantic love of Orlando and Rosalind. Unlike Audrey and Touchstone, who are totally mismatched, Orlando and Rosalind are well suited for one another, both in background and in personality. Theirs will be a holy and permanent union, in contrast to the sexual one between Audrey and Touchstone.

Act III, Scene 4

Summary

This scene opens with Rosalind and Celia in the forest. Rosalind is highly disappointed and angry that Orlando has not kept his appointment with her for his "love cure." Celia teases her by making uncomplimentary comments about Orlando; she says his hair is probably "browner than Judas." When Rosalind wonders why he has not turned up after promising to come, Celia says, "There is no truth in him." Then becoming serious, Celia tells Rosalind that Orlando has probably been helping Duke Senior.

Rosalind tells how she has seen her father, the duke, but he failed to recognise her in disguise. When he asked about her parentage, she replied that her parentage was as good as his, causing the duke to laugh. Rosalind then says she would prefer to talk of Orlando, not of her father.

Corin enters and invites Celia and Rosalind to watch the scene between the love-sick Silvius and the disdainful Phebe. Rosalind readily agrees to go with Corin for "the sight of lovers feedeth those in love." She also decides to "prove a busy actor in their play."

Notes

This scene presents another side of Rosalind not seen before. When Orlando fails to come for his first love cure, the impatient Rosalind becomes irritated and angry. It is obvious she had been looking forward to his visit. Celia tries to calm her down by teasing her about Orlando, saying he is untruthful, much like a Judas. Her light-hearted humour lightens the entire mood of the scene. Then on a serious note, she reminds her friend that Orlando has been helping Duke Senior, Rosalind's father. Rosalind does not seem to care; she asks Celia, "Why talk we of fathers, when there is such a man as Orlando?"

Rosalind's attention is diverted by the arrival of Corin, who asks the two ladies to come and watch the love-sick scene between the eager Silvius and the disdainful Phebe. Rosalind is eager to watch any two lovers, hoping it will nourish her own love for Orlando. What she does not know is that the relationship between Silvius and Phebe is not at all romantic or emotional.

Act III, Scene 5

Summary

This scene opens with Silvius pleading with Phebe for her love; when she does not respond, he says she is more stern than an executioner. Phebe, who feels neither love nor pity for Silvius, then orders him not to come near her and mocks his suggestion that her eyes have wounded him. Rosalind and Celia, still in their disguises, have been listening to their exchange. Finally Rosalind can stand it no more; she advances towards the couple and admonishes Phebe for being proud and pitiless. She tells her that she cannot possibly hope for a better spouse than Silvius, especially since she is no beauty. In the end, she tells Phebe she should kneel before Silvius and accept his love. If Phebe refuses, she warns Silvius that he should not follow after her any longer, pleading for her love.

As Rosalind, dressed as Ganymede, lectures the couple, Phebe begins to flirt with "him," thinking him very attractive and calling him "sweet youth;" she even says she may be in love with Ganymede. A concerned Ganymede (really

Rosalind) warns Phebe not to fall in love with "him," for "he" is falser than vows made in wine.

Rosalind and Celia depart, leaving Phebe to dream about Ganymede. She decides she must write him a love note and have Silvius deliver it. She falsely tells Silvius that she is going to write a very angry letter to that peevish youth and hopes that he will deliver it for her. Silvius considers it an honour to do such a favour for his beloved.

Notes

Just as Rosalind felt snubbed by Orlando in the last scene, Silvius feels snubbed by Phebe in this one. As he tells her of his love and pleads for hers in return, Phebe tells him never to come near her. The sentiments of the wooing shepherd and the contempt of the woman he loves are intentionally exaggerated by Shakespeare to make a mockery of untrue love.

Rosalind, who has been watching the whole scene while still in disguise, cannot believe that Phebe is acting so callous and rude in matters of love. She interrupts the couple and pointedly tells the girl that she will never find a better husband than Silvius. She says she should kneel before him immediately and accept his love. Ironically, as "Ganymede" scolds Phebe, the country wench falls in love with the fair youth. It is humourous that she loves Gànymede, who calls her ugly, and scorns Silvius, who calls her sweet and beautiful. Shakespeare is pointing out that there is no logic in love, only emotion. A horrified Rosalind warns Phebe that Ganymede is false and cannot be trusted. She is also distressed that her efforts to make things better for Silvius have really made things worse.

Act IV, Scene 1

Summary

This scene is set in a clearing in the forest. Jaques and Rosalind (still disguised as Ganymede) are arguing about his melancholic attitude. He insists that his melancholy is special, not the "melancholy of a scholar's, which is emulation; nor the musician's, which is fantastical; nor the courtier's, which is proud; nor the soldier's, which is ambitious; nor the lawyer's which is politic; nor the lady's which is nice; nor the lover's which is all these." He further states that he has come by his melancholy through his many travels. Rosalind responds that a traveller has nothing much to show, other than rich eyes. He argues that his travels have given him a great deal of important experience. She answers that she would rather have a fool to make her merry than a man of experience to make her sad.

The banter between Rosalind and Jaques is interrupted by the arrival of Orlando, who has finally come for his appointment. When he greets Rosalind warmly, she pretends to take no note of him, acting angry about his tardiness. After Jaques leaves the scene, however, Rosalind turns to Orlando and rebukes him severely for being late. She reminds him that he should be acting like a true lover, who would never be tardy, even by a fraction of a minute, when calling on his lady love. She says he is worse than a snail, for at least a snail has an excuse for being slow, since it carries its house and its destiny on its back.

In order to practice how to woo the real Rosalind, Ganymede invites Orlando to woo "him." Ganymede inquires how Orlando would begin. He replies that he would kiss Rosalind before speaking to her. Ganymede says that he should speak first and when there is nothing else to talk about, he should then kiss Rosalind. Ganymede asks Orlando what he would do if Rosalind rejected him. Orlando replies that he would die. Rosalind contradicts him, stating that men do not die from love.

Orlando asks Ganymede if he would love him if he were Rosalind. Ganymede replies, "Ay, Twenty such." When Orlando says he is bewildered by this response, Ganymede says that one cannot "desire too much of a good thing." Ganymede then asks Celia to pretend to be a priest and conduct a mock wedding. After the exchange of vows, Ganymede, now playing the part of Rosalind, demands to know how long Orlando would have her; he responds he would love her forever. Ganymede reminds him that men and women change after they are wed; he claims that he will probably become "more jealous than a Barbary Cock Pigeon, more clamorous than a Parrot." Ganymede also claims that Rosalind will probably weep when Orlando is merry and laugh when he wants to sleep.

After a while, Orlando says he must leave to help Duke Senior at lunchtime, but he promises to return in two hours. Before he leaves, Rosalind chides him severely, saying his departure is another indication of his not being a true lover. After he leaves, Celia rebukes Rosalind for criticizing womanhood to Orlando. She apologises and admits she is not thinking straight, for her head is filled with thoughts of true love. When he is out of sight, Rosalind says that life becomes impossible; therefore, she decides to go and chase Orlando's shadow.

Notes

The first part of this scene presents Rosalind and Jaques in an entertaining conversation. The meeting between the vivacious Rosalind and melancholy Jaques is like a meeting of sunshine and cloud. But Jaques' sad mood cannot cloud Rosalind's sunny wit, which comes shining through in this scene; she humourously mocks everything about Jaques — his travels, his experience, and his explanation of his melancholy. When Rosalind makes fun of Jaques' travels, Shakespeare is really ridiculing the Elizabethans' craze for going abroad, usually to Italy, the cradle of the Renaissance. Although Shakespeare's contemporaries claimed to be traveling to gain an education, they usually brought back more vices than culture.

The banter between Jaques and Rosalind is brought to an end by the arrival of the tardy Orlando, who has come for his love-sick treatment. The wooing scene is filled with dramatic irony, for everyone in the audience knows about Rosalind's disguise, while Orlando is in the dark. The whole scene is delightful to view or read, as Rosalind turns every moment into merriment and mockery. She comments on the transitory nature of love, the faithlessness of men, and the unpredictable and capricious nature of women. Underneath her wit, there is really great wisdom.

In the conversation, Rosalind says, "Men are April when they woo, December when they wed." While courting a woman, men show themselves at their best, full of lively spirit, politeness, and tenderness; however, when they get married, they become as serious and gloomy as the month of December. Like men, "Maids are May when they are maids, but the sky changes when they are wives." Before they marry, women are as cheerful and pleasing as the spring season, but their temperament changes for the worse after marriage. Rosalind, as Ganymede, admits that after she marries she will be more jealous than a Barbary cock-pigeon over his hen, more noisy than a parrot, more fond of the novel things than an ape, and more sensual than a monkey.

When Orlando goes to attend Duke Senior, promising to return in two hours, Celia scolds her friend for talking so negatively about women. Rosalind admits that she must sound foolish, for her head is filled only with thoughts of Orlando. Even though he has just left, she misses him so much that she decides to follow him.

Act IV, Scene 2

Summary

The scene is again set near the cave of Duke Senior, where several of the lords have gathered after they have been hunting. One of them has killed a deer, and Jaques suggests that he pretend to be a Roman conqueror and present the slaughtered creature to the duke. Following Jaques' suggestion, the lord who killed the deer is raised aloft by the rest. The others sing a song that glorifies the hunter and the horns worn by him. Since a horned man is a symbol of a cuckold (a man married to an unfaithful wife), the lords are really singing in jest and merriment.

Notes

This scene is a brief one that does not advance the action of the plot; instead, it is used to fill up the time while Orlando is away and to add humour to the play. The hunters are in a jolly mood and sing a racy song. Even the melancholy Jaques joins in the merriment. In an earlier scene, he was weeping over a wounded deer; now Jaques thinks that the hunter who killed the deer should be presented to the Duke like a victorious Roman general entering the city of Rome in triumph. He should wear the deer's horns as a symbol of his victory. The image of a horned man on stage was a source of comedy for the Elizabethans, for it symbolised a husband who was misused by his wife.

Act IV, Scene 3

Summary

This scene returns to Rosalind and Celia. As Rosalind impatiently waits for the return of Orlando, Celia teases that perhaps he has gone to sleep. Silvius enters, carrying Phebe's letter for Ganymede. Not knowing he has carried a love letter, Silvius warns that it is probably an angry criticism of Ganymede. Rosalind reads aloud the verses of love that Phebe has written. Poor Silvius is totally shocked. Rosalind chides him for his timidity and directs him to tell Phebe, "If she loves me, I charge her to love thee." Rosalind is trying to make the best of a bad situation.

After Silvius' exit, a stranger (Orlando's brother Oliver) hastily enters. He says that he has a message for Ganymede from Orlando and asks for directions to his cottage. Celia gives him the directions, but states that no one is there at present. Because of Orlando's description, Oliver guesses that he is speaking to Ganymede and begins to explain Orlando's absence. After Orlando parted from Ganymede, he found a man asleep in the forest, unaware that there was a snake near his neck. On seeing Orlando, the snake slithered away into a bush. Orlando approached the sleeping man and discovered that it was his brother, Oliver. He was happy to see him, even though Oliver had been cruel to him in the past.

The brothers were unaware that under the shade of the bush, there was a hungry lioness waiting for something to eat. To protect Oliver, the noble Orlando battled with the lioness. Although he overpowered the lioness, Orlando was wounded in the fight. After going back to the duke's cave, Orlando discovered that the lioness had torn apart his arm. Because of the loss of blood, Orlando fainted, and Oliver took care of his brother.

Oliver then reveals to Rosalind and Celia that he is Orlando's brother. Celia accuses him of trying to kill his brother. Oliver replies, "Twas I; but 'tis not I," implying that he is a changed man. Oliver explains that his brother has forgiven him and that everything is now harmonious between them. He then produces Orlando's bloody handkerchief and explains that his brother has asked him to bring it to Ganymede with an explanation of his absence.

Looking at the blood-stained handkerchief, Ganymede faints. When he recovers, Oliver comments that Ganymede lacks a man's heart. With characteristic presence of mind, Ganymede claims that he only pretended to faint, playing the role of Rosalind. Ganymede makes Oliver promise to tell Orlando how well the youth has acted the part. Because Oliver is shrewd, he senses that something is wrong about Ganymede's story

Notes

This scene can be divided into two sections. The first part deals with the ironic and humourous situation where Phebe makes Silvius carry her love message to Ganymede. When Silvius delivers the letter, he genuinely believes that it is probably an angry one, filled with criticism, and warns Ganymede about it. When the disguised Rosalind reads the love verses a loud, Silvius is embarrassed and shocked to learn the truth. The kind Ganymede tries to save the day. He sends a message to Phebe stating that in order to prove her love for Ganymede, Phebe must love Silvius.

In the second part of the scene, the focus is entirely on Oliver and his reconciliation with his brother, Orlando. Oliver comes on stage searching for Ganymede, for he has a message for the youth from his brother. When he realises he is talking to Ganymede, he tells about what has happened to Orlando. After finding his brother in the forest, Orlando saves him two different times. First he frightens away a snake that was about to strike the sleeping Oliver. Then he fights a lioness that was about to attack. Although Orlando was wounded in the battle, he was able to overpower the animal and save his brother and himself. Orlando is now resting in the duke's cave and has sent Oliver to explain what has happened and to give Ganymede the bloody handkerchief as proof. When Rosalind sees the handkerchief, she faints, almost giving away the fact that she is not a man; however, her quick thinking rescues her. When Oliver says she does not act like a man, she claims that she was only role- playing, acting as Rosalind would have done.

The outspoken Celia accuses Oliver of having tried to kill his brother in the past; he admits that it is true. Oliver then explains that he is a changed man; appropriately, the change has occurred in the Forest of Arden, far away from the pretentious court. As a result of Oliver's conversion, Orlando has forgiven him, and they have a new harmonious relationship. Oliver has seen the error of his ways and now recognises and praises the compassion and heroism of Orlando. When Rosalind hears her lover being praised, she loves Orlando even more.

There are several important things to notice about this scene. Orlando's being wounded in a battle with a lioness is only reported by Oliver. In Elizabethan times, it would have been impossible to act out such a battle on stage. Also it is important to notice that Shakespeare is foreshadowing the future relationship between Oliver and Celia. When Oliver asks a question, it is always Celia who answers, not Rosalind.

She is obviously attracted to the man. Finally it is important to notice that Rosalind is not always in control. When she looks at the bloody handkerchief, she does faint; however, as soon as she recovers, she is her old quick-witted self, making up a marvelous excuse about pretending to faint. Her explanation is filled with dramatic irony and humour.

Act V, Scene 1

Summary

This scene opens with Touchstone and Audrey on stage. Audrey is whining about the fact that their marriage has been delayed by Touchstone. He tries to change the conversation, asking her about the other young man who claims to love her. At that moment, William, the other young man, enters. Touchstone interrogates him about his age, upbringing, and education. Then with a pompous flurry of words, he threatens to kill William if he does not "abandon the society of this female." The poor country shepherd is thoroughly terrified and quickly departs. Corin then enters and tells them that the master and mistress (Ganymede and Aliena) have sent for them. Audrey and Touchstone rush towards their cottage.

Notes

This scene is filled with humour. As it opens, Audrey frets about her postponed wedding and fears she will never get Touchstone to the altar. Touchstone tries to change the subject by asking Audrey about the other young man who supposedly loves her. Then William himself enters, and Touchstone verbally attacks him. His use of exaggerated metaphors in threatening the poor shepherd is totally unwarranted and creates effective humour. The dull-witted Audrey, however, is impressed by Touchstone's performance.

It is obvious that Shakespeare intentionally creates the real country characters, like Audrey, William, and Corin, to be totally naïve and unsophisticated. They rarely speak, and when they do their sentences are short and terse. They are a complete contrast to the "foreigners" in the forest, like Orlando,

Rosalind, Celia, and Duke Senior, who are simply enamored with pastoral living, but retain the sophistication that they learned at court.

Act V, Scene 2

Summary

Oliver and Orlando (with a bandaged arm) are seated on a bank. Oliver tells his brother about his love for Aliena (Celia). Orlando is surprised at the suddenness of Oliver's emotions. Oliver tries to convince him of the seriousness of his love. He will hand over all the family property to Orlando, marry Aliena, and live forever in the forest with her.

When Ganymede arrives, Oliver greets him as "fair sister" and departs. Orlando tells the youth about Oliver's love for Aliena and reveals that Oliver is planning on marrying her the next day. Ganymede compares the suddenness of Oliver's emotions to the rapidity of Caesar, who "came, saw, and conquered." As he talks of his brother's impending marriage, Orlando expresses his longing to be united with Rosalind. Ganymede says that he can still play the part of Rosalind, but Orlando declines; he says, "I can live no longer by thinking." A clever Ganymede then claims to have trained with a magician since childhood. He promises to use his magic and produce the real Rosalind tomorrow. If Orlando finds that he still loves her, he can marry Rosalind at the same time that Oliver weds Aliena. Ganymede tells him to wear his best clothes the next day and be prepared for a wedding.

Silvius and Phebe enter. She is angry that Ganymede has read her letter to Silvius. Ganymede reminds her that Silvius is a much better choice of husband than he is and again suggests that Phebe reciprocate Silvius' love. Phebe insists that she loves only Ganymede, but he responds that he loves no woman.

Before the couple departs, Ganymede asks them to come to the forest the next day for a meeting, suggesting that Silvius may be able to marry Phebe at that time. Ganymede then turns to Phebe and makes her promise to marry Silvius if she finds a reason not to marry Ganymede. Phebe, thinking nothing will change her mind about Ganymede, agrees to the proposal.

Notes

The suddenness of Oliver's love for Aliena (Celia) surprises both Orlando and Rosalind; but they are both convinced that it is true love, for Oliver has agreed to give up his fortune and live in the forest with Aliena forever. It is ironic that Orlando and Rosalind should be surprised, for both of them fell in love with each other after only one meeting

Rosalind begins to work her magic in this scene to bring everyone together. After hearing that Oliver will wed Aliena the next day, she plans for several other people to be united at the same time. First she offers to produce Rosalind through her magician's power so that Orlando may marry her. Next she makes Phebe promise to marry Silvius if she finds a reason not to marry Ganymede; of course, Phebe will not want to marry "him" when she finds out Ganymede is a "her."

It is important to notice that Oliver calls Rosalind "fair sister," even though she is still disguised as the young man, Ganymede. Most critics believe that Oliver uses this greeting because he has seen through Rosalind's disguise. It is also possible that since Ganymede is playing Rosalind, Oliver addresses her as sister simply to humour both Ganymede and Orlando. It is also important to see the humour behind Ganymede's statement that he loves "no woman." Obviously, Rosalind is referencing the fact that as a female herself, she does not love another woman. However, the original Ganymede was homosexual and loved only men, "no women."

Act V, Scene 3

Summary

As the play opens, Touchstone and Audrey are discussing the fact that they are finally to be married the next day. Audrey is delighted, thinking she will become a real woman of the world. As they talk, two of Duke Senior's pages arrive, singing a merry song about "a lover and his lass." Always the fool, Touchstone, the anti- romantic, criticizes the song as being silly. He tells the singers to go and improve their voices.

Notes

The primary purpose of this scene is to set the stage for the finale of the play, in which all of the weddings will take place. Oliver and Aliena plan to wed tomorrow. In addition, Rosalind has orchestrated the marriage of Orlando and herself and the marriage of Phebe and Silvius. In this short scene, the audience learns that Touchstone and Audrey also plan to wed the next day.

It is appropriate that the pages arrive singing a beautiful love song about a lad and his lass; the words warn the young couple to seize the day and live for the moment, just as the key characters have learned to do in the pastoral setting. Throughout the play, Shakespeare has used music and song to symbolise the freedom of the forest and the beauty of love and romance. Touchstone, always the fool, objects to the music and sends the singers, telling them that they need to work on their voices.

Act V, Scene 5

Summary

Duke Senior, Orlando, Oliver, Celia and others are waiting in the forest for the Ganymede, who has claimed he will perform miracles and produce Rosalind. The duke asks Orlando if he believes the youth's promise; Orlando admits that he vacillates between hope and fear.

Rosalind, still disguised as Ganymede, enters with Silvius and Phebe. She immediately turns to her father, Duke Senior, and asks if he would allow his daughter to marry Orlando if she is indeed produced by magic. The duke assures her that he would be delighted to have Rosalind marry Orlando. He adds that if he had kingdoms to give, he would bestow them on Ganymede if he succeeds in producing Rosalind. She then turns to Orlando and asks if he would marry Rosalind. and he says he would. Then Phebe tells of her plans to marry Ganymede, but if she changes her mind, she will give herself to Silvius.

Having made all these bargains, Rosalind beckons to Celia, still disguised as Aliena, and the two of them leave the scene. After they exit, the duke confesses that there are some things about Ganymede that remind him of his own lively daughter. Orlando also says he can see some similarity.

Touchstone and Audrey arrive to be wed. Touchstone tells the duke that he has consented to marry the "poor virgin," for no other man will. Then at Jaques' prompting, Touchstone launches into a long account of the codes of quarreling. The duke comments that the fool uses his folly like a stalking horse and under the presentation of that he shoots his wit.

Rosalind and Celia enter without their disguises. They are accompanied by Hymen, the god of marriage. The duke, Orlando, and Phebe are wonderstruck at the sight of Rosalind. Hymen sings about the glory of marriage and greets the lovers who are to wed: Orlando and Rosalind, Oliver and Celia, Audrey and Touchstone. Upon realizing the truth about Ganymede, Phebe also decides to marry Silvius, as promised.

Jaques de Boys, the middle brother of Orlando and Oliver, makes his entry. He informs them that Duke Frederick, jealous of the flowering popularity of his brother, has set out for the forest of Arden with the purpose of killing Duke Senior. On the way, he has met an old religious man, who works a miracle and reforms him. The evil in Duke Frederick is truly gone. Because of his conversion, he has decided to restore the dukedom to his brother and return all confiscated properties back to the rightful owners.

Now there is more to celebrate than just the four marriages. Duke Senior welcomes the "good of our returned fortune." The play ends in happiness, with music and dancing. Even Jaques gives each set of newlyweds a good word of greeting.

Notes

The final scene ends in total happiness, with the resolution of all conflict. Rosalind sheds her disguise to reunite with her father and to wed Orlando. Oliver is delighted to find out that he is really marrying Celia instead of the poor Aliena. Phebe accepts that she cannot marry Ganymede, who is really a woman, and decides to wed Silvius instead. Touchstone and Audrey are also able to finally tie the knot. Amidst the wedding bells, the middle brother of Orlando and Oliver arrives to give more good news. Duke Frederick is a changed man and has decided to restore the dukedom to Duke Senior and return all confiscated lands to the rightful owners. The religious and moral conversion of Duke Frederick is totally contrived and hard to accept, but it allows Shakespeare to resolve all of the conflict in the play and tie up all of the loose ends.

The appearance of Hymen at the weddings is very significant. He is the advocate of marriage and procreation as the basic bonds of society. Shakespeare wanted to make it clear that he was not advocating free love in this romantic comedy; instead, like Hymen, he supports true love, commitment, and responsibility in marriage. It is also significant that Hymen sings about love. Music has been a motif throughout the play.

Although all of the happiness in the play has been brought about in the Forest of Arden, the visitors are now ready to return to life in the city. Duke Senior is particularly excited to get back his dukedom, and Oliver seems relieved that he is marrying a city girl rather than a poor country maiden, who would keep him in the forest. Only the melancholy Jaques will not be returning. He will inhabit the "abandoned cave" of Duke Senior. It is ironic that throughout most of the play, he criticized pastoral life, yet he is the only one from the city who chooses to remain in the Forest of Arden.

At the end of the play, there is music and dancing. In truth, the whole play has been a dance between characters. Shakespeare carefully developed the relationships between

Rosalind and Celia, between Rosalind and Duke Senior, between Rosalind and Orlando, between Celia and Oliver, between Oliver and

Orlando, between Audrey and Touchstone, and between Phebe and Silvius. The master of drama orchestrated these relationships with perfect harmony until the finale of the music is reached in the last scene of the play. As always, Shakespeare has created a masterpiece.

EPILOGUE

Summary

The epilogue of the play is spoken by Rosalind. She agrees that it is not in fashion for a lady to speak the epilogue but it is no more "unhandsome" than a lord speaking the prologue. She urges the women in the audience to show the love they have for men by applauding the play if they like it. She makes a similar exhortation to the men in the audience. If she were a woman, she would kiss as many men as pleased her. Saying so, she makes her curtsy and bids farewell.

Notes

The main purpose of the epilogue is to encourage applause from the audience. It also seems to throw some light on the title of the play itself. When Rosalind comes out and addresses the audience personally, she implies that the audience should applaud "as you like it." Since she feels that there is something in the play for everyone to like, she expects that the applause will be loud and strong.

It should be remembered that in Elizabethan times, Rosalind would really have been played by a young man, for women were not allowed to be actresses. As a result, the boy actor who spoke the epilogue was correct when he said that if he were a woman, he would kiss any man he pleased.

Chapter 15

Complete Text

Act I Scene I: Orchard of Oliver's House

Enter Orlando and Adam Orlando

As I remember, Adam, it was upon this fashion bequeathed me by will but poor a thousand crowns, and, as thou sayest, charged my brother, on his blessing, to breed me well: and there begins my sadness. My brother Jaques he keeps at school, and report speaks goldenly of his profit: for my part, he keeps me rustically at home, or, to speak more properly, stays me here at home unkept; for call you that keeping for a gentleman of my birth, that differs not from the stalling of an ox? His horses are bred better; for, besides that they are fair with their feeding, they are taught their manage, and to that end riders dearly hired: but I, his brother, gain nothing under him but growth; for the which his animals on his dunghills are as much bound to him as I. Besides this nothing that he so plentifully gives me, the something that nature gave me his countenance seems to take from me: he lets me feed with his hinds, bars me the place of a brother, and, as much as in him lies, mines my gentility with my education. This is it, Adam, that grieves me; and the spirit of my father, which I think is within me, begins to mutiny against this servitude: I will no longer endure it, though yet I know no wise remedy how to avoid it.

Adam: Yonder comes my master, your brother.

Orlando: Go apart, Adam, and thou shalt hear how he will shake me up.

Enter Oliver

Oliver: Now, sir! what make you here?

Orlando: Nothing: I am not taught to make any thing.

Oliver: What mar you then, sir?

Orlando: Marry, sir, I am helping you to mar that which God made, a poor unworthy brother of yours, with idleness.

Oliver: Marry, sir, be better employed, and be naught awhile.

Orlando: Shall I keep your hogs and eat husks with them?

What prodigal portion have I spent, that I should come to such penury?

Oliver: Know you where your are, sir?

Orlando: O, sir, very well; here in your orchard.

Oliver: Know you before whom, sir?

Orlando: Ay, better than him I am before knows me. I know you are my eldest brother; and, in the gentle condition of blood, you should so know me. The courtesy of nations allows you my better, in that you are the first-born; but the same tradition takes not away my blood, were there twenty brothers betwixt us: I have as much of my father in me as you; albeit, I confess, your coming before me is nearer to his reverence.

Oliver: What, boy!

Orlando: Come, come, elder brother, you are too young in this.

Oliver: Wilt thou lay hands on me, villain?

Orlando: I am no villain; I am the youngest son of Sir Rowland de Boys; he was my father, and he is thrice a villain that says such a father begot villains.

Wert thou not my brother, I would not take this hand from thy throat till this other had pulled out thy tongue for saying so: thou hast railed on thyself.

Adam: Sweet masters, be patient: for your father's remembrance, be at accord.

Oliver: Let me go, I say.

Orlando: I will not, till I please: you shall hear me. My father charged you in his will to give me good education: you have trained me like a peasant, obscuring and hiding from me all gentleman-like qualities. The spirit of my father grows strong in me, and I will no longer endure it: therefore allow me such exercises as may become a gentleman, or give me the poor allottery my father left me by testament; with that I will go buy my fortunes.

Oliver: And what wilt thou do? beg, when that is spent? Well, sir, get you in: I will not long be troubled with you; you shall have some part of your will: I pray you, leave me.

Orlando: I will no further offend you than becomes me for my good.

Oliver: Get you with him, you old dog.

Adam: Is 'old dog' my reward? Most true, I have lost my teeth in your service. God be with my old master! he would not have spoke such a word.

Exeunt *Orlando* and *Adam*

Oliver: Is it even so? begin you to grow upon me? I will physic your rankness, and yet give no thousand crowns neither. Holla, Dennis!

Enter *Dennis*

Dennis: Calls your worship?

Oliver: Was not Charles, the duke's wrestler, here to speak with me?

Dennis: So please you, he is here at the door and importunes access to you.

Oliver: Call him in.

Exit *Dennis*

'Twill be a good way; and to-morrow the wrestling is.

Enter *Charles*

Charles: Good morrow to your worship.

Oliver: Good Monsieur Charles, what's the new news at the new court?

Charles: There's no news at the court, sir, but the old news: that is, the old duke is banished by his younger brother the new duke; and three or four loving lords have put themselves into voluntary exile with him, whose lands and revenues enrich the new duke; therefore he gives them good leave to wander.

Oliver: Can you tell if Rosalind, the duke's daughter, be banished with her father?

Charles: O, no; for the duke's daughter, her cousin, so loves her, being ever from their cradles bred together, that she would have followed her exile, or have died to stay behind her. She is at the court, and no less beloved of her uncle than his own daughter; and never two ladies loved as they do.

Oliver: Where will the old duke live?

Charles: They say he is already in the forest of Arden, and a many merry men with him; and there they live like the old Robin Hood of England: they say many young gentlemen flock to him every day, and fleet the time carelessly, as they did in the golden world.

Oliver: What, you wrestle to-morrow before the new duke?

Charles: Marry, do I, sir; and I came to acquaint you with a matter. I am given, sir, secretly to understand that your younger brother Orlando hath a disposition to come in disguised against me to try a fall. To-morrow, sir, I wrestle for my credit; and he that escapes me without some broken limb shall acquit him well. Your brother is but young and tender; and, for your love, I would be loath to foil him, as I must, for my own honour, if he come in: therefore, out of my love to you, I came hither to acquaint you withal, that either you might stay him from his intendment or brook such disgrace well as he shall run into, in that it is a thing of his own search and altogether against my will.

Oliver: Charles, I thank thee for thy love to me, which thou shalt find I will most kindly requite. I had myself notice of my brother's purpose herein and have by underhand means laboured to dissuade him from it, but he is resolute. I'll tell thee, Charles: it is the stubbornest young fellow of France, full of ambition, an envious emulator of every man's good parts, a secret and villanous contriver against me his natural brother: therefore use thy discretion; I had as lief thou didst break his neck as his finger. And thou wert best look to't; for if thou dost him any slight disgrace or if he do not mightily grace himself on thee, he will practise against thee by poison, entrap thee by some treacherous device and never leave thee till he hath ta'en thy life by some indirect means or other; for, I assure thee, and almost with tears I speak it, there is not one so young and so villanous this day living. I speak but brotherly of him; but should I anatomize him to thee as he is, I must blush and weep and thou must look pale and wonder.

Charles: I am heartily glad I came hither to you. If he come to-morrow, I'll give him his payment: if ever he go alone again, I'll never wrestle for prize more: and so God keep your worship!

Oliver: Farewell, good Charles.

Exit *Charles*

Now will I stir this gamester: I hope I shall see an end of him; for my soul, yet I know not why, hates nothing more than he. Yet he's gentle, never schooled and yet learned, full of noble device, of all sorts enchantingly beloved, and indeed so much in the heart of the world, and especially of my own people, who best know him, that I am altogether misprised: but it shall not be so long; this wrestler shall clear all: nothing remains but that I kindle the boy thither; which now I'll go about.

Exit

Scene II: Lawn before the Duke's Palace

Enter Celia and Rosalind

Celia: I pray thee, Rosalind, sweet my coz, be merry.

Rosalind: Dear Celia, I show more mirth than I am mistress of; and would you yet I were merrier? Unless you could teach me to forget a banished father, you must not learn me how to remember any extraordinary pleasure.

Celia: Herein I see thou lovest me not with the full weight that I love thee. If my uncle, thy banished father, had banished thy uncle, the duke my father, so thou hadst been still with me, I could have taught my love to take thy father for mine: so wouldst thou, if the truth of thy love to me were so righteously tempered as mine is to thee.

*Rosalind:*Well, I will forget the condition of my estate, to rejoice in yours.

Celia: You know my father hath no child but I, nor none is like to have: and, truly, when he dies, thou shalt be his heir, for what he hath taken away from thy father perforce, I will render thee again in affection; by mine honour, I will; and when I break that oath, let me turn monster: therefore, my sweet Rose, my dear Rose, be merry.

Rosalind: From henceforth I will, coz, and devise sports. Let me see; what think you of falling in love?

Celia: Marry, I prithee, do, to make sport withal: but love no man in good earnest; nor no further in sport neither than with safety of a pure blush thou mayst in honour come off again.

Rosalind: What shall be our sport, then?

Celia: Let us sit and mock the good housewife Fortune from her wheel, that her gifts may henceforth be bestowed equally.

Rosalind: I would we could do so, for her benefits are mightily misplaced, and the bountiful blind woman doth most mistake in her gifts to women.

Celia: 'Tis true; for those that she makes fair she scarce makes honest, and those that she makes honest she makes very ill-favouredly.

Rosalind: Nay, now thou goest from Fortune's office to Nature's: Fortune reigns in gifts of the world, not in the lineaments of Nature.

Enter *Touchstone*

Celia: No? when Nature hath made a fair creature, may she not by Fortune fall into the fire? Though Nature hath given us wit to flout at Fortune, hath not Fortune sent in this fool to cut off the argument?

Rosalind: Indeed, there is Fortune too hard for Nature, when Fortune makes Nature's natural the cutter-off of Nature's wit.

Celia: Peradventure this is not Fortune's work neither, but Nature's; who perceiveth our natural wits too dull to reason of such goddesses and hath sent this natural for our whetstone; for always the dulness of the fool is the whetstone of the wits. How now, wit! whither wander you?

Touchstone: Mistress, you must come away to your father.

Celia: Were you made the messenger?

Touchstone: No, by mine honour, but I was bid to come for you.

Rosalind: Where learned you that oath, fool?

Touchstone: Of a certain knight that swore by his honour they were good pancakes and swore by his honour the mustard was naught: now I'll stand to it, the pancakes were naught and the mustard was good, and yet was not the knight forsworn.

Celia: How prove you that, in the great heap of your knowledge?

Rosalind: Ay, marry, now unmuzzle your wisdom.

Touchstone: Stand you both forth now: stroke your chins, and swear by your beards that I am a knave.

Celia: By our beards, if we had them, thou art.

Touchstone: By my knavery, if I had it, then I were; but if you swear by that that is not, you are not forsworn: no more was this knight swearing by his honour, for he never had any; or if he had, he had sworn it away before ever he saw those pancakes or that mustard.

Celia: Prithee, who is't that thou meanest?

Touchstone: One that old Frederick, your father, loves.

Celia: My father's love is enough to honour him: enough! speak no more of him; you'll be whipped for taxation one of these days.

Touchstone: The more pity, that fools may not speak wisely what wise men do foolishly.

Celia: By my troth, thou sayest true; for since the little wit that fools have was silenced, the little foolery that wise men have makes a great show. Here comes Monsieur Le Beau.

Rosalind: With his mouth full of news.

Celia: Which he will put on us, as pigeons feed their young.

Rosalind: Then shall we be news-crammed.

Celia: All the better; we shall be the more marketable.

Enter *Le Beau*

Bon jour, Monsieur Le Beau: what's the news?

Le Beau: Fair princess, you have lost much good sport.

Celia: Sport! of what colour?

Le Beau: What colour, madam! how shall I answer you?

Rosalind: As wit and fortune will.

Touchstone: Or as the Destinies decree.

Celia: Well said: that was laid on with a trowel.

Touchstone: Nay, if I keep not my rank,—

Rosalind: Thou losest thy old smell.

Le Beau: You amaze me, ladies: I would have told you of good wrestling, which you have lost the sight of.

Rosalind: You tell us the manner of the wrestling.

Le Beau: I will tell you the beginning; and, if it please your ladyships, you may see the end; for the best is yet to do; and here, where you are, they are coming to perform it.

Celia: Well, the beginning, that is dead and buried.

Le Beau: There comes an old man and his three sons,—

Celia: I could match this beginning with an old tale.

Le Beau: Three proper young men, of excellent growth and presence.

Rosalind: With bills on their necks, 'Be it known unto all men by these presents.'

Le Beau: The eldest of the three wrestled with Charles, the duke's wrestler; which Charles in a moment threw him and broke three of his ribs, that there is little hope of life in him: so he served the second, and so the third. Yonder they lie; the poor old man, their father, making such pitiful dole over them that all the beholders take his part with weeping.

Rosalind Alas!

Touchstone: But what is the sport, monsieur, that the ladies have lost?

Le Beau: Why, this that I speak of.

*Touchstone:*Thus men may grow wiser every day: it is the first time that ever I heard breaking of ribs was sport for ladies.

Celia: Or I, I promise thee.

Rosalind: But is there any else longs to see this broken music in his sides? is there yet another dotes upon rib-breaking? Shall we see this wrestling, cousin?

Le Beau: You must, if you stay here; for here is the place appointed for the wrestling, and they are ready to perform it.

Celia: Yonder, sure, they are coming: let us now stay and see it.

Flourish. Enter Duke Frederick, Lords, Orlando, Charles, and Attendants

Duke Frederick: Come on: since the youth will not be entreated, his own peril on his forwardness.

Rosalind: Is yonder the man?

Le Beau: Even he, madam.

Celia: Alas, he is too young! yet he looks successfully.

Duke Frederick: How now, daughter and cousin! are you crept hither to see the wrestling?

Rosalind: Ay, my liege, so please you give us leave.

Duke Frederick: You will take little delight in it, I can tell you; there is such odds in the man. In pity of the challenger's youth I would fain dissuade him, but he will not be entreated. Speak to him, ladies; see if you can move him.

Celia: Call him hither, good Monsieur Le Beau.

Duke Frederick: Do so: I'll not be by.

Le Beau: Monsieur the challenger, the princesses call for you.

Orlando: I attend them with all respect and duty.

Rosalind: Young man, have you challenged Charles the wrestler?

Orlando: No, fair princess; he is the general challenger: I come but in, as others do, to try with him the strength of my youth.

Celia: Young gentleman, your spirits are too bold for your years. You have seen cruel proof of this man's strength: if you saw yourself with your eyes or knew yourself with your judgment, the fear of your adventure would counsel you to a more equal enterprise. We pray you, for your own sake, to embrace your own safety and give over this attempt.

Rosalind: Do, young sir; your reputation shall not therefore be misprised: we will make it our suit to the duke that the wrestling might not go forward.

Orlando: I beseech you, punish me not with your hard thoughts; wherein I confess me much guilty, to deny so fair and excellent ladies any thing. But let your fair eyes and gentle wishes go with me to my trial: wherein if I be foiled, there is but one shamed that was never gracious; if killed, but one dead that was willing to be so: I shall do my friends no wrong, for I have none to lament me, the world no injury, for in it I have nothing; only in the world I fill up a place, which may be better supplied when I have made it empty.

Rosalind: The little strength that I have, I would it were with you.

Celia: And mine, to eke out hers.

Rosalind: Fare you well: pray heaven I be deceived in you!

Celia: Your heart's desires be with you!

Charles: Come, where is this young gallant that is so desirous to lie with his mother earth?

Orlando: Ready, sir; but his will hath in it a more modest working.

Duke Frederick: You shall try but one fall.

Charles: No, I warrant your grace, you shall not entreat him to a second, that have so mightily persuaded him from a first.

Orlando: An you mean to mock me after, you should not have mocked me before: but come your ways.

Rosalind: Now Hercules be thy speed, young man!

Celia: I would I were invisible, to catch the strong fellow by the leg.

They wrestle

Rosalind: O excellent young man!

Celia: If I had a thunderbolt in mine eye, I can tell who should down.

Shout. *Charles* is thrown

Duke Frederick: No more, no more.

Orlando: Yes, I beseech your grace: I am not yet well breathed.

Duke Frederick: How dost thou, Charles?

Le Beau: He cannot speak, my lord.

Duke Frederick: Bear him away. What is thy name, young man?

Orlando: Orlando, my liege; the youngest son of Sir Rowland de Boys.

Duke Frederick: I would thou hadst been son to some man else:

The world esteem'd thy father honourable, But I did find him still mine enemy: Thou shouldst have better pleased me with this deed, Hadst thou descended from another house. But fare thee well; thou art a gallant youth:

I would thou hadst told me of another father. Exeunt Duke Frederick, train, and *Le Beau*

Celia: Were I my father, coz, would I do this?

Orlando: I am more proud to be Sir Rowland's son, His youngest son; and would not change that calling, To be adopted heir to Frederick.

Rosalind: My father loved Sir Rowland as his soul, And all the world was of my father's mind: Had I before known this young man his son, I should have given him tears unto entreaties, Ere he should thus have ventured.

Celia: Gentle cousin, Let us go thank him and encourage him. My father's rough and envious disposition Sticks me at heart. Sir, you have well deserved. If you do keep your promises in love. But justly, as you have exceeded all promise, Your mistress shall be happy.

Rosalind: Gentleman, Giving him a chain from her neck. Wear this for me, one out of suits with fortune, That could give more, but that her hand lacks means. Shall we go, coz?

Celia: Ay. Fare you well, fair gentleman.

Orlando:

Can I not say, I thank you? My better parts
Are all thrown down, and that which here stands up
Is but a quintain, a mere lifeless block.

Rosalind:

He calls us back: my pride fell with my fortunes;
I'll ask him what he would. Did you call, sir?
Sir, you have wrestled well and overthrown
More than your enemies.

Celia: Will you go, coz?

Rosalind: Have with you. Fare you well.

Exeunt *Rosalind* and *Celia*

Orlando:

What passion hangs these weights upon my tongue?
I cannot speak to her, yet she urged conference.
O poor Orlando, thou art overthrown!
Or Charles or something weaker masters thee.
Re-enter *Le Beau*

Le Beau:

Good sir, I do in friendship counsel you
To leave this place. Albeit you have deserved
High commendation, true applause and love,
Yet such is now the duke's condition
That he misconstrues all that you have done.
The duke is humourous; what he is indeed,
More suits you to conceive than I to speak of.

Orlando:

I thank you, sir: and, pray you, tell me this:
Which of the two was daughter of the duke
That here was at the wrestling?

Le Beau:

Neither his daughter, if we judge by manners;
But yet indeed the lesser is his daughter

The other is daughter to the banish'd duke,
And here detain'd by her usurping uncle,
To keep his daughter company; whose loves
Are dearer than the natural bond of sisters.
But I can tell you that of late this duke
Hath ta'en displeasure 'gainst his gentle niece,
Grounded upon no other argument
But that the people praise her for her virtues
And pity her for her good father's sake;
And, on my life, his malice 'gainst the lady
Will suddenly break forth. Sir, fare you well:
Hereafter, in a better world than this,
I shall desire more love and knowledge of you.

Orlando

I rest much bounden to you: fare you well.

Exit *Le Beau*

Thus must I from the smoke into the smother;
From tyrant duke unto a tyrant brother:
But heavenly Rosalind!

Exit

Scene III: A Room in the Palace

Enter *Celia* and *Rosalind*

Celia: Why, cousin! why, Rosalind! Cupid have mercy! not a word?

Rosalind: Not one to throw at a dog.

Celia: No, thy words are too precious to be cast away upon curs; throw some of them at me; come, lame me with reasons.

Rosalind: Then there were two cousins laid up; when the one should be lamed with reasons and the other mad without any.

Celia: But is all this for your father?

Rosalind: No, some of it is for my child's father. O, how full of briers is this working-day world!

Celia: They are but burs, cousin, thrown upon thee in holiday foolery: if we walk not in the trodden paths our very petticoats will catch them.

Rosalind: I could shake them off my coat: these burs are in my heart.

Celia: Hem them away.

Rosalind: I would try, if I could cry 'hem' and have him.

Celia: Come, come, wrestle with thy affections.

Rosalind: O, they take the part of a better wrestler than myself!

Celia: O, a good wish upon you! you will try in time, in despite of a fall. But, turning these jests out of service, let us talk in good earnest: is it possible, on such a sudden, you should fall into so strong a liking with old Sir Rowland's youngest son?

Rosalind: The duke my father loved his father dearly.

Celia: Doth it therefore ensue that you should love his son dearly? By this kind of chase, I should hate him, for my father hated his father dearly; yet I hate not Orlando.

Rosalind: No, faith, hate him not, for my sake.

Celia: Why should I not? doth he not deserve well?

Rosalind: Let me love him for that, and do you love him because I do. Look, here comes the duke.

Celia: With his eyes full of anger.

Enter Duke Frederick, with Lords

Duke Frederick: Mistress, dispatch you with your safest haste And get you from our court.

Rosalind: Me, uncle?

Duke Frederick: You, cousin Within these ten days if that thou be'st found So near our public court as twenty miles, Thou diest for it.

Rosalind: I do beseech your grace,
Let me the knowledge of my fault bear with me:
If with myself I hold intelligence
Or have acquaintance with mine own desires,
If that I do not dream or be not frantic,—
As I do trust I am not—then, dear uncle,
Never so much as in a thought unborn
Did I offend your highness.

Duke Frederick

Thus do all traitors:
If their purgation did consist in words,
They are as innocent as grace itself:
Let it suffice thee that I trust thee not.

Rosalind

Yet your mistrust cannot make me a traitor:
Tell me whereon the likelihood depends.

Duke Frederick

Thou art thy father's daughter; there's enough.

Rosalind

So was I when your highness took his dukedom;
So was I when your highness banish'd him:
Treason is not inherited, my lord;
Or, if we did derive it from our friends,
What's that to me? my father was no traitor:
Then, good my liege, mistake me not so much
To think my poverty is treacherous.
Celia: Dear sovereign, hear me speak.
Duke Frederick: Ay, Celia; we stay'd her for your sake,
Else had she with her father ranged along.

Celia:

I did not then entreat to have her stay;
It was your pleasure and your own remorse:
I was too young that time to value her;
But now I know her: if she be a traitor,
Why so am I; we still have slept together,

Rose at an instant, learn'd, play'd, eat together,
And wheresoever we went, like Juno's swans,
Still we went coupled and inseparable.

Duke Frederick

She is too subtle for thee; and her smoothness,
Her very silence and her patience
Speak to the people, and they pity her.
Thou art a fool: she robs thee of thy name;
And thou wilt show more bright and seem more virtuous
When she is gone. Then open not thy lips:
Firm and irrevocable is my doom
Which I have pass'd upon her; she is banish'd.

Celia:

Pronounce that sentence then on me, my liege:
I cannot live out of her company.

Duke Frederick

You are a fool. You, niece, provide yourself:
If you outstay the time, upon mine honour,
And in the greatness of my word, you die.
Exeunt *Duke Frederick* and Lords

Celia

O my poor Rosalind, whither wilt thou go?
Wilt thou change fathers? I will give thee mine.
I charge thee, be not thou more grieved than I am.
Rosalind: I have more cause.

Celia

Thou hast not, cousin;
Prithee be cheerful: know'st thou not, the duke
Hath banish'd me, his daughter?

Rosalind: That he hath not.

Celia: No, hath not? Rosalind lacks then the love
Which teacheth thee that thou and I am one:
Shall we be sunder'd? shall we part, sweet girl?
No: let my father seek another heir.

Therefore devise with me how we may fly,
Whither to go and what to bear with us;
And do not seek to take your change upon you,
To bear your griefs yourself and leave me out;
For, by this heaven, now at our sorrows pale,
Say what thou canst, I'll go along with thee.

Rosalind: Why, whither shall we go?

Celia: To seek my uncle in the forest of Arden.

Rosalind: Alas, what danger will it be to us,
Maids as we are, to travel forth so far!
Beauty provoketh thieves sooner than gold.

Celia: I'll put myself in poor and mean attire
And with a kind of umber smirch my face;
The like do you: so shall we pass along
And never stir assailants.

Rosalind:

Were it not better,
Because that I am more than common tall,
That I did suit me all points like a man?
A gallant curtle-axe upon my thigh,
A boar-spear in my hand; and—in my heart
Lie there what hidden woman's fear there will—
We'll have a swashing and a martial outside,
As many other mannish cowards have
That do outface it with their semblances.

Celia: What shall I call thee when thou art a man?

Rosalind:

I'll have no worse a name than Jove's own page;
And therefore look you call me Ganymede.
But what will you be call'd?

Celia:

Something that hath a reference to my state
No longer Celia, but Aliena.

Rosalind:

But, cousin, what if we assay'd to steal
The clownish fool out of your father's court?
Would he not be a comfort to our travel?

Celia:

He'll go along o'er the wide world with me;
Leave me alone to woo him. Let's away,
And get our jewels and our wealth together,
Devise the fittest time and safest way
To hide us from pursuit that will be made
After my flight. Now go we in content
To liberty and not to banishment.
Exeunt

ACT II

Scene I: The Forest of Arden

Enter Duke Senior, Amiens, and two or three Lords, like foresters

Duke Senior

Now, my co-mates and brothers in exile,
Hath not old custom made this life more sweet
Than that of painted pomp? Are not these woods
More free from peril than the envious court?
Here feel we but the penalty of Adam,
The seasons' difference, as the icy fang
And churlish chiding of the winter's wind,
Which, when it bites and blows upon my body,
Even till I shrink with cold, I smile and say
'This is no flattery: these are counsellors
That feelingly persuade me what I am.'
Sweet are the uses of adversity,
Which, like the toad, ugly and venomous,
Wears yet a precious jewel in his head;
And this our life exempt from public haunt
Finds tongues in trees, books in the running brooks,
Sermons in stones and good in every thing.
I would not change it.

Amiens

Happy is your grace,
That can translate the stubbornness of fortune
Into so quiet and so sweet a style.

Duke Senior

Come, shall we go and kill us venison?
And yet it irks me the poor dappled fools,
Being native burghers of this desert city,
Should in their own confines with forked heads
Have their round haunches gored.

First Lord

Indeed, my lord,
The melancholy Jaques grieves at that,
And, in that kind, swears you do more usurp
Than doth your brother that hath banish'd you.
To-day my Lord of Amiens and myself
Did steal behind him as he lay along
Under an oak whose antique root peeps out
Upon the brook that brawls along this wood:
To the which place a poor sequester'd stag,
That from the hunter's aim had ta'en a hurt,
Did come to languish, and indeed, my lord,
The wretched animal heaved forth such groans
That their discharge did stretch his leathern coat
Almost to bursting, and the big round tears
Coursed one another down his innocent nose
In piteous chase; and thus the hairy fool
Much marked of the melancholy Jaques,
Stood on the extremest verge of the swift brook,
Augmenting it with tears.

Duke Senior

But what said Jaques?
Did he not moralize this spectacle?

First Lord

O, yes, into a thousand similes.
First, for his weeping into the needless stream;
'Poor deer,' quoth he, 'thou makest a testament

As worldlings do, giving thy sum of more
To that which had too much:' then, being there alone,
Left and abandon'd of his velvet friends,
''Tis right:' quoth he; 'thus misery doth part
The flux of company:' anon a careless herd,
Full of the pasture, jumps along by him
And never stays to greet him; 'Ay' quoth Jaques,
'Sweep on, you fat and greasy citizens;
'Tis just the fashion: wherefore do you look
Upon that poor and broken bankrupt there?'
Thus most invectively he pierceth through
The body of the country, city, court,
Yea, and of this our life, swearing that we
Are mere usurpers, tyrants and what's worse,
To fright the animals and to kill them up
In their assign'd and native dwelling-place.

Duke Senior

And did you leave him in this contemplation?

Second Lord

We did, my lord, weeping and commenting
Upon the sobbing deer.

Duke Senior

Show me the place:
I love to cope him in these sullen fits,
For then he's full of matter.

First Lord

I'll bring you to him straight.
Exeunt

SCENE II. A room in the palace.

Enter Duke Senior, with Lords

Duke Senior

Can it be possible that no man saw them?
It cannot be: some villains of my court
Are of consent and sufferance in this.

First Lord

I cannot hear of any that did see her.
The ladies, her attendants of her chamber,
Saw her abed, and in the morning early
They found the bed untreasured of their mistress.

Second Lord

My lord, the roynish clown, at whom so oft
Your grace was wont to laugh, is also missing.
Hisperia, the princess' gentlewoman,
Confesses that she secretly o'erheard
Your daughter and her cousin much commend
The parts and graces of the wrestler
That did but lately foil the sinewy Charles;
And she believes, wherever they are gone,
That youth is surely in their company.

Duke Frederick

Send to his brother; fetch that gallant hither;
If he be absent, bring his brother to me;
I'll make him find him: do this suddenly,
And let not search and inquisition quail
To bring again these foolish runaways.
Exeunt

SCENE III. Before OLIVER'S house.

Enter Orlando and Adam, meeting

Orlando: Who's there?

Adam: What, my young master? O, my gentle master!
O my sweet master! O you memory
Of old Sir Rowland! why, what make you here?
Why are you virtuous? why do people love you?
And wherefore are you gentle, strong and valiant?
Why would you be so fond to overcome
The bonny priser of the humourous duke?
Your praise is come too swiftly home before you.
Know you not, master, to some kind of men

Their graces serve them but as enemies?
No more do yours: your virtues, gentle master,
Are sanctified and holy traitors to you.
O, what a world is this, when what is comely
Envenoms him that bears it!

Orlando: Why, what's the matter?

Adam

O unhappy youth!
Come not within these doors; within this roof
The enemy of all your graces lives:
Your brother—no, no brother; yet the son—
Yet not the son, I will not call him son
Of him I was about to call his father—
Hath heard your praises, and this night he means
To burn the lodging where you use to lie
And you within it: if he fail of that,
He will have other means to cut you off.
I overheard him and his practises.
This is no place; this house is but a butchery:
Abhor it, fear it, do not enter it.

Orlando:

Why, whither, Adam, wouldst thou have me go?

Adam:

No matter whither, so you come not here.

Orlando:

What, wouldst thou have me go and beg my food?
Or with a base and boisterous sword enforce
A thievish living on the common road?
This I must do, or know not what to do:
Yet this I will not do, do how I can;
I rather will subject me to the malice
Of a diverted blood and bloody brother.

Adam:

But do not so. I have five hundred crowns,
The thrifty hire I saved under your father,
Which I did store to be my foster-nurse
When service should in my old limbs lie lame
And unregarded age in corners thrown:
Take that, and He that doth the ravens feed,
Yea, providently caters for the sparrow,
Be comfort to my age! Here is the gold;
And all this I give you. Let me be your servant:
Though I look old, yet I am strong and lusty;
For in my youth I never did apply
Hot and rebellious liquors in my blood,
Nor did not with unbashful forehead woo
The means of weakness and debility;
Therefore my age is as a lusty winter,
Frosty, but kindly: let me go with you;
I'll do the service of a younger man
In all your business and necessities.

Orlando:

O good old man, how well in thee appears
The constant service of the antique world,
When service sweat for duty, not for meed!
Thou art not for the fashion of these times,
Where none will sweat but for promotion,
And having that, do choke their service up
Even with the having: it is not so with thee.
But, poor old man, thou prunest a rotten tree,
That cannot so much as a blossom yield
In lieu of all thy pains and husbandry
But come thy ways; well go along together,
And ere we have thy youthful wages spent,
We'll light upon some settled low content.

Adam:

Master, go on, and I will follow thee,
To the last gasp, with truth and loyalty.

From seventeen years till now almost fourscore
Here lived I, but now live here no more.
At seventeen years many their fortunes seek;
But at fourscore it is too late a week:
Yet fortune cannot recompense me better
Than to die well and not my master's debtor.

Exeunt

Scene IV: The Forest of Arden

Enter *Rosalind* for Ganymede, *Celia* for Aliena, and *Touchstone*

Rosalind: O Jupiter, how weary are my spirits!

Touchstone: I care not for my spirits, if my legs were not weary.

Rosalind: I could find in my heart to disgrace my man's apparel and to cry like a woman; but I must comfort the weaker vessel, as doublet and hose ought to show itself courageous to petticoat: therefore courage, good Aliena!

Celia: I pray you, bear with me; I cannot go no further.

Touchstone: For my part, I had rather bear with you than bear you; yet I should bear no cross if I did bear you, for I think you have no money in your purse.

Rosalind: Well, this is the forest of Arden.

Touchstone: Ay, now am I in Arden; the more fool I; when I was at home, I was in a better place: but travellers must be content.

Rosalind: Ay, be so, good Touchstone.

Enter Corin and Silvius

Look you, who comes here; a young man and an old in solemn talk.

Corin: That is the way to make her scorn you still.

Silvius: O Corin, that thou knew'st how I do love her!

Corin: I partly guess; for I have loved ere now.

Silvius: No, Corin, being old, thou canst not guess,
Though in thy youth thou wast as true a lover
As ever sigh'd upon a midnight pillow:
But if thy love were ever like to mine—
As sure I think did never man love so—
How many actions most ridiculous
Hast thou been drawn to by thy fantasy?

Corin:

Into a thousand that I have forgotten.

Silvius:

O, thou didst then ne'er love so heartily!
If thou remember'st not the slightest folly
That ever love did make thee run into,
Thou hast not loved:
Or if thou hast not sat as I do now,
Wearying thy hearer in thy mistress' praise,
Thou hast not loved:
Or if thou hast not broke from company
Abruptly, as my passion now makes me,
Thou hast not loved.
O Phebe, Phebe, Phebe!
Exit

Rosalind:

Alas, poor shepherd! searching of thy wound,
I have by hard adventure found mine own.

Touchstone:

And I mine. I remember, when I was in love I broke my sword upon a stone and bid him take that for coming a-night to Jane Smile; and I remember the kissing of her batlet and the cow's dugs that her pretty chopt hands had milked; and I remember the wooing of a peascod instead of her, from whom I took two cods and, giving her them again, said with weeping tears 'Wear these for my sake.' We that are true lovers run into strange capers; but as all is mortal in nature, so is all nature in love mortal in folly.

Rosalind: Thou speakest wiser than thou art ware of.

Touchstone:

Nay, I shall ne'er be ware of mine own wit till I
break my shins against it.
Rosalind: Jove, Jove! this shepherd's passion
Is much upon my fashion.

Touchstone: And mine; but it grows something stale with me.

Celia:

I pray you, one of you question yond man
If he for gold will give us any food:
I faint almost to death.

*Touchstone:*Holla, you clown!

Rosalind: Peace, fool: he's not thy kinsman.

Corin: Who calls?

Touchstone: Your betters, sir.

Corin: Else are they very wretched.

Rosalind: Peace, I say. Good even to you, friend.

Corin: And to you, gentle sir, and to you all.

Rosalind: I prithee, shepherd, if that love or gold
Can in this desert place buy entertainment,
Bring us where we may rest ourselves and feed:
Here's a young maid with travel much oppress'd
And faints for succor.

Corin: Fair sir, I pity her
And wish, for her sake more than for mine own,
My fortunes were more able to relieve her;
But I am shepherd to another man
And do not shear the fleeces that I graze:
My master is of churlish disposition
And little recks to find the way to heaven
By doing deeds of hospitality:
Besides, his cote, his flocks and bounds of feed
Are now on sale, and at our sheepcote now,

By reason of his absence, there is nothing
That you will feed on; but what is, come see.
And in my voice most welcome shall you be.

Rosalind: What is he that shall buy his flock and pasture?

Corin:

That young swain that you saw here but erewhile,
That little cares for buying any thing.

Rosalind:

I pray thee, if it stand with honesty,
Buy thou the cottage, pasture and the flock,
And thou shalt have to pay for it of us.

Celia:

And we will mend thy wages. I like this place.
And willingly could waste my time in it.

Corin:

Assuredly the thing is to be sold:
Go with me: if you like upon report
The soil, the profit and this kind of life,
I will your very faithful feeder be
And buy it with your gold right suddenly.

Exeunt

Scene V: The Forest

Enter Amiens, Jaques, and others

Song

Amiens:

Under the greenwood tree
Who loves to lie with me,
And turn his merry note
Unto the sweet bird's throat,
Come hither, come hither, come hither:
Here shall he see No enemy
But winter and rough weather.

Jaques: More, more, I prithee, more.

Amiens:

It will make you melancholy, Monsieur Jaques.

Jaques:

I thank it. More, I prithee, more. I can suck
melancholy out of a song, as a weasel sucks eggs.
More, I prithee, more.

Amiens: My voice is ragged: I know I cannot please you.

Jaques: I do not desire you to please me;
I do desire you to sing. Come, more;
another stanzo: call you 'em stanzos?

Amiens: What you will, Monsieur Jaques.

Jaques: Nay, I care not for their names;
they owe me nothing. Will you sing?

Amiens: More at your request than to please myself.

Jaques: Well then, if ever I thank any man, I'll thank you; but that they call compliment is like the encounter of two dog-apes, and when a man thanks me heartily, methinks I have given him a penny and he renders me the beggarly thanks. Come, sing; and you that will not, hold your tongues.

Amiens: Well, I'll end the song. Sirs, cover the while; the duke will drink under this tree. He hath been all this day to look you.

Jaques: And I have been all this day to avoid him. He is too disputable for my company: I think of as many matters as he, but I give heaven thanks and make no boast of them. Come, warble, come.

Song: Who doth ambition shun
All together here
And loves to live i' the sun,
Seeking the food he eats
And pleased with what he gets,
Come hither, come hither, come hither:
Here shall he see No enemy
But winter and rough weather.

Jaques:

I'll give you a verse to this note that I made
yesterday in despite of my invention.

Amiens: And I'll sing it.

Jaques:

Thus it goes:
If it do come to pass
That any man turn ass,
Leaving his wealth and ease,
A stubborn will to please,
Ducdame, ducdame, ducdame:
Here shall he see
Gross fools as he,
An if he will come to me.

Amiens: What's that 'ducdame'?

Jaques: 'Tis a Greek invocation, to call fools into a circle. I'll go sleep, if I can; if I cannot, I'll rail against all the first-born of Egypt.

Amiens: And I'll go seek the duke: his banquet is prepared.

Exeunt severally

Scene VI: The Forest

Enter Orlando and Adam

Adam:

Dear master, I can go no further. O, I die for food!

Here lie I down, and measure out my grave. Farewell,

kind master.

Orlando: Why, how now, Adam! no greater heart in thee? Live a little; comfort a little; cheer thyself a little.

If this uncouth forest yield any thing savage, I will either be food for it or bring it for food to thee. Thy conceit is nearer death than thy powers.

For my sake be comfortable; hold death awhile at the arm's end: I will here be with thee presently; and if I bring thee not something to eat, I will give thee leave to die: but if thou diest before I come, thou art a mocker of my labour. Well said! thou lookest cheerly, and I'll be with thee quickly.

Yet thou liest in the bleak air: come, I will bear thee to some shelter; and thou shalt not die for lack of a dinner, if there live any thing in this desert. Cheerly, good Adam!

Exeunt

Scene VII: The Forest

A table set out. Enter Duke Senior, Amiens, and Lords like outlaws

Duke Senior

I think he be transform'd into a beast;
For I can no where find him like a man.

First Lord

My lord, he is but even now gone hence:
Here was he merry, hearing of a song.

Duke Senior

If he, compact of jars, grow musical,
We shall have shortly discord in the spheres.
Go, seek him: tell him I would speak with him.

Enter Jaques

First Lord

He saves my labour by his own approach.

Duke Senior

Why, how now, monsieur! what a life is this,
That your poor friends must woo your company?
What, you look merrily!

Jaques

A fool, a fool! I met a fool i' the forest,
A motley fool; a miserable world!

As I do live by food, I met a fool
Who laid him down and bask'd him in the sun,
And rail'd on Lady Fortune in good terms,
In good set terms and yet a motley fool.
'Good morrow, fool,' quoth I. 'No, sir,' quoth he,
'Call me not fool till heaven hath sent me fortune:'
And then he drew a dial from his poke,
And, looking on it with lack-lustre eye,
Says very wisely, 'It is ten o'clock:
Thus we may see,' quoth he, 'how the world wags:
'Tis but an hour ago since it was nine,
And after one hour more 'twill be eleven;
And so, from hour to hour, we ripe and ripe,
And then, from hour to hour, we rot and rot;
And thereby hangs a tale.' When I did hear
The motley fool thus moral on the time,
My lungs began to crow like chanticleer,
That fools should be so deep-contemplative,
And I did laugh sans intermission
An hour by his dial. O noble fool!
A worthy fool! Motley's the only wear.

Duke Senior: What fool is this?

Jaques

O worthy fool! One that hath been a courtier,
And says, if ladies be but young and fair,
They have the gift to know it: and in his brain,
Which is as dry as the remainder biscuit
After a voyage, he hath strange places cramm'd
With observation, the which he vents
In mangled forms. O that I were a fool!
I am ambitious for a motley coat.

Duke Senior: Thou shalt have one.

Jaques:

It is my only suit;
Provided that you weed your better judgments
Of all opinion that grows rank in them

That I am wise. I must have liberty
Withal, as large a charter as the wind,
To blow on whom I please; for so fools have;
And they that are most galled with my folly,
They most must laugh. And why, sir, must they so?
The 'why' is plain as way to parish church:
He that a fool doth very wisely hit
Doth very foolishly, although he smart,
Not to seem senseless of the bob: if not,
The wise man's folly is anatomised
Even by the squandering glances of the fool.
Invest me in my motley; give me leave
To speak my mind, and I will through and through
Cleanse the foul body of the infected world,
If they will patiently receive my medicine.

Duke Senior:

Fie on thee! I can tell what thou wouldst do.

Jaques:

What, for a counter, would I do but good?

Duke Senior:

Most mischievous foul sin, in chiding sin:
For thou thyself hast been a libertine,
As sensual as the brutish sting itself;
And all the embossed sores and headed evils,
That thou with licence of free foot hast caught,
Wouldst thou disgorge into the general world.

Jaques:

Why, who cries out on pride,
That can therein tax any private party?
Doth it not flow as hugely as the sea,
Till that the weary very means do ebb?
What woman in the city do I name,
When that I say the city-woman bears
The cost of princes on unworthy shoulders?
Who can come in and say that I mean her,

When such a one as she such is her neighbour?
Or what is he of basest function
That says his bravery is not of my cost,
Thinking that I mean him, but therein suits
His folly to the mettle of my speech?
There then; how then? what then? Let me see wherein
My tongue hath wrong'd him: if it do him right,
Then he hath wrong'd himself; if he be free,
Why then my taxing like a wild-goose flies,
Unclaim'd of any man. But who comes here?

Enter *Orlando*, with his sword drawn

Orlando: Forbear, and eat no more.

Jaques: Why, I have eat none yet.

Orlando: Nor shalt not, till necessity be served.

Jaques: Of what kind should this cock come of?

Duke Senior:

Art thou thus bolden'd, man, by thy distress,
Or else a rude despiser of good manners,
That in civility thou seem'st so empty?

Orlando:

You touch'd my vein at first: the thorny point
Of bare distress hath ta'en from me the show
Of smooth civility: yet am I inland bred
And know some nurture. But forbear, I say:
He dies that touches any of this fruit
Till I and my affairs are answered.

Jaques: An you will not be answered with reason, I must die.

Duke Senior:

What would you have? Your gentleness shall force
More than your force move us to gentleness.

Orlando: I almost die for food; and let me have it.

Duke Senior:

Sit down and feed, and welcome to our table.

Orlando:

Speak you so gently? Pardon me, I pray you:
I thought that all things had been savage here;
And therefore put I on the countenance
Of stern commandment. But whate'er you are
That in this desert inaccessible,
Under the shade of melancholy boughs,
Lose and neglect the creeping hours of time
If ever you have look'd on better days,
If ever been where bells have knoll'd to church,
If ever sat at any good man's feast,
If ever from your eyelids wiped a tear
And know what 'tis to pity and be pitied,
Let gentleness my strong enforcement be:
In the which hope I blush, and hide my sword.

Duke Senior:

True is it that we have seen better days,
And have with holy bell been knoll'd to church
And sat at good men's feasts and wiped our eyes
Of drops that sacred pity hath engender'd:
And therefore sit you down in gentleness
And take upon command what help we have
That to your wanting may be minister'd.

Orlando:

Then but forbear your food a little while,
Whiles, like a doe, I go to find my fawn
And give it food. There is an old poor man,
Who after me hath many a weary step
Limp'd in pure love: till he be first sufficed,
Oppress'd with two weak evils, age and hunger,
I will not touch a bit.

Duke Senior:

Go find him out,
And we will nothing waste till you return.

Orlando:

I thank ye; and be blest for your good comfort!

Exit

Duke Senior:

Thou seest we are not all alone unhappy:
This wide and universal theatre
Presents more woeful pageants than the scene
Wherein we play in.

Jaques:

All the world's a stage,
And all the men and women merely players:
They have their exits and their entrances;
And one man in his time plays many parts,
His acts being seven ages. At first the infant,
Mewling and puking in the nurse's arms.
And then the whining school-boy, with his satchel
And shining morning face, creeping like snail
Unwillingly to school. And then the lover,
Sighing like furnace, with a woeful ballad
Made to his mistress' eyebrow. Then a soldier,
Full of strange oaths and bearded like the pard,
Jealous in honour, sudden and quick in quarrel,
Seeking the bubble reputation
Even in the cannon's mouth. And then the justice,
In fair round belly with good capon lined,
With eyes severe and beard of formal cut,
Full of wise saws and modern instances;
And so he plays his part. The sixth age shifts
Into the lean and slipper'd pantaloon,
With spectacles on nose and pouch on side,
His youthful hose, well saved, a world too wide
For his shrunk shank; and his big manly voice,

Turning again toward childish treble, pipes
And whistles in his sound. Last scene of all,
That ends this strange eventful history,
Is second childishness and mere oblivion,
Sans teeth, sans eyes, sans taste, sans everything.
Re-enter Orlando, with Adam

Duke Senior:

Welcome. Set down your venerable burthen,
And let him feed.

Orlando:

I thank you most for him.

Adam:

So had you need:
I scarce can speak to thank you for myself.

Duke Senior:

Welcome; fall to: I will not trouble you
As yet, to question you about your fortunes.
Give us some music; and, good cousin, sing.

Song:

Amiens:

Blow, blow, thou winter wind.
Thou art not so unkind
As man's ingratitude;
Thy tooth is not so keen,
Because thou art not seen,
Although thy breath be rude.
Heigh-ho! sing, heigh-ho! unto the green holly:
Most friendship is feigning, most loving mere folly:
Then, heigh-ho, the holly!
This life is most jolly.
Freeze, freeze, thou bitter sky,
That dost not bite so nigh
As benefits forgot:
Though thou the waters warp,

Thy sting is not so sharp
As friend remember'd not.
Heigh-ho! sing, & c.

Duke Senior:

If that you were the good Sir Rowland's son,
As you have whisper'd faithfully you were,
And as mine eye doth his effigies witness
Most truly limn'd and living in your face,
Be truly welcome hither: I am the duke
That loved your father: the residue of your fortune,
Go to my cave and tell me. Good old man,
Thou art right welcome as thy master is.
Support him by the arm. Give me your hand,
And let me all your fortunes understand.
Exeunt

Act III

Scene I: A Room in the Palace

Enter Duke Frederick, Lords, and Oliver

Duke Frederick:

Not see him since? Sir, sir, that cannot be:
But were I not the better part made mercy,
I should not seek an absent argument
Of my revenge, thou present. But look to it:
Find out thy brother, wheresoe'er he is;
Seek him with candle; bring him dead or living
Within this twelvemonth, or turn thou no more
To seek a living in our territory.
Thy lands and all things that thou dost call thine
Worth seizure do we seize into our hands,
Till thou canst quit thee by thy brothers mouth
Of what we think against thee.

Oliver:

O that your highness knew my heart in this!
I never loved my brother in my life.

Duke Frederick:

More villain thou. Well, push him out of doors;
And let my officers of such a nature
Make an extent upon his house and lands:
Do this expediently and turn him going.

Exeunt

Scene II: The Forest

Enter Orlando, with a paper

Orlando:

Hang there, my verse, in witness of my love:
And thou, thrice-crowned queen of night, survey
With thy chaste eye, from thy pale sphere above,
Thy huntress' name that my full life doth sway.
O Rosalind! these trees shall be my books
And in their barks my thoughts I'll character;
That every eye which in this forest looks
Shall see thy virtue witness'd every where.
Run, run, Orlando; carve on every tree
The fair, the chaste and unexpressive she.
Exit

Enter Corin and Touchstone

Corin: And how like you this shepherd's life, Master Touchstone?

Touchstone: Truly, shepherd, in respect of itself, it is a good life, but in respect that it is a shepherd's life, it is naught. In respect that it is solitary, I like it very well; but in respect that it is private, it is a very vile life. Now, in respect it is in the fields, it pleaseth me well; but in respect it is not in the court, it is tedious. As is it a spare life, look you, it fits my humour well; but as there is no more plenty in it, it goes much against my stomach. Hast any philosophy in thee, shepherd?

Corin: No more but that I know the more one sickens the worse at ease he is; and that he that wants money, means and content is without three good friends; that the property of rain is to wet and fire to burn; that good pasture makes fat sheep, and that a great cause of the night is lack of the sun; that he that hath learned no wit by nature nor art may complain of good breeding or comes of a very dull kindred.

Touchstone: Such a one is a natural philosopher. Wast ever in court, shepherd?

Corin: No, truly.

Touchstone: Then thou art damned.

Corin: Nay, I hope.

Touchstone: Truly, thou art damned like an ill-roasted egg, all on one side.

Corin: For not being at court? Your reason.

Touchstone: Why, if thou never wast at court, thou never sawest good manners; if thou never sawest good manners, then thy manners must be wicked; and wickedness is sin, and sin is damnation. Thou art in a parlous state, shepherd.

Corin: Not a whit, Touchstone: those that are good manners at the court are as ridiculous in the country as the behaviour of the country is most mockable at the court. You told me you salute not at the court, but you kiss your hands: that courtesy would be uncleanly, if courtiers were shepherds.

Touchstone: Instance, briefly; come, instance.

Corin: Why, we are still handling our ewes, and their fells, you know, are greasy.

Touchstone: Why, do not your courtier's hands sweat? and is not the grease of a mutton as wholesome as the sweat of a man? Shallow, shallow. A better instance, I say; come.

Corin: Besides, our hands are hard.

Touchstone: Your lips will feel them the sooner. Shallow again. A more sounder instance, come.

Corin: And they are often tarred over with the surgery of our sheep: and would you have us kiss tar? The courtier's hands are perfumed with civet.

Touchstone: Most shallow man! thou worms-meat, in respect of a good piece of flesh indeed! Learn of the wise, and perpend: civet is of a baser birth than tar, the very uncleanly flux of a cat. Mend the instance, shepherd.

Corin: You have too courtly a wit for me: I'll rest.

Touchstone: Wilt thou rest damned? God help thee, shallow man!

God make incision in thee! thou art raw.

Corin: Sir, I am a true labourer: I earn that I eat, get that I wear, owe no man hate, envy no man's happiness, glad of other men's good, content with my harm, and the greatest of my pride is to see my ewes graze and my lambs suck.

Touchstone: That is another simple sin in you, to bring the ewes and the rams together and to offer to get your living by the copulation of cattle; to be bawd to a bell-wether, and to betray a she-lamb of a twelvemonth to a crooked-pated, old, cuckoldly ram, out of all reasonable match. If thou beest not damned for this, the devil himself will have no shepherds; I cannot see else how thou shouldst 'scape.

Corin: Here comes young Master Ganymede, my new mistress's brother.

Enter Rosalind, with a paper, reading

Rosalind:

From the east to western Ind,
No jewel is like Rosalind.
Her worth, being mounted on the wind,
Through all the world bears Rosalind.
All the pictures fairest lined
Are but black to Rosalind.
Let no fair be kept in mind
But the fair of Rosalind.

Touchstone: I'll rhyme you so eight years together, dinners and suppers and sleeping-hours excepted: it is the right butter-women's rank to market.

Rosalind: Out, fool!

Touchstone:

For a taste:
If a hart do lack a hind,
Let him seek out Rosalind.
If the cat will after kind,
So be sure will Rosalind.
Winter garments must be lined,
So must slender Rosalind.
They that reap must sheaf and bind;
Then to cart with Rosalind.
Sweetest nut hath sourest rind,
Such a nut is Rosalind.
He that sweetest rose will find
Must find love's prick and Rosalind.
This is the very false gallop of verses: why do you infect yourself with them?

Rosalind: Peace, you dull fool! I found them on a tree.

Touchstone: Truly, the tree yields bad fruit.

Rosalind: I'll graff it with you, and then I shall graff it with a medlar: then it will be the earliest fruit i' the country; for you'll be rotten ere you be half ripe, and that's the right virtue of the medlar.

Touchstone: You have said; but whether wisely or no, let the forest judge.

Enter Celia, with a writing

Rosalind: Peace! Here comes my sister, reading: stand aside.

Celia:

[Reads]

Why should this a desert be?
For it is unpeopled? No:
Tongues I'll hang on every tree,
That shall civil sayings show:

Some, how brief the life of man
Runs his erring pilgrimage,
That the stretching of a span
Buckles in his sum of age;
Some, of violated vows
'Twixt the souls of friend and friend:
But upon the fairest boughs,
Or at every sentence end,
Will I Rosalinda write,
Teaching all that read to know
The quintessence of every sprite
Heaven would in little show.
Therefore Heaven Nature charged
That one body should be fill'd
With all graces wide-enlarged:
Nature presently distill'd
Helen's cheek, but not her heart,
Cleopatra's majesty,
Atalanta's better part,
Sad Lucretia's modesty.
Thus Rosalind of many parts
By heavenly synod was devised,
Of many faces, eyes and hearts,
To have the touches dearest prized.
Heaven would that she these gifts should have,
And I to live and die her slave.

Rosalind: O most gentle pulpiter! what tedious homily of love have you wearied your parishioners withal, and never cried 'Have patience, good people!'

Celia:

How now! back, friends! Shepherd, go off a little.

Go with him, sirrah.

Touchstone: Come, shepherd, let us make an honourable retreat; though not with bag and baggage, yet with scrip and scrippage.

Exeunt Corin and *Touchstone*

Celia: Didst thou hear these verses?

Rosalind: O, yes, I heard them all, and more too; for some of them had in them more feet than the verses would bear.

Celia: That's no matter: the feet might bear the verses.

Rosalind: Ay, but the feet were lame and could not bear themselves without the verse and therefore stood lamely in the verse.

Celia: But didst thou hear without wondering how thy name should be hanged and carved upon these trees?

Rosalind: I was seven of the nine days out of the wonder before you came; for look here what I found on a palm-tree. I was never so be-rhymed since Pythagoras' time, that I was an Irish rat, which I can hardly remember.

Celia: Trow you who hath done this?

Rosalind: Is it a man?

Celia: And a chain, that you once wore, about his neck.

Change you colour?

Rosalind: I prithee, who?

Celia: O Lord, Lord! it is a hard matter for friends to meet; but mountains may be removed with earthquakes and so encounter.

Rosalind: Nay, but who is it?

Celia: Is it possible?

Rosalind: Nay, I prithee now with most petitionary vehemence, tell me who it is.

Celia: O wonderful, wonderful, and most wonderful wonderful! and yet again wonderful, and after that, out of all hooping!

Rosalind: Good my complexion! dost thou think, though I am caparisoned like a man, I have a doublet and hose in my disposition? One inch of delay more is a South-sea of discovery; I prithee, tell me who is it quickly, and speak apace. I would thou couldst stammer, that thou mightst pour this concealed man out of thy mouth, as wine comes out of a narrow- mouthed bottle, either too much at once, or none at all. I prithee, take the cork out of thy mouth that may drink thy tidings.

Celia: So you may put a man in your belly.

Rosalind: Is he of God's making? What manner of man? Is his head worth a hat, or his chin worth a beard?

Celia: Nay, he hath but a little beard.

Rosalind: Why, God will send more, if the man will be thankful: let me stay the growth of his beard, if thou delay me not the knowledge of his chin.

Celia: It is young Orlando, that tripped up the wrestler's

heels and your heart both in an instant.

Rosalind: Nay, but the devil take mocking: speak, sad brow and true maid.

Celia: I' faith, coz, 'tis he.

Rosalind: Orlando?

Celia: Orlando.

Rosalind: Alas the day! what shall I do with my doublet and hose? What did he when thou sawest him? What said he? How looked he? Wherein went he? What makes him here? Did he ask for me? Where remains he? How parted he with thee? and when shalt thou see him again? Answer me in one word.

Celia: You must borrow me Gargantua's mouth first: 'tis a word too great for any mouth of this age's size. To say ay and no to these particulars is more than to answer in a catechism.

Rosalind: But doth he know that I am in this forest and in man's apparel? Looks he as freshly as he did the day he wrestled?

Celia: It is as easy to count atomies as to resolve the propositions of a lover; but take a taste of my finding him, and relish it with good observance. I found him under a tree, like a dropped acorn.

Rosalind: It may well be called Jove's tree, when it drops

forth such fruit.

Celia: Give me audience, good madam.

Rosalind: Proceed.

Celia: There lay he, stretched along, like a wounded knight.

Rosalind: Though it be pity to see such a sight, it well becomes the ground.

Celia: Cry 'holla' to thy tongue, I prithee; it curvets unseasonably. He was furnished like a hunter.

Rosalind: O, ominous! he comes to kill my heart.

Celia: I would sing my song without a burden: thou bringest me out of tune.

Rosalind: Do you not know I am a woman? when I think, I must speak. Sweet, say on.

Celia: You bring me out. Soft! comes he not here?

Enter Orlando and Jaques

Rosalind: 'Tis he: slink by, and note him.

Jaques: I thank you for your company; but, good faith, I had as lief have been myself alone.

Orlando: And so had I; but yet, for fashion sake, I thank you too for your society.

Jaques: God be wi' you: let's meet as little as we can.

Orlando: I do desire we may be better strangers.

Jaques: I pray you, mar no more trees with writing love-songs in their barks.

Orlando: I pray you, mar no more of my verses with reading them ill-favouredly.

Jaques: Rosalind is your love's name?

Orlando: Yes, just.

Jaques: I do not like her name.

Orlando: There was no thought of pleasing you when she was christened.

Jaques: What stature is she of?

Orlando: Just as high as my heart.

Jaques: You are full of pretty answers. Have you not been acquainted with goldsmiths' wives, and conned them out of rings?

Orlando: Not so; but I answer you right painted cloth, from whence you have studied your questions.

Jaques: You have a nimble wit: I think 'twas made of Atalanta's heels. Will you sit down with me? and we two will rail against our mistress the world and all our misery.

Orlando: I will chide no breather in the world but myself, against whom I know most faults.

Jaques: The worst fault you have is to be in love.

Orlando: 'Tis a fault I will not change for your best virtue. I am weary of you.

Jaques: By my troth, I was seeking for a fool when I found you.

Orlando: He is drowned in the brook: look but in, and you shall see him.

Jaques: There I shall see mine own figure.

Orlando: Which I take to be either a fool or a cipher.

Jaques: I'll tarry no longer with you: farewell, good Signior Love.

Orlando: I am glad of your departure: adieu, good Monsieur Melancholy.

Exit *Jaques*

Rosalind: [Aside to *Celia*] I will speak to him, like a saucy lackey and under that habit play the knave with him.

Do you hear, forester?

Orlando: Very well: what would you?

Rosalind: I pray you, what is't o'clock?

Orlando: You should ask me what time o' day: there's no clock in the forest.

Rosalind: Then there is no true lover in the forest; else sighing every minute and groaning every hour would detect the lazy foot of Time as well as a clock.

Orlando: And why not the swift foot of Time? had not that been as proper?

Rosalind: By no means, sir: Time travels in divers paces with divers persons. I'll tell you who Time ambles withal, who Time trots withal, who Time gallops withal and who he stands still withal.

Orlando: I prithee, who doth he trot withal?

Rosalind: Marry, he trots hard with a young maid between the contract of her marriage and the day it is solemnised: if the interim be but a se'nnight, Time's pace is so hard that it seems the length of seven year.

Orlando: Who ambles Time withal?

Rosalind: With a priest that lacks Latin and a rich man that hath not the gout, for the one sleeps easily because he cannot study, and the other lives merrily because he feels no pain, the one lacking the burden of lean and wasteful learning, the other knowing no burden of heavy tedious penury; these Time ambles withal.

Orlando: Who doth he gallop withal?

Rosalind: With a thief to the gallows, for though he go as softly as foot can fall, he thinks himself too soon there.

Orlando: Who stays it still withal?

Rosalind: With lawyers in the vacation, for they sleep between term and term and then they perceive not how Time moves.

Orlando: Where dwell you, pretty youth?

Rosalind: With this shepherdess, my sister; here in the skirts of the forest, like fringe upon a petticoat.

Orlando: Are you native of this place?

Rosalind: As the cony that you see dwell where she is kindled.

Orlando: Your accent is something finer than you could purchase in so removed a dwelling.

Rosalind: I have been told so of many: but indeed an old religious uncle of mine taught me to speak, who was in his youth an inland man; one that knew courtship too well, for there he fell in love. I have heard him read many lectures against it, and I thank God I am not a woman, to be touched with so many giddy offences as he hath generally taxed their whole sex withal.

Orlando: Can you remember any of the principal evils that he laid to the charge of women?

Rosalind: There were none principal; they were all like one another as half-pence are, every one fault seeming monstrous till his fellow fault came to match it.

Orlando: I prithee, recount some of them.

Rosalind: No, I will not cast away my physic but on those that are sick. There is a man haunts the forest, that abuses our young plants with carving 'Rosalind' on their barks; hangs odes upon hawthorns and elegies on brambles, all, forsooth, deifying the name of Rosalind: if I could meet that fancy-monger I would give him some good counsel, for he seems to have the quotidian of love upon him.

Orlando: I am he that is so love-shaked: I pray you tell me your remedy.

Rosalind: There is none of my uncle's marks upon you: he taught me how to know a man in love; in which cage of rushes I am sure you are not prisoner.

Orlando: What were his marks?

Rosalind: A lean cheek, which you have not, a blue eye and sunken, which you have not, an unquestionable spirit, which you have not, a beard neglected, which you have not; but I pardon you for that, for simply your having in beard is a younger brother's revenue: then your hose should be ungartered, your bonnet unbanded, your sleeve unbuttoned, your shoe untied and every thing about you demonstrating a careless desolation; but you are no such man; you are rather point-device in your accoutrements as loving yourself than seeming the lover of any other.

Orlando: Fair youth, I would I could make thee believe I love.

Rosalind: Me believe it! you may as soon make her that you love believe it; which, I warrant, she is apter to do than to confess she does: that is one of the points in the which women still give the lie to their consciences. But, in good sooth, are you he that hangs the verses on the trees, wherein Rosalind is so admired?

Orlando: I swear to thee, youth, by the white hand of Rosalind, I am that he, that unfortunate he.

Rosalind: But are you so much in love as your rhymes speak?

Orlando: Neither rhyme nor reason can express how much.

Rosalind: Love is merely a madness, and, I tell you, deserves as well a dark house and a whip as madmen do: and the reason why they are not so punished and cured is, that the lunacy is so ordinary that the whippers are in love too. Yet I profess curing it by counsel.

Orlando: Did you ever cure any so?

Rosalind: Yes, one, and in this manner. He was to imagine me his love, his mistress; and I set him every day to woo me:

at which time would I, being but a moonish youth, grieve, be effeminate, changeable, longing and liking, proud, fantastical, apish, shallow, inconstant, full of tears, full of smiles, for every passion something and for no passion truly any thing, as boys and women are for the most part cattle of this colour; would now like him, now loathe him; then entertain him, then forswear him; now weep for him, then spit at him; that I drave my suitor from his mad humour of love to a living humour of madness; which was, to forswear the full stream of the world, and to live in a nook merely monastic. And thus I cured him; and this way will I take upon me to wash your liver as clean as a sound sheep's heart, that there shall not be one spot of love in't.

Orlando: I would not be cured, youth.

Rosalind: I would cure you, if you would but call me Rosalind and come every day to my cote and woo me.

Orlando: Now, by the faith of my love, I will: tell me where it is.

Rosalind: Go with me to it and I'll show it you and by the way you shall tell me where in the forest you live.

Will you go?

Orlando: With all my heart, good youth.

Rosalind: Nay you must call me Rosalind. Come, sister, will you go?

Exeunt

Scene III: The Forest

Enter *Touchstone* and Audrey; Jaques behind

Touchstone: Come apace, good Audrey: I will fetch up your goats, Audrey. And how, Audrey? am I the man yet? doth my simple feature content you?

Audrey: Your features! Lord warrant us! what features!

Touchstone: I am here with thee and thy goats, as the most capricious poet, honest Ovid, was among the Goths.

Jaques: [Aside] O knowledge ill-inhabited, worse than Jove in a thatched house!

Touchstone: When a man's verses cannot be understood, nor a man's good wit seconded with the forward child Understanding, it strikes a man more dead than a great reckoning in a little room. Truly, I would the gods had made thee poetical.

Audrey: I do not know what 'poetical' is: is it honest in deed and word? is it a true thing?

Touchstone: No, truly; for the truest poetry is the most feigning; and lovers are given to poetry, and what they swear in poetry may be said as lovers they do feign.

Audrey: Do you wish then that the gods had made me poetical?

Touchstone: I do, truly; for thou swearest to me thou art honest: now, if thou wert a poet, I might have some hope thou didst feign.

Audrey: Would you not have me honest?

Touchstone: No, truly, unless thou wert hard-favoured; for honesty coupled to beauty is to have honey a sauce to sugar.

Jaques: [Aside] A material fool!

Audrey: Well, I am not fair; and therefore I pray the gods make me honest.

Touchstone: Truly, and to cast away honesty upon a foul slut were to put good meat into an unclean dish.

Audrey: I am not a slut, though I thank the gods I am foul.

Touchstone: Well, praised be the gods for thy foulness! sluttishness may come hereafter. But be it as it may be, I will marry thee, and to that end I have been with Sir Oliver Martext, the vicar of the next village, who hath promised to meet me in this place of the forest and to couple us.

Jaques: [Aside] I would fain see this meeting.

Audrey: Well, the gods give us joy!

Touchstone: Amen. A man may, if he were of a fearful heart, stagger in this attempt; for here we have no temple but the wood, no assembly but horn-beasts. But what though? C ourage! As horns are odious, they are necessary. It is said, 'many a man knows no end of his goods:' right; many a man has good horns, and knows no end of them. Well, that is the dowry of his wife; 'tis none of his own getting. Horns?

Even so. Poor men alone? No, no; the noblest deer hath them as huge as the rascal. Is the single man therefore blessed? No: as a walled town is more worthier than a village, so is the forehead of a married man more honourable than the bare brow of a bachelor; and by how much defence is better than no skill, by so much is a horn more precious than to want. Here comes Sir Oliver.

Enter Sir Oliver Martext

Sir Oliver Martext, you are well met: will you dispatch us here under this tree, or shall we go with you to your chapel?

Sir Oliver Martext: Is there none here to give the woman?

Touchstone: I will not take her on gift of any man.

Sir Oliver Martext: Truly, she must be given, or the marriage is not lawful.

Jaques: [Advancing] Proceed, proceed I'll give her.

Touchstone: Good even, good Master What-ye-call't: how do you, sir? You are very well met: God 'ild you for your last company: I am very glad to see you: even a toy in hand here, sir: nay, pray be covered.

Jaques: Will you be married, motley?

Touchstone: As the ox hath his bow, sir, the horse his curb and the falcon her bells, so man hath his desires; and as pigeons bill, so wedlock would be nibbling.

Jaques: And will you, being a man of your breeding, be married under a bush like a beggar? Get you to church, and have a good priest that can tell you what marriage is: this fellow will but join you together as they join wainscot; then one of you will prove a shrunk panel and, like green timber, warp, warp.

Touchstone: [Aside] I am not in the mind but I were better to be married of him than of another: for he is not like to marry me well; and not being well married, it will be a good excuse for me hereafter to leave my wife.

Jaques: Go thou with me, and let me counsel thee.

Touchstone:

'Come, sweet Audrey:
We must be married, or we must live in bawdry.
Farewell, good Master Oliver: not,—
O sweet Oliver,
O brave Oliver,
Leave me not behind thee: but,—
Wind away,
Begone, I say,
I will not to wedding with thee.
Exeunt Jaques, Touchstone and Audrey

Sir Oliver Martext: 'Tis no matter: ne'er a fantastical knave of them all shall flout me out of my calling.

Exit

Scene IV : The Forest

Enter *Rosalind* and *Celia*

Rosalind: Never talk to me; I will weep.

Celia: Do, I prithee; but yet have the grace to consider that tears do not become a man.

Rosalind: But have I not cause to weep?

Celia: As good cause as one would desire; therefore weep.

Rosalind: His very hair is of the dissembling colour.

Celia: Something browner than Judas's marry, his kisses are Judas's own children.

Rosalind: I' faith, his hair is of a good colour.

Celia: An excellent colour: your chestnut was ever the only colour.

Rosalind: And his kissing is as full of sanctity as the touch of holy bread.

Celia: He hath bought a pair of cast lips of Diana: a nun of winter's sisterhood kisses not more religiously; the very ice of chastity is in them.

Rosalind: But why did he swear he would come this morning, and comes not?

Celia: Nay, certainly, there is no truth in him.

Rosalind: Do you think so?

Celia: Yes; I think he is not a pick-purse nor a horse-stealer, but for his verity in love, I do think him as concave as a covered goblet or a worm-eaten nut.

Rosalind: Not true in love?

Celia: Yes, when he is in; but I think he is not in.

Rosalind: You have heard him swear downright he was.

Celia: 'Was' is not 'is:' besides, the oath of a lover is no stronger than the word of a tapster; they are both the confirmer of false reckonings. He attends here in the forest on the duke your father.

Rosalind: I met the duke yesterday and had much question with him: he asked me of what parentage I was; I told him, of as good as he; so he laughed and let me go. But what talk we of fathers, when there is such a man as Orlando?

Celia: O, that's a brave man! he writes brave verses, speaks brave words, swears brave oaths and breaks them bravely, quite traverse, athwart the heart of his lover; as a puisny tilter, that spurs his horse but on one side, breaks his staff like a noble goose: but all's brave that youth mounts and folly guides. Who comes here?

Enter *Corin*

Corin: Mistress and master, you have oft inquired
After the shepherd that complain'd of love,
Who you saw sitting by me on the turf,
Praising the proud disdainful shepherdess
That was his mistress.
Celia: Well, and what of him?
Corin: If you will see a pageant truly play'd,
Between the pale complexion of true love
And the red glow of scorn and proud disdain,
Go hence a little and I shall conduct you,
If you will mark it.

Rosalind:

O, come, let us remove:
The sight of lovers feedeth those in love.
Bring us to this sight, and you shall say
I'll prove a busy actor in their play.

Exeunt

Scene V. Another part of the forest.

Enter Silvius and Phebe

Silvius: Sweet Phebe, do not scorn me; do not, Phebe;
Say that you love me not, but say not so
In bitterness. The common executioner,
Whose heart the accustom'd sight of death makes hard,
Falls not the axe upon the humbled neck
But first begs pardon: will you sterner be
Than he that dies and lives by bloody drops?
Enter *Rosalind, Celia,* and *Corin,* behind
Phebe: I would not be thy executioner:
I fly thee, for I would not injure thee.
Thou tell'st me there is murder in mine eye:
'Tis pretty, sure, and very probable,
That eyes, that are the frail'st and softest things,
Who shut their coward gates on atomies,
Should be call'd tyrants, butchers, murderers!
Now I do frown on thee with all my heart;
And if mine eyes can wound, now let them kill thee:

Now counterfeit to swoon; why now fall down;
Or if thou canst not, O, for shame, for shame,
Lie not, to say mine eyes are murderers!
Now show the wound mine eye hath made in thee:
Scratch thee but with a pin, and there remains
Some scar of it; lean but upon a rush,
The cicatrice and capable impressure
Thy palm some moment keeps; but now mine eyes,
Which I have darted at thee, hurt thee not,
Nor, I am sure, there is no force in eyes
That can do hurt.

Silvius: O dear Phebe,
If ever,—as that ever may be near,—
You meet in some fresh cheek the power of fancy,
Then shall you know the wounds invisible
That love's keen arrows make.

Phebe: But till that time
Come not thou near me: and when that time comes,
Afflict me with thy mocks, pity me not;
As till that time I shall not pity thee.

Rosalind: And why, I pray you? Who might be your mother,
That you insult, exult, and all at once,
Over the wretched? What though you have no beauty,—
As, by my faith, I see no more in you
Than without candle may go dark to bed—
Must you be therefore proud and pitiless?
Why, what means this? Why do you look on me?
I see no more in you than in the ordinary
Of nature's sale-work. 'Od's my little life,
I think she means to tangle my eyes too!
No, faith, proud mistress, hope not after it:
'Tis not your inky brows, your black silk hair,
Your bugle eyeballs, nor your cheek of cream,
That can entame my spirits to your worship.
You foolish shepherd, wherefore do you follow her,
Like foggy south puffing with wind and rain?
You are a thousand times a properer man

Than she a woman: 'tis such fools as you
That makes the world full of ill-favour'd children:
'Tis not her glass, but you, that flatters her;
And out of you she sees herself more proper
Than any of her lineaments can show her.
But, mistress, know yourself: down on your knees,
And thank heaven, fasting, for a good man's love:
For I must tell you friendly in your ear,
Sell when you can: you are not for all markets:
Cry the man mercy; love him; take his offer:
Foul is most foul, being foul to be a scoffer.
So take her to thee, shepherd: fare you well.

Phebe: Sweet youth, I pray you, chide a year together:

I had rather hear you chide than this man woo.

Rosalind: He's fallen in love with your foulness and she'll fall in love with my anger. If it be so, as fast as she answers thee with frowning looks, I'll sauce her with bitter words. Why look you so upon me?

Phebe: For no ill will I bear you.

Rosalind: I pray you, do not fall in love with me,
For I am falser than vows made in wine:
Besides, I like you not. If you will know my house,
'Tis at the tuft of olives here hard by.
Will you go, sister? Shepherd, ply her hard.
Come, sister. Shepherdess, look on him better,
And be not proud: though all the world could see,
None could be so abused in sight as he.
Come, to our flock.

Exeunt *Rosalind, Celia* and *Corin*

Phebe:

Dead Shepherd, now I find thy saw of might,
'Who ever loved that loved not at first sight?'

Silvius

Sweet Phebe,—

Phebe: Ha, what say'st thou, Silvius?

Silvius: Sweet Phebe, pity me.

Phebe: Why, I am sorry for thee, gentle Silvius.

Silvius: Wherever sorrow is, relief would be:
If you do sorrow at my grief in love,
By giving love your sorrow and my grief
Were both extermined.

Phebe: Thou hast my love: is not that neighbourly?

Silvius: I would have you.

Phebe: Why, that were covetousness.
Silvius, the time was that I hated thee,
And yet it is not that I bear thee love;
But since that thou canst talk of love so well,
Thy company, which erst was irksome to me,
I will endure, and I'll employ thee too:
But do not look for further recompense
Than thine own gladness that thou art employ'd.

Silvius: So holy and so perfect is my love,
And I in such a poverty of grace,
That I shall think it a most plenteous crop
To glean the broken ears after the man
That the main harvest reaps: loose now and then
A scatter'd smile, and that I'll live upon.

Phebe: Know'st now the youth that spoke to me erewhile?

Silvius: Not very well, but I have met him oft;
And he hath bought the cottage and the bounds
That the old carlot once was master of.
Phebe: Think not I love him, though I ask for him:
'Tis but a peevish boy; yet he talks well;
But what care I for words? yet words do well
When he that speaks them pleases those that hear.
It is a pretty youth: not very pretty:
But, sure, he's proud, and yet his pride becomes him:
He'll make a proper man: the best thing in him
Is his complexion; and faster than his tongue

Did make offence his eye did heal it up.
He is not very tall; yet for his years he's tall:
His leg is but so so; and yet 'tis well:
There was a pretty redness in his lip,
A little riper and more lusty red
Than that mix'd in his cheek; 'twas just the difference
Between the constant red and mingled damask.
There be some women, Silvius, had they mark'd him
In parcels as I did, would have gone near
To fall in love with him; but, for my part,
I love him not nor hate him not; and yet
I have more cause to hate him than to love him:
For what had he to do to chide at me?
He said mine eyes were black and my hair black:
And, now I am remember'd, scorn'd at me:
I marvel why I answer'd not again:
But that's all one; omittance is no quittance.
I'll write to him a very taunting letter,
And thou shalt bear it: wilt thou, Silvius?

Silvius: Phebe, with all my heart.

Phebe: I'll write it straight;
The matter's in my head and in my heart:
I will be bitter with him and passing short.
Go with me, Silvius.

Exeunt

Act IV Scene I. The forest.

Enter *Rosalind, Celia,* and *Jaques*

Jaques: I prithee, pretty youth, let me be better acquainted with thee.

Rosalind: They say you are a melancholy fellow.

Jaques: I am so; I do love it better than laughing.

Rosalind: Those that are in extremity of either are abominable fellows and betray themselves to every modern censure worse than drunkards.

Jaques: Why, 'tis good to be sad and say nothing.

Rosalind: Why then, 'tis good to be a post.

Jaques: I have neither the scholar's melancholy, which is emulation, nor the musician's, which is fantastical, nor the courtier's, which is proud, nor the soldier's, which is ambitious, nor the lawyer's, which is politic, nor the lady's, which is nice, nor the lover's, which is all these: but it is a melancholy of mine own, compounded of many simples, extracted from many objects, and indeed the sundry's contemplation of my travels, in which my often rumination wraps me m a most humourous sadness.

Rosalind: A traveller! By my faith, you have great reason to be sad. I fear you have sold your own lands to see other men's; then, to have seen much and to have nothing, is to have rich eyes and poor hands.

Jaques: Yes, I have gained my experience.

Rosalind: And your experience makes you sad: I had rather have a fool to make me merry than experience to make me sad; and to travel for it too!

Enter Orlando

Orlando: Good day and happiness, dear Rosalind!

Jaques: Nay, then, God be wi' you, an you talk in blank verse.

Exit

Rosalind: Farewell, Monsieur Traveller: look you lisp and wear strange suits, disable all the benefits of your own country, be out of love with your nativity and almost chide God for making you that countenance you are, or I will scarce think you have swam in a gondola. Why, how now, Orlando! where have you been all this while? You a lover! An you serve me such another trick, never come in my sight more.

Orlando: My fair Rosalind, I come within an hour of my promise.

Rosalind: Break an hour's promise in love! He that will divide a minute into a thousand parts and break but a part of the thousandth part of a minute in the affairs of love, it may be said of him that Cupid hath clapped him o' the shoulder, but I'll warrant him heart-whole.

Orlando: Pardon me, dear Rosalind.

Rosalind: Nay, an you be so tardy, come no more in my sight: I had as lief be wooed of a snail.

Orlando: Of a snail?

Rosalind: Ay, of a snail; for though he comes slowly, he carries his house on his head; a better jointure, I think, than you make a woman: besides he brings his destiny with him.

Orlando: What's that?

Rosalind: Why, horns, which such as you are fain to be beholding to your wives for: but he comes armed in his fortune and prevents the slander of his wife.

Orlando: Virtue is no horn-maker; and my Rosalind is virtuous.

Rosalind: And I am your Rosalind.

Celia: It pleases him to call you so; but he hath a Rosalind of a better leer than you.

Rosalind: Come, woo me, woo me, for now I am in a holiday humour and like enough to consent. What would you say to me now, an I were your very very Rosalind?

Orlando: I would kiss before I spoke.

Rosalind: Nay, you were better speak first, and when you were gravelled for lack of matter, you might take occasion to kiss. Very good orators, when they are out, they will spit; and for lovers lacking—God warn us!—matter, the cleanliest shift is to kiss.

Orlando: How if the kiss be denied?

Rosalind: Then she puts you to entreaty, and there begins new matter.

Orlando: Who could be out, being before his beloved mistress?

Rosalind: Marry, that should you, if I were your mistress, or I should think my honesty ranker than my wit.

Orlando: What, of my suit?

Rosalind: Not out of your apparel, and yet out of your suit. Am not I your Rosalind?

Orlando: I take some joy to say you are, because I would be talking of her.

Rosalind: Well in her person I say I will not have you.

Orlando: Then in mine own person I die.

Rosalind: No, faith, die by attorney. The poor world is almost six thousand years old, and in all this time there was not any man died in his own person, videlicit, in a love-cause. Troilus had his brains dashed out with a Grecian club; yet he did what he could to die before, and he is one of the patterns of love. Leander, he would have lived many a fair year, though Hero had turned nun, if it had not been for a hot midsummer night; for, good youth, he went but forth to wash him in the Hellespont and being taken with the cramp was drowned and the foolish coroners of that age found it was 'Hero of Sestos.'

But these are all lies: men have died from time to time and worms have eaten them, but not for love.

Orlando: I would not have my right Rosalind of this mind, for, I protest, her frown might kill me.

Rosalind: By this hand, it will not kill a fly. But come, now I will be your Rosalind in a more coming-on disposition, and ask me what you will. I will grant it.

Orlando: Then love me, Rosalind.

Rosalind: Yes, faith, will I, Fridays and Saturdays and all.

Orlando: And wilt thou have me?

Rosalind: Ay, and twenty such.

Orlando: What sayest thou?

Rosalind: Are you not good?

Orlando: I hope so.

Rosalind: Why then, can one desire too much of a good thing? Come, sister, you shall be the priest and marry us. Give me your hand, Orlando. What do you say, sister?

Orlando: Pray thee, marry us.

Celia: I cannot say the words.

Rosalind: You must begin, 'Will you, Orlando—'

Celia: Go to. Will you, Orlando, have to wife this Rosalind?

Orlando: I will.

Rosalind: Ay, but when?

Orlando: Why now; as fast as she can marry us.

Rosalind: Then you must say 'I take thee, Rosalind, for wife.'

Orlando: I take thee, Rosalind, for wife.

Rosalind: I might ask you for your commission; but I do take thee, Orlando, for my husband: there's a girl goes before the priest; and certainly a woman's thought runs before her actions.

Orlando: So do all thoughts; they are winged.

Rosalind: Now tell me how long you would have her after you have possessed her.

Orlando: For ever and a day.

Rosalind: Say 'a day,' without the 'ever.' No, no, Orlando; men are April when they woo, December when they wed: maids are May when they are maids, but the sky changes when they are wives. I will be more jealous of thee than a Barbary cock-pigeon over his hen, more clamorous than a parrot against rain, more new-fangled than an ape, more giddy in my desires than a monkey: I will weep for nothing, like Diana in the fountain, and I will do that when you are disposed to be merry; I will laugh like a hyen, and that when thou art inclined to sleep.

Orlando: But will my Rosalind do so?

Rosalind: By my life, she will do as I do.

Orlando: O, but she is wise.

Rosalind: Or else she could not have the wit to do this: the wiser, the waywarder: make the doors upon a woman's wit and it will out at the casement; shut that and 'twill out at the key-hole; stop that, 'twill fly with the smoke out at the chimney.

Orlando: A man that had a wife with such a wit, he might say 'Wit, whither wilt?'

Rosalind: Nay, you might keep that cheque for it till you met your wife's wit going to your neighbour's bed.

Orlando: And what wit could wit have to excuse that?

Rosalind: Marry, to say she came to seek you there. You shall never take her without her answer, unless you take her without her tongue. O, that woman that cannot make her fault her husband's occasion, let her never nurse her child herself, for she will breed it like a fool!

Orlando: For these two hours, Rosalind, I will leave thee.

Rosalind: Alas! dear love, I cannot lack thee two hours.

Orlando: I must attend the duke at dinner: by two o'clock I will be with thee again.

Rosalind: Ay, go your ways, go your ways; I knew what you would prove: my friends told me as much, and I thought no less: that flattering tongue of yours won me: 'tis but one cast away, and so, come, death! Two o'clock is your hour?

Orlando: Ay, sweet Rosalind.

Rosalind: By my troth, and in good earnest, and so God mend me, and by all pretty oaths that are not dangerous, if you break one jot of your promise or come one minute behind your hour, I will think you the most pathetical break-promise and the most hollow lover and the most unworthy of her you call Rosalind that may be chosen out of the gross band of the unfaithful: therefore beware my censure and keep your promise.

Orlando: With no less religion than if thou wert indeed my Rosalind: so adieu.

Rosalind: Well, Time is the old justice that examines all such offenders, and let Time try: adieu.

Exit *Orlando*

Celia: You have simply misused our sex in your love-prate: we must have your doublet and hose plucked over your head, and show the world what the bird hath done to her own nest.

Rosalind: O coz, coz, coz, my pretty little coz, that thou didst know how many fathom deep I am in love! But it cannot be sounded: my affection hath an unknown bottom, like the bay of Portugal.

Celia: Or rather, bottomless, that as fast as you pour affection in, it runs out.

Rosalind: No, that same wicked bastard of Venus that was begot of thought, conceived of spleen and born of madness, that blind rascally boy that abuses every one's eyes because his own are out, let him be judge how deep I am in love. I'll tell thee, Aliena, I cannot be out of the sight of Orlando: I'll go find a shadow and sigh till he come.

Celia: And I'll sleep.

Exeunt

Scene II: The Forest.

Enter Jaques, Lords, and Foresters

Jaques: Which is he that killed the deer?

A Lord

Sir, it was I.

Jaques: Let's present him to the duke, like a Roman conqueror; and it would do well to set the deer's horns upon his head, for a branch of victory. Have you no song, forester, for this purpose?

Forester

Yes, sir.

Jaques: Sing it: 'tis no matter how it be in tune, so it make noise enough.

Song

Forester
What shall he have that kill'd the deer?
His leather skin and horns to wear.
Then sing him home;
The rest shall bear this burden
Take thou no scorn to wear the horn;
It was a crest ere thou wast born:
Thy father's father wore it,
And thy father bore it:
The horn, the horn, the lusty horn
Is not a thing to laugh to scorn.

Exeunt

Scene III: The Forest

Enter Rosalind and *Celia*

Rosalind: How say you now? Is it not past two o'clock? and here much Orlando!

Celia: I warrant you, with pure love and troubled brain, he hath ta'en his bow and arrows and is gone forth to sleep. Look, who comes here.

Enter Silvius

Silvius:

My errand is to you, fair youth;
My gentle Phebe bid me give you this:
I know not the contents; but, as I guess
By the stern brow and waspish action
Which she did use as she was writing of it,

It bears an angry tenor: pardon me:
I am but as a guiltless messenger.

Rosalind:

Patience herself would startle at this letter
And play the swaggerer; bear this, bear all:
She says I am not fair, that I lack manners;
She calls me proud, and that she could not love me,
Were man as rare as phoenix. 'Od's my will!
Her love is not the hare that I do hunt:
Why writes she so to me? Well, shepherd, well,
This is a letter of your own device.

Silvius:

No, I protest, I know not the contents:
Phebe did write it.

Rosalind:

Come, come, you are a fool
And turn'd into the extremity of love.
I saw her hand: she has a leathern hand.
A freestone-colour'd hand; I verily did think
That her old gloves were on, but 'twas her hands:
She has a huswife's hand; but that's no matter:
I say she never did invent this letter;
This is a man's invention and his hand.

Silvius: Sure, it is hers.

Rosalind:

Why, 'tis a boisterous and a cruel style.
A style for-challengers; why, she defies me,
Like Turk to Christian: women's gentle brain
Could not drop forth such giant-rude invention
Such Ethiope words, blacker in their effect
Than in their countenance. Will you hear the letter?

Silvius:

So please you, for I never heard it yet;
Yet heard too much of Phebe's cruelty.

Rosalind: She Phebes me: mark how the tyrant writes.

Reads

Art thou god to shepherd turn'd,
That a maiden's heart hath burn'd?
Can a woman rail thus?

Silvius: Call you this railing?

Rosalind: [Reads]

Why, thy godhead laid apart,
Warr'st thou with a woman's heart?
Did you ever hear such railing?
Whiles the eye of man did woo me,
That could do no vengeance to me.
Meaning me a beast.
If the scorn of your bright eyne
Have power to raise such love in mine,
Alack, in me what strange effect
Would they work in mild aspect!
Whiles you chid me, I did love;
How then might your prayers move!
He that brings this love to thee
Little knows this love in me:
And by him seal up thy mind;
Whether that thy youth and kind
Will the faithful offer take
Of me and all that I can make;
Or else by him my love deny,
And then I'll study how to die.

Silvius: Call you this chiding?

Celia: Alas, poor shepherd!

Rosalind: Do you pity him? no, he deserves no pity. Wilt thou love such a woman? What, to make thee an instrument and play false strains upon thee! not to be endured! Well, go your way to her, for I see love hath made thee a tame snake, and say this to her: that if she love me, I charge her to love thee; if she will not, I will never have her unless thou entreat for her. If you be a true lover, hence, and not a word; for here comes more company.

Exit *Silvius*

Enter Oliver

Oliver: Good morrow, fair ones: pray you, if you know,
Where in the purlieus of this forest stands
A sheep-cote fenced about with olive trees?

Celia:

West of this place, down in the neighbour bottom:
The rank of osiers by the murmuring stream
Left on your right hand brings you to the place.
But at this hour the house doth keep itself;
There's none within.

Oliver:

If that an eye may profit by a tongue,
Then should I know you by description;
Such garments and such years: 'The boy is fair,
Of female favour, and bestows himself
Like a ripe sister: the woman low
And browner than her brother.' Are not you
The owner of the house I did inquire for?
Celia: It is no boast, being ask'd, to say we are.

Oliver:

Orlando doth commend him to you both,
And to that youth he calls his Rosalind
He sends this bloody napkin. Are you he?

Rosalind: I am: what must we understand by this?

Oliver:

Some of my shame; if you will know of me
What man I am, and how, and why, and where
This handkercher was stain'd.

Celia: I pray you, tell it.

Oliver:

When last the young Orlando parted from you
He left a promise to return again
Within an hour, and pacing through the forest,
Chewing the food of sweet and bitter fancy,
Lo, what befell! he threw his eye aside,
And mark what object did present itself:
Under an oak, whose boughs were moss'd with age
And high top bald with dry antiquity,
A wretched ragged man, o'ergrown with hair,
Lay sleeping on his back: about his neck
A green and gilded snake had wreathed itself,
Who with her head nimble in threats approach'd
The opening of his mouth; but suddenly,
Seeing Orlando, it unlink'd itself,
And with indented glides did slip away
Into a bush: under which bush's shade
A lioness, with udders all drawn dry,
Lay couching, head on ground, with catlike watch,
When that the sleeping man should stir; for 'tis
The royal disposition of that beast
To prey on nothing that doth seem as dead:
This seen, Orlando did approach the man
And found it was his brother, his elder brother.

Celia:

O, I have heard him speak of that same brother;
And he did render him the most unnatural
That lived amongst men.

Orlando:

And well he might so do,
For well I know he was unnatural.

Rosalind:

But, to Orlando: did he leave him there,
Food to the suck'd and hungry lioness?

Oliver:

Twice did he turn his back and purposed so;
But kindness, nobler ever than revenge,
And nature, stronger than his just occasion,
Made him give battle to the lioness,
Who quickly fell before him: in which hurtling
From miserable slumber I awaked.

Celia: Are you his brother?

Rosalind: Wast you he rescued?

Celia: Was't you that did so oft contrive to kill him?

Oliver:

'Twas I; but 'tis not I I do not shame
To tell you what I was, since my conversion
So sweetly tastes, being the thing I am.

Rosalind: But, for the bloody napkin?

Oliver: By and by.
When from the first to last betwixt us two
Tears our recountments had most kindly bathed,
As how I came into that desert place:—
In brief, he led me to the gentle duke,
Who gave me fresh array and entertainment,
Committing me unto my brother's love;
Who led me instantly unto his cave,
There stripp'd himself, and here upon his arm
The lioness had torn some flesh away,
Which all this while had bled; and now he fainted
And cried, in fainting, upon Rosalind.
Brief, I recover'd him, bound up his wound;
And, after some small space, being strong at heart,
He sent me hither, stranger as I am,
To tell this story, that you might excuse
His broken promise, and to give this napkin
Dyed in his blood unto the shepherd youth
That he in sport doth call his Rosalind.

Rosalind: Swoons

Celia: Why, how now, Ganymede! sweet Ganymede!

Oliver: Many will swoon when they do look on blood.

Celia: There is more in it. Cousin Ganymede!

Oliver: Look, he recovers.

Rosalind: I would I were at home.

Celia: We'll lead you thither.

I pray you, will you take him by the arm?

Oliver: Be of good cheer, youth: you a man! you lack a man's heart.

Rosalind: I do so, I confess it. Ah, sirrah, a body would think this was well counterfeited! I pray you, tell your brother how well I counterfeited. Heigh-ho!

Oliver: This was not counterfeit: there is too great testimony in your complexion that it was a passion of earnest.

Rosalind: Counterfeit, I assure you.

Oliver: Well then, take a good heart and counterfeit to be a man.

Rosalind: So I do: but, i' faith, I should have been a woman by right.

Celia: Come, you look paler and paler: pray you, draw homewards. Good sir, go with us.

Oliver: That will I, for I must bear answer back

How you excuse my brother, Rosalind.

Rosalind: I shall devise something: but, I pray you, commend my counterfeiting to him. Will you go?

Exeunt

Act V Scene I The Forest

Enter *Touchstone* and *Audrey*

Touchstone: We shall find a time, Audrey; patience, gentle Audrey.

Audrey: Faith, the priest was good enough, for all the old gentleman's saying.

Touchstone: A most wicked Sir Oliver, Audrey, a most vile Martext. But, Audrey, there is a youth here in the forest lays claim to you.

Audrey: Ay, I know who 'tis; he hath no interest in me in the world: here comes the man you mean.

Touchstone: It is meat and drink to me to see a clown: by my troth, we that have good wits have much to answer for; we shall be flouting; we cannot hold.

Enter William

William: Good even, Audrey.

Audrey: God ye good even, William.

William: And good even to you, sir.

Touchstone: Good even, gentle friend. Cover thy head, cover thy head; nay, prithee, be covered. How old are you, friend?

William: Five and twenty, sir.

Touchstone: A ripe age. Is thy name William?

William: William, sir.

Touchstone: A fair name. Wast born i' the forest here?

William: Ay, sir, I thank God.

Touchstone: 'Thank God;' a good answer. Art rich?

William: Faith, sir, so so.

Touchstone: 'So so' is good, very good, very excellent good; and yet it is not; it is but so so. Art thou wise?

William: Ay, sir, I have a pretty wit.

Touchstone: Why, thou sayest well. I do now remember a saying, 'The fool doth think he is wise, but the wise man knows himself to be a fool.' The heathen philosopher, when he had a desire to eat a grape, would open his lips when he put it into his mouth; meaning thereby that grapes were made to eat and lips to open. You do love this maid?

William: I do, sir.

Touchstone: Give me your hand. Art thou learned?

William: No, sir.

Touchstone: Then learn this of me: to have, is to have; for it is a figure in rhetoric that drink, being poured out of a cup into a glass, by filling the one doth empty the other; for all your writers do consent that ipse is he: now, you are not ipse, for I am he.

William: Which he, sir?

Touchstone: He, sir, that must marry this woman. Therefore, you clown, abandon,—which is in the vulgar leave,—the society,—which in the boorish is company,—of this female,—which in the common is woman; which together is, abandon the society of this female, or, clown, thou perishest; or, to thy better understanding, diest; or, to wit I kill thee, make thee away, translate thy life into death, thy liberty into bondage: I will deal in poison with thee, or in bastinado, or in steel; I will bandy with thee in faction; I will o'errun thee with policy; I will kill thee a hundred and fifty ways: therefore tremble and depart.

Audrey: Do, good William.

William: God rest you merry, sir.

Exit

Enter *Corin*

Corin: Our master and mistress seeks you; come, away, away!

Touchstone: Trip, Audrey! trip, Audrey! I attend, I attend.

Exeunt

Scene II: The Forest

Enter *Orlando* and *Oliver*

Orlando: Is't possible that on so little acquaintance you should like her? that but seeing you should love her? and loving woo? and, wooing, she should grant? and will you persever to enjoy her?

Oliver: Neither call the giddiness of it in question, the poverty of her, the small acquaintance, my sudden wooing, nor her sudden consenting; but say with me, I love Aliena; say with her that she loves me; consent with both that we may enjoy each other: it shall be to your good; for my father's house and all the revenue that was old Sir Rowland's will I estate upon you, and here live and die a shepherd.

Orlando: You have my consent. Let your wedding be to-morrow: thither will I invite the duke and all's contented followers. Go you and prepare Aliena; for look you, here comes my Rosalind.

Enter *Rosalind*

Rosalind: God save you, brother.

Oliver: And you, fair sister.

Exit

Rosalind: O, my dear Orlando, how it grieves me to see thee wear thy heart in a scarf!

Orlando: It is my arm.

Rosalind: I thought thy heart had been wounded with the claws of a lion.

Orlando: Wounded it is, but with the eyes of a lady.

Rosalind: Did your brother tell you how I counterfeited to swoon when he showed me your handkerchief?

Orlando: Ay, and greater wonders than that.

Rosalind: O, I know where you are: nay, 'tis true: there was never any thing so sudden but the fight of two rams and

Caesar's thrasonical brag of 'I came, saw, and overcame:' for your brother and my sister no sooner met but they looked, no sooner looked but they loved, no sooner loved but they sighed, no sooner sighed but they asked one another the reason, no sooner knew the reason but they sought the remedy; and in these degrees have they made a pair of stairs to marriage which they will climb incontinent, or else be incontinent before marriage: they are in the very wrath of love and they will together; clubs cannot part them.

Orlando: They shall be married to-morrow, and I will bid the duke to the nuptial. But, O, how bitter a thing it is to look into happiness through another man's eyes! By so much the more shall I to-morrow be at the height of heart-heaviness, by how much I shall think my brother happy in having what he wishes for.

Rosalind: Why then, to-morrow I cannot serve your turn for Rosalind?

Orlando: I can live no longer by thinking.

Rosalind: I will weary you then no longer with idle talking. Know of me then, for now I speak to some purpose, that I know you are a gentleman of good conceit: I speak not this that you should bear a good opinion of my knowledge, insomuch I say I know you are; neither do I labour for a greater esteem than may in some little measure draw a belief from you, to do yourself good and not to grace me. Believe then, if you please, that I can do strange things: I have, since I was three year old, conversed with a magician, most profound in his art and yet not damnable. If you do love Rosalind so near the heart as your gesture cries it out, when your brother marries Aliena, shall you marry her: I know into what straits of fortune she is driven; and it is not impossible to me, if it appear not inconvenient to you, to set her before your eyes tomorrow human as she is and without any danger.

Orlando: Speakest thou in sobre meanings?

Rosalind: By my life, I do; which I tender dearly, though I say I am a magician. Therefore, put you in your best array:

bid your friends; for if you will be married to-morrow, you shall, and to Rosalind, if you will.

Enter Silvius and Phebe

Look, here comes a lover of mine and a lover of hers.

Phebe: Youth, you have done me much ungentleness, To show the letter that I writ to you.

Rosalind: I care not if I have: it is my study
To seem despiteful and ungentle to you:
You are there followed by a faithful shepherd;
Look upon him, love him; he worships you.

Phebe: Good shepherd, tell this youth what 'tis to love.

Silvius: It is to be all made of sighs and tears; And so am I for Phebe.

Phebe: And I for Ganymede.

*Orlando:*And I for Rosalind.

Rosalind: And I for no woman.

Silvius: It is to be all made of faith and service; And so am I for Phebe.

Phebe: And I for Ganymede.

Orlando: And I for Rosalind.

Rosalind: And I for no woman.

Silvius:

It is to be all made of fantasy,
All made of passion and all made of wishes,
All adoration, duty, and observance,
All humbleness, all patience and impatience,
All purity, all trial, all observance;
And so am I for Phebe.

Phebe: And so am I for Ganymede.

Orlando: And so am I for Rosalind.

Rosalind: And so am I for no woman.

Phebe: If this be so, why blame you me to love you?

Silvius: If this be so, why blame you me to love you?

Orlando: If this be so, why blame you me to love you?

Rosalind: Who do you speak to, 'Why blame you me to love you?'

Orlando: To her that is not here, nor doth not hear.

Rosalind: Pray you, no more of this; 'tis like the howling of Irish wolves against the moon.

To *Silvius:* I will help you, if I can:

To *Phebe:* I would love you, if I could. To-morrow meet me all together.

To *Phebe:* I will marry you, if ever I marry woman, and I'll be married to-morrow:

To *Orlando:* I will satisfy you, if ever I satisfied man, and you shall be married to-morrow:

To *Silvius:* I will content you, if what pleases you contents you, and you shall be married to-morrow.

To *Orlando:* As you love Rosalind, meet:

To *Silvius:* As you love Phebe, meet: and as I love no woman, I'll meet. So fare you well: I have left you commands.

Silvius: I'll not fail, if I live.

Phebe: Nor I.

Orlando: Nor I.

Exeunt

Scene III: The Forest

Enter *Touchstone* and *Audrey*

Touchstone: To-morrow is the joyful day, Audrey; to-morrow will we be married.

Audrey: I do desire it with all my heart; and I hope it is no dishonest desire to desire to be a woman of the world. Here comes two of the banished duke's pages.

Enter two Pages

First Page: Well met, honest gentleman.

Touchstone: By my troth, well met. Come, sit, sit, and a song.

Second Page: We are for you: sit i' the middle.

First Page: Shall we clap into't roundly, without hawking or spitting or saying we are hoarse, which are the only prologues to a bad voice?

Second Page: I'faith, i'faith; and both in a tune, like two gipsies on a horse.

Song

It was a lover and his lass,
With a hey, and a ho, and a hey nonino,
That o'er the green corn-field did pass
In the spring time, the only pretty ring time,
When birds do sing, hey ding a ding, ding:
Sweet lovers love the spring.
Between the acres of the rye,
With a hey, and a ho, and a hey nonino
These pretty country folks would lie,
In spring time, & c.
This carol they began that hour,
With a hey, and a ho, and a hey nonino,
How that a life was but a flower
In spring time, & c.
And therefore take the present time,
With a hey, and a ho, and a hey nonino;
For love is crowned with the prime
In spring time, & c.

Touchstone: Truly, young gentlemen, though there was no great matter in the ditty, yet the note was very untuneable.

First Page : You are deceived, sir: we kept time, we lost not our time.

Touchstone: By my troth, yes; I count it but time lost to hear such a foolish song. God be wi' you; and God mend your voices! Come, Audrey.

Exeunt

Scene IV: The Forest

Enter Duke Senior, Amiens, Jaques, Orlando, Oliver, and Celia

Duke Senior: Dost thou believe, Orlando, that the boy Can do all this that he hath promised?

Orlando: I sometimes do believe, and sometimes do not; As those that fear they hope, and know they fear.

Enter Rosalind, Silvius, and Phebe

Rosalind: Patience once more, whiles our compact is urged:
You say, if I bring in your Rosalind,
You will bestow her on Orlando here?

Duke Senior: That would I, had I kingdoms to give with her.

Rosalind: And you say, you will have her, when I bring her?

Orlando: That would I, were I of all kingdoms king.

Rosalind: You say, you'll marry me, if I be willing?

Phebe: That will I, should I die the hour after.

Rosalind: But if you do refuse to marry me, You'll give yourself to this most faithful shepherd?

Phebe: So is the bargain.

Rosalind: You say, that you'll have Phebe, if she will?

Silvius: Though to have her and death were both one thing.

Rosalind:

I have promised to make all this matter even.
Keep you your word, O duke, to give your daughter;
You yours, Orlando, to receive his daughter:

Keep your word, Phebe, that you'll marry me,
Or else refusing me, to wed this shepherd:
Keep your word, Silvius, that you'll marry her.
If she refuse me: and from hence I go,
To make these doubts all even.
Exeunt Rosalind and Celia

Duke Senior:

I do remember in this shepherd boy
Some lively touches of my daughter's favour.

Orlando:

My lord, the first time that I ever saw him
Methought he was a brother to your daughter:
But, my good lord, this boy is forest-born,
And hath been tutor'd in the rudiments
Of many desperate studies by his uncle,
Whom he reports to be a great magician,
Obscured in the circle of this forest.
Enter Touchstone and Audrey

Jaques: There is, sure, another flood toward, and these couples are coming to the ark. Here comes a pair of very strange beasts, which in all tongues are called fools.

Touchstone: Salutation and greeting to you all!

Jaques: Good my lord, bid him welcome: this is the motley-minded gentleman that I have so often met in the forest: he hath been a courtier, he swears.

Touchstone: If any man doubt that, let him put me to my purgation. I have trod a measure; I have flattered a lady; I have been politic with my friend, smooth with mine enemy; I have undone three tailors; I have had four quarrels, and like to have fought one.

Jaques: And how was that ta'en up?

Touchstone: Faith, we met, and found the quarrel was upon the seventh cause.

Jaques: How seventh cause? Good my lord, like this fellow.

Duke Senior: I like him very well.

Touchstone: God 'ild you, sir; I desire you of the like. I press in here, sir, amongst the rest of the country copulatives, to swear and to forswear: according as marriage binds and blood breaks: a poor virgin, sir, an ill-favoured thing, sir, but mine own; a poor humour of mine, sir, to take that that no man else will: rich honesty dwells like a miser, sir, in a poor house; as your pearl in your foul oyster.

Duke Senior: By my faith, he is very swift and sententious.

Touchstone: According to the fool's bolt, sir, and such dulcet diseases.

Jaques: But, for the seventh cause; how did you find the quarrel on the seventh cause?

Touchstone: Upon a lie seven times removed:—bear your body more seeming, Audrey:—as thus, sir. I did dislike the cut of a certain courtier's beard: he sent me word, if I said his beard was not cut well, he was in the mind it was: this is called the Retort Courteous.

If I sent him word again 'it was not well cut,' he would send me word, he cut it to please himself: this is called the Quip Modest. If again 'it was not well cut,' he disabled my judgment: this is called the Reply Churlish. If again 'it was not well cut,' he would answer, I spake not true: this is called the Reproof Valiant. If again 'it was not well cut,' he would say I lied: this is called the Counter-cheque Quarrelsome: and so to the Lie Circumstantial and the Lie Direct.

Jaques: And how oft did you say his beard was not well cut?

Touchstone: I durst go no further than the Lie Circumstantial, nor he durst not give me the Lie Direct; and so we measured swords and parted.

Jaques: Can you nominate in order now the degrees of the lie?

Touchstone: O sir, we quarrel in print, by the book; as you have books for good manners: I will name you the degrees. The first, the Retort Courteous; the second, the Quip Modest; the third, the Reply Churlish; the fourth, the Reproof Valiant; the fifth, the Countercheque Quarrelsome; the sixth, the Lie with Circumstance; the seventh, the Lie Direct. All these you may avoid but the Lie Direct; and you may avoid that too, with an If. I knew when seven justices could not take up a quarrel, but when the parties were met themselves, one of them thought but of an If, as, 'If you said so, then I said so;' and they shook hands and swore brothers. Your If is the only peacemaker; much virtue in If.

Jaques: Is not this a rare fellow, my lord? he's as good at any thing and yet a fool.

Duke Senior: He uses his folly like a stalking-horse and under the presentation of that he shoots his wit.

Enter Hymen, Rosalind, and Celia

Still Music

Hymen:

Then is there mirth in heaven,
When earthly things made even
Atone together.
Good duke, receive thy daughter
Hymen from heaven brought her,
Yea, brought her hither,
That thou mightst join her hand with his
Whose heart within his bosom is.

Rosalind: [To Duke Senior] To you I give myself, for I am yours.

To Orlando

To you I give myself, for I am yours.

Duke Senior: If there be truth in sight, you are my daughter.

Orlando: If there be truth in sight, you are my Rosalind.

Phebe:

If sight and shape be true,
Why then, my love adieu!

Rosalind:

I'll have no father, if you be not he:
I'll have no husband, if you be not he:
Nor ne'er wed woman, if you be not she.

Hymen:

Peace, ho! I bar confusion:
'Tis I must make conclusion
Of these most strange events:
Here's eight that must take hands
To join in Hymen's bands,
If truth holds true contents.
You and you no cross shall part:
You and you are heart in heart
You to his love must accord,
Or have a woman to your lord:
You and you are sure together,
As the winter to foul weather.
Whiles a wedlock-hymn we sing,
Feed yourselves with questioning;
That reason wonder may diminish,
How thus we met, and these things finish.

Song

Wedding is great Juno's crown:
O blessed bond of board and bed!
'Tis Hymen peoples every town;
High wedlock then be honoured:
Honour, high honour and renown,
To Hymen, god of every town!

Duke Senior:

O my dear niece, welcome thou art to me!
Even daughter, welcome, in no less degree.

Phebe:

I will not eat my word, now thou art mine;
Thy faith my fancy to thee doth combine.

Enter Jaques De Boys

Jaques De Boys

Let me have audience for a word or two:
I am the second son of old Sir Rowland,
That bring these tidings to this fair assembly.
Duke Frederick, hearing how that every day
Men of great worth resorted to this forest,
Address'd a mighty power; which were on foot,
In his own conduct, purposely to take
His brother here and put him to the sword:
And to the skirts of this wild wood he came;
Where meeting with an old religious man,
After some question with him, was converted
Both from his enterprise and from the world,
His crown bequeathing to his banish'd brother,
And all their lands restored to them again
That were with him exiled. This to be true,
I do engage my life.

Duke Senior:

Welcome, young man;
Thou offer'st fairly to thy brothers' wedding:
To one his lands withheld, and to the other
A land itself at large, a potent dukedom.
First, in this forest, let us do those ends
That here were well begun and well begot:
And after, every of this happy number
That have endured shrewd days and nights with us
Shall share the good of our returned fortune,
According to the measure of their states.
Meantime, forget this new-fall'n dignity
And fall into our rustic revelry.
Play, music! And you, brides and bridegrooms all,
With measure heap'd in joy, to the measures fall.

Jaques:

Sir, by your patience. If I heard you rightly,
The duke hath put on a religious life
And thrown into neglect the pompous court?

Jaques De Boys:

He hath.

Jaques:

To him will I: out of these convertites
There is much matter to be heard and learn'd.

To *Duke Senior:*

You to your former honour I bequeath;
Your patience and your virtue well deserves it:

To *Orlando:*

You to a love that your true faith doth merit:

To *Oliver:*

You to your land and love and great allies:

To *Silvius:*

You to a long and well-deserved bed:

To *Touchstone:*

And you to wrangling; for thy loving voyage
Is but for two months victuall'd. So, to your pleasures:
I am for other than for dancing measures.

Duke Senior:

Stay, Jaques, stay.

Jaques:

To see no pastime I what you would have
I'll stay to know at your abandon'd cave.

Exit

Duke Senior:

Proceed, proceed: we will begin these rites,
As we do trust they'll end, in true delights.

A dance

Epilogue

Rosalind

It is not the fashion to see the lady the epilogue; but it is no more unhandsome than to see the lord the prologue. If it be true that good wine needs no bush, 'tis true that a good play needs no epilogue; yet to good wine they do use good bushes, and good plays prove the better by the help of good epilogues. What a case am I in then, that am neither a good epilogue nor cannot insinuate with you in the behalf of a good play! I am not furnished like a beggar, therefore to beg will not become me: my way is to conjure you; and I'll begin with the women. I charge you, O women, for the love you bear to men, to like as much of this play as please you: and I charge you, O men, for the love you bear to women—as I perceive by your simpering, none of you hates them—that between you and the women the play may please. If I were a woman I would kiss as many of you as had beards that pleased me, complexions that liked me and breaths that I defied not: and, I am sure, as many as have good beards or good faces or sweet breaths will, for my kind offer, when I make curtsy, bid me farewell.

Exeunt

Chapter 16

Theme

The Delights of Love

As You Like It spoofs many of the conventions of poetry and literature dealing with love, such as the idea that love is a disease that brings suffering and torment to the lover, or the assumption that the male lover is the slave or servant of his mistress. These ideas are central features of the courtly love tradition, which greatly influenced European literature for hundreds of years before Shakespeare's time. In *As You Like It,* characters lament the suffering caused by their love, but these laments are all unconvincing and ridiculous. While Orlando's metrically incompetent poems conform to the notion that he should "live and die [Rosalind's] slave," these sentiments are roundly ridiculed (III.ii.142). Even Silvius, the untutored shepherd, assumes the role of the tortured lover, asking his beloved Phoebe to notice "the wounds invisible / That love's keen arrows make" (III.v.31–32). But Silvius's request for Phoebe's attention implies that the enslaved lover can loosen the chains of love and that all romantic wounds can be healed—otherwise, his request for notice would be pointless. In general, *As You Like It* breaks with the courtly love tradition by portraying love as a force for happiness and fulfillment and ridicules those who revel in their own suffering.

Celia speaks to the curative powers of love in her introductory scene with Rosalind, in which she implores her cousin to allow "the full weight" of her love to push aside Rosalind's unhappy thoughts. As soon as Rosalind takes to

Ardenne, she displays her own copious knowledge of the ways of love. Disguised as Ganymede, she tutors Orlando in how to be a more attentive and caring lover, counsels Silvius against prostrating himself for the sake of the all-too-human Phoebe, and scolds Phoebe for her arrogance in playing the shepherd's disdainful love object. When Rosalind famously insists that "[m]en have died from time to time, and worms have eaten them, but not for love," she argues against the notion that love concerns the perfect, mythic, or unattainable. Unlike Jaques and Touchstone, both of whom have keen eyes and biting tongues trained on the follies of romance, Rosalind does not mean to disparage love. On the contrary, she seeks to teach a version of love that not only can survive in the real world, but can bring delight as well. By the end of the play, having successfully orchestrated four marriages and ensured the happy and peaceful return of a more just government, Rosalind proves that love is a source of incomparable delight.

The Malleability of the Human Experience

In Act II, scene vii, Jaques philosophises on the stages of human life: man passes from infancy into boyhood; becomes a lover, a soldier, and a wise civic leader; and then, year by year, becomes a bit more foolish until he is returned to his "second childishness and mere oblivion" (II.vii.164). Jaques's speech remains an eloquent commentary on how quickly and thoroughly human beings can change, and, indeed, *do* change in *As You Like It*. Whether physically, emotionally, or spiritually, those who enter the Forest of Ardenne are often remarkably different when they leave. The most dramatic and unmistakable change, of course, occurs when Rosalind assumes the disguise of Ganymede. As a young man, Rosalind demonstrates how vulnerable to change men and women truly are. Orlando, of course, is putty in her hands; more impressive, however, is her ability to manipulate Phoebe's affections, which move from Ganymede to the once despised Silvius with amazing speed.

In *As You Like It,* Shakespeare dispenses with the time—consuming and often hard-won processes involved in change.

The characters do not struggle to become more pliant—their changes are instantaneous. Oliver, for instance, learns to love both his brother Orlando and a disguised Celia within moments of setting foot in the forest. Furthermore, the vengeful and ambitious Duke Frederick abandons all thoughts of fratricide after a single conversation with a religious old man. Certainly, these transformations have much to do with the restorative, almost magical effects of life in the forest, but the consequences of the changes also matter in the real world: the government that rules the French duchy, for example, will be more just under the rightful ruler Duke Senior, while the class structures inherent in court life promise to be somewhat less rigid after the courtiers sojourn in the forest. These social reforms are a clear improvement and result from the more private reforms of the play's characters. *As You Like It* not only insists that people can and do change, but also celebrates their ability to change for the better.

City Life Versus Country Life

Pastoral literature thrives on the contrast between life in the city and life in the country. Often, it suggests that the oppressions of the city can be remedied by a trip into the country's therapeutic woods and fields, and that a person's sense of balance and rightness can be restored by conversations with uncorrupted shepherds and shepherdesses. This type of restoration, in turn, enables one to return to the city a better person, capable of making the most of urban life. Although Shakespeare tests the bounds of these conventions—his shepherdess Audrey, for instance, is neither articulate nor pure—he begins *As You Like It* by establishing the city/country dichotomy on which the pastoral mood depends. In Act I, scene i, Orlando rails against the injustices of life with Oliver and complains that he "know[s] no wise remedy how to avoid it". Later in that scene, as Charles relates the whereabouts of Duke Senior and his followers, the remedy is clear: "in the forest of Ardenne... many young gentlemen... fleet the time carelessly, as they did in the golden world". Indeed, many are healed in the forest—the lovesick are coupled with their lovers, and the usurped duke returns to his throne—but Shakespeare reminds us that life in Ardenne is a temporary affair. As the characters prepare to return to life at court, the play does not laud country over city or vice versa, but instead suggests a delicate and necessary balance between the two. The simplicity of the forest provides shelter from the strains of the court, but it also creates the need for urban style and sophistication: one would not do, or even matter, without the other.

Motifs

Artifice

As Orlando runs through the forest decorating every tree with love poems for Rosalind, and as Silvius pines for Phoebe and compares her cruel eyes to a murderer, we cannot help but notice the importance of artifice to life in Ardenne. Phoebe decries such artificiality when she laments that her eyes lack the power to do the devoted shepherd any real harm, and Rosalind similarly puts a stop to Orlando's romantic fussing when she reminds him that "[m]en have died from time to time, and worms have eaten them, but not for love". Although Rosalind is susceptible to the contrivances of romantic love, as when her composure crumbles when Orlando is only minutes late for their appointment, she does her best to move herself and the others toward a more realistic understanding of love. Knowing that the excitement of the first days of courtship will flag, she warns Orlando that "[m]aids are May when they are maids, but the sky changes when they are wives". Here, Rosalind cautions against any love that sustains itself on artifice alone. She advocates a love that, while delightful, can survive in the real world. During the Epilogue, Rosalind returns the audience to reality by stripping away not only the artifice of Ardenne, but of her character as well. As the Elizabethan actor stands on the stage and reflects on this temporary foray into the unreal, the audience's experience comes to mirror the experience of the characters. The theater becomes Ardenne, the artful means of edifying us for our journey into the world in which we live.

Homoeroticism

Like many of Shakespeare's plays and poems, *As You Like It* explores different kinds of love between members of the same sex. Celia and Rosalind, for instance, are extremely close friends—almost sisters—and the profound intimacy of their relationship seems at times more intense than that of ordinary friends. Indeed, Celia's words in Act I, scenes ii and iii echo the protestations of lovers. But to assume that Celia or Rosalind possesses a sexual identity as clearly defined as our modern understandings of *heterosexual* or *homosexual* would be to work against the play's celebration of a range of intimacies and sexual possibilities.

The other kind of homoeroticism within the play arises from Rosalind's cross-dressing. Everybody, male and female, seems to love Ganymede, the beautiful boy who looks like a woman because he is really Rosalind in disguise. The name Rosalind chooses for her alter ego, Ganymede, traditionally belonged to a beautiful boy who became one of Jove's lovers, and the name carries strong homosexual connotations. Even though Orlando is supposed to be in love with Rosalind, he seems to enjoy the idea of acting out his romance with the beautiful, young boy Ganymede—almost as if a boy who looks like the woman he loves is even more appealing than the woman herself. Phoebe, too, is more attracted to the feminine Ganymede than to the real male, Silvius.

In drawing on the motif of homoeroticism, *As You Like It* is influenced by the pastoral tradition, which typically contains elements of same-sex love. In the Forest of Ardenne, as in pastoral literature, homoerotic relationships are not necessarily antithetical to heterosexual couplings, as modern readers tend to assume. Instead, homosexual and heterosexual love exist on a continuum across which, as the title of the play suggests, one can move as one likes.

Exile

As You Like It abounds in banishment. Some characters have been forcibly removed or threatened from their homes, such as Duke Senior, Rosalind, and Orlando. Some have voluntarily abandoned their positions out of a sense of rightness, such as Senior's loyal band of lords, Celia, and the noble servant Adam. It is, then, rather remarkable that the play ends with four marriages—a ceremony that unites individuals into couples and ushers these couples into the community. The community that sings and dances its way through Ardenne at the close of Act V, scene iv, is the same community that will return to the dukedom in order to rule and be ruled. This event, where the poor dance in the company of royalty, suggests a utopian world in which wrongs can be righted and hurts healed. The sense of restoration with which the play ends depends upon the formation of a community of exiles in politics and love coming together to soothe their various wounds.

Symbols

Orlando's Poems

The poems that Orlando nails to the trees of Ardenne are a testament to his love for Rosalind. In comparing her to the romantic heroines of classical literature—Helen, Cleopatra, Lucretia—Orlando takes his place among a long line of poets who regard the love object as a bit of earthbound perfection. Much to the amusement of Rosalind, Celia, and Touchstone, Orlando's efforts are far less accomplished than, say, Ovid's, and so bring into sharp focus the silliness of which all lovers are guilty. Orlando's "tedious homil[ies] of love" stand as a reminder of the wide gap that exists between the fancies of literature and the kind of love that exists in the real world.

The Slain Deer

In Act IV, scene ii, Jaques and other lords in Duke Senior's party kill a deer. Jaques proposes to "set the deer's horns upon [the hunter's] head for a branch of victory". To an Elizabethan audience, however, the slain deer would have signaled more than just an accomplished archer. As the song that follows the lord's return to camp makes clear, the deer placed atop the hunter's head is a symbol of cuckoldry, commonly represented by a man with horns atop his head. Allusions to the cuckolded man run throughout the play, betraying one of the dominant anxieties of the age—that women are sexually uncontrollable—and pointing out the schism between ideal and imperfect love.

Ganymede

Rosalind's choice of alternative identities is significant. Ganymede is the cupbearer and beloved of Jove and is a standard symbol of homosexual love. In the context of the play, her choice of an alter ego contributes to a continuum of sexual possibilities.

Chapter 17

Quotes to be Quoted

Quotation

Now, my co-mates and brothers in exile,
Hath not old custom made this life more sweet
Than that of painted pomp? Are not these woods
More free from peril than the envious court?
Here feel we not the penalty of Adam,
The seasons' difference, as the icy fang
And churlish chiding of the winter's wind,
Which when it bites and blows upon my body
Even till I shrink with cold, I smile, and say
'This is no flattery. These are counsellors
That feelingly persuade me what I am.'
Sweet are the uses of adversity
Which, like the toad, ugly and venomous,
Wears yet a precious jewel in his head;
And this our life, exempt from public haunt,
Finds tongues in trees, books in the running brooks,
Sermons in stones, and good in everything. (II.i.1–17)

Explanation

These lines, spoken by Duke Senior upon his introduction in Act II, scene i, establish the pastoral mode of the play. With great economy, Shakespeare draws a dividing line between the "painted pomp" of court—with perils great enough to drive the duke and his followers into exile—and the safe and restorative Forest of Ardenne (II.i.3). The woods are romanticised, as they typically are in pastoral literature, and the mood is set for the remainder of the play. Although perils may present themselves, they remain distant, and, in the end, there truly is "good in everything" (II.i.17). This passage, more than any other in the play, presents the conceits of the pastoral mode. Here, the corruptions of life at court are left behind in order to learn the simple and valuable lessons of the country.

Shakespeare highlights the educational, edifying, and enlightening nature of this foray into the woods by employing language that invokes the classroom, the library, and the church: in the trees, brooks, and stones surrounding him, the duke finds tongues, books, and sermons. As is his wont, Shakespeare goes on to complicate the literary conventions upon which he depends. His shepherds and shepherdesses, for instance, ultimately prove too lovesick or dim-witted to dole out the kind of wisdom the pastoral form demands of them, but for now Shakespeare merely sets up the opposition between city and country that provides the necessary tension to drive his story forward.

Quotation

As I do live by food, I met a fool,
Who laid him down and basked him in the sun,
And railed on Lady Fortune in good terms,
In good set terms, and yet a motley fool.
'Good morrow, fool,' quoth I. 'No, sir,' quoth he,
'Call me not fool till heaven hath sent me fortune.'
And then he drew a dial from his poke,
And looking on it with lack-lustre eye
Says very wisely 'It is ten o'clock.'
'Thus we may see', quoth he, 'how the world wags.
'Tis but an hour ago since it was nine,
And after one hour more 'twill be eleven.
And so from hour to hour we ripe and ripe,
And then from hour to hour we rot and rot;
And thereby hangs a tale.' (II.vii.14–28)

Explanation

In Act II, scene vii, melancholy Jaques displays an uncharacteristic burst of delight. While wandering through the forest, he relates, he met a fool, who entertained him with rather nihilistic musings on the passage of time and man's life. According to Touchstone, time ensures nothing other than man's own decay: "from hour to hour we rot and rot" (II.vii.27). That this speech appeals to Jaques says much about his character: he delights not only in the depressing, but also in the rancid. Practically all of Touchstone's lines contain some bawdy innuendo, and these are no exception. Here, by punning the word "hour" with "whore," he transforms the general notion of man's decay into the unpleasant specifics of a man dying from venereal disease. Touchstone appropriately, if distastefully, confirms this hidden meaning by ending his speech with the words "thereby hangs a tale," for tale was Elizabethan slang for penis (II.vii.28).

Quotation

> *No, faith; die by attorney. The poor world is almost six thousand years old, and in all this time there was not any man died in his own person, videlicet, in a love-cause. Troilus had his brains dashed out with a Grecian club, yet he did what he could to die before, and he is one of the patterns of love. Leander, he would have lived many a fair year though Hero had turned nun if it had not been for a hot midsummer night, for, good youth, he went but forth to wash him in the Hellespont and, being taken with the cramp, was drowned; and the foolish chroniclers of that age found it was Hero of Sestos. But these are all lies. Men have died from time to time, and worms have eaten them, but not for love.* (IV.i.81–92)

Explanation

In Act IV, scene i, Rosalind rejects Orlando's claim that he would die if Rosalind should fail to return his love. Rosalind's insistence that "[m]en have died from time to time, and worms have eaten them, but not for love" is one of the most recognizable lines from the play and perhaps the wisest (IV.i.91–92). Here, Rosalind takes on one of the most dominant interpretations of romantic love, an understanding that is sustained by mythology and praised in literature, and insists on its unreality. She holds to the light the stories of Troilus and Leander, both immortal lovers, in order to expose their falsity. Men are, according to Rosalind, much more likely to die by being hit with a club or drowning than in a fatal case of heartbreak. Rosalind does not mean to deny the existence of love. On the contrary, she delights in loving Orlando. Instead, her criticism comes from an unwillingness to let affection cloud or warp her sense of reality. By casting aside the conventions of the standard—and usually tragic—romance, Rosalind advocates a kind of love that belongs and can survive in the real world that she inhabits.

Quotation

> *O sir, we quarrel in print, by the book, as you have books for good manners. I will name you the degrees. The first, the Retort Courteous; the second, the Quip Modest; the third, the Reply Churlish; the fourth, the Reproof Valiant; the fifth, the Countercheck Quarrelsome; the sixth, the Lie with Circumstance; the seventh, the Lie Direct. All these you may avoid but the Lie Direct; and you may avoid that, too, with an 'if'. I knew when seven justices could not take up a quarrel, but when the parties were met themselves, one of them thought but of an 'if', as 'If you said so, then I said so', and they shook hands and swore brothers. Your 'if' is the only peacemaker; much virtue in 'if'.* (V.iv.81-92)

Explanation

In Act V, scene iv, Touchstone delivers an account of a recent argument he has had. His anatomy of the quarrel, as this speech might be called, is a deftly comic moment that skewers all behaviour that is "by the book," whether it be rules for engaging an enemy or a lover (V.iv.81). The end of the speech, in which Touchstone turns his attentions to the powers of the word "if," is particularly fine and fitting. "If" points to the potential of events in possible worlds. "If" allows slights to be forgiven, wounds to be salved, and promising opportunities to be taken. Notably, within a dozen lines of this speech, Duke Senior, Orlando, and Phoebe each usher in a new stage of life with a simple sentence that begins with that simple word.

Quotation

> *It is not the fashion to see the lady the epilogue; but it is no more unhandsome than to see the lord the prologue. If it be true that good wine needs no bush, 'tis true that a good play needs no epilogue. Yet to good wine they do use good bushes, and good plays prove the better by the help of good epilogues. What a case am I in then, that am neither a good epilogue nor cannot insinuate with you in the behalf of a good play! I am not furnished like a beggar, therefore to beg will not become me. My way is to conjure you; and I'll begin with the women. I charge you, O women, for the love you bear to men, to like as much of this play as please you. And I charge you, O men, for the love you bear to women—as I perceive by your simpering none of you hates them— that between you and the women the play may please. If I were a woman I would kiss as many of you as had beards that pleased me, complexions that liked me, and breaths that I defied not. And I am sure, as many as have good beards, or good faces, or sweet breaths will for my kind offer, when I make curtsy, bid me farewell.* (Epilogue, 1–19).

Explanation

The Epilogue was a standard component of Elizabethan drama. One actor remains onstage after the play has ended to ask the audience for applause. As Rosalind herself notes, it is odd that she has been chosen to deliver the Epilogue, as that task is usually assigned to a male character. By the time she addresses the audience directly, Rosalind has discarded her

Ganymede disguise. She is again a woman and has married a man. Although we may think the play of gender has come to an end with the fall of the curtain, we must remember that women were forbidden to perform onstage in Shakespeare's England. Rosalind would have been played by a man, which further obscures the boundaries of gender. Rosalind emerges as a man who pretends to be a woman who pretends to be a man who pretends to be a woman to win the love of a man. When the actor solicits the approval of the men in the audience, he says, "If I were a woman I would kiss as many of you as had beards that pleased me"— returning us to the dizzying intermingling of homosexual and heterosexual affections that govern life in the Forest of Ardenne (Epilogue, 14–16). The theater, like Ardenne, is an escape from reality where the wonderful, sometimes overwhelmingcomplexities of human life can be witnessed, contemplated, enjoyed, and studied.

- "All the world 's a stage, and all the men and women merely players. They have their exits and their entrances; And one man in his time plays many parts" As You Like It - (Act II, Scene VII).
- "Can one desire too much of a good thing?". As You Like It (Act IV, Scene I).
- "True is it that we have seen better days". As You Like It - Act II, Scene VII).
- "For ever and a day". As You Like It - (Act IV, Scene I).
- "The fool doth think he is wise, but the wise man knows himself to be a fool". (Act V, Scene I).

Chapter 18

Study Questions

Q1. Critically examine Character Transformation in Shakespeare's As You Like It.

Many characters undergo a change in William Shakespeare's play, "As You Like It". Duke Senior goes from being a member of a court to being a member of a forest and Orlando changes from a bitter, younger brother, to a love-struck young man. The most obvious transformation undergone, is undoubtedly that of Rosalind. Her change from a woman to a man, not only alters her mood, candor, and gender, but also allows her to be the master of ceremonies.

Celia and Rosalind are fairly happy in the court of Celia's father, Duke Frederick. However, much to her surprise, the Duke banishes Rosalind from his court because of his dislike for her. Celia, not allowing her beloved cousin to "go it alone", decides to accompany her to where ever she may roam. They decide to search out Rosalind's father, Duke Senior, in the forest of Arden. Before they depart, Rosalind decides that the forest, being a treacherous place full of danger, demands that she dresses as a man, while Celia remained a woman.

"Were it not better, Because that I am more than common tall,

That I did suit me all points like a man? A gallant curtal ax upon my thigh,

A boar spear in my hand, and- in my hear Lie there what hidden woman's fear there will-

We'll have a swashing and a martial outside, As many other mannish cowards have

That do outface it with their semblances."

At first glance, this transformation is a mere change of clothes and the addition of weapons, but it goes much deeper. To Rosalind, the taking on of a man's appearance requires certain things. She believes that while dressed as a man, she cannot bring shame to the image of men. A good example of this is in Act 2, Scene 4, where she says, "I could find in my heart to disgrace my man's apparel and to cry like a woman; but I must comfort the weaker vessel, as doublet and hose ought to show itself courageous to petticoat. This is not the only time she mentions a doublet and hose. It seems almost that the doublet and hose are the actual source of strength for a man, as in the next example when Rosalind is begging Celia for an answer, saying, "Good my complexion! Dost thou think, / though I am caparisoned like a man, I have a Doublet and hose in my disposition?"

Shakespeare's play "As you like it," is a comedy about the changes the characters undergo. Although several characters undergo significant changes, the most apparent are in the character Rosalind, who is kicked out of her uncle's kingdom and is forced to dress as a man, and falls in love with Orlando.

Q2. Discuss the problems faced by readers while reading "As You Like It".

As You Like It will be for many of you a rather difficult play to appreciate and interpret simply on the basis of a reading. The reasons for this are not difficult to ascertain. The play is, as I have observed, a pastoral comedy, that is, a comedy which involves a traditional literary style of moving sophisticated urban courtiers out into the countryside, where they have to deal with life in a very different manner from that of the aristocratic court. This play, like others in the Pastoral tradition, freely departs from naturalism, and in As You Like It (certainly by comparison with the History plays) there is little attempt to maintain any consistently naturalistic style.

This can create problems for readers unfamiliar with the conventions of pastoral, especially those who find it just too artificial and incredible to grasp imaginatively. After all, how are we to understand the unmotivated family hatreds which launch the action? We are simply not given any sufficiently detailed look at why Oliver hates Orlando (he himself does not understand the reason) or why Duke Frederick hates Duke Senior and turns on Rosalind so suddenly or, what is most surprising of all, why the nasty people whose animosities have given rise to the plot so suddenly and so conveniently convert and become nice people just in time to wind the plot up happily under the supervision of the goddess Hymen, the Greek deity of marriage, who arrives as an unexpected but welcome guest.

But these features of the plot which we might find unconvincing if we demand naturalism (that is, if we insist on treating the play as a "Hence" story) are little more than standard plot devices in "And then" stories, common in a genre like pastoral, which makes no claims to naturalistic motivation. Such plotting serves to launch and to conclude the comic confusion. The main point of the play here, after all, is not the working out of a carefully constructed plot, but rather the various encounters which take place in the Forest of Ardenne. In fact, the structure of the play is less a carefully complex and unfolding plot than a series of conversations between characters who happen to run into each other amid the trees.

You will notice, for example, that most of the central part of As You Like It consists of often random encounters between different characters in the forest. In many cases, they have no particular reason to talk to each other. What these serve to bring out is a series of conversations about life (and particularly about love) in which we witness different attitudes clashing. The effect is to take us through a variety of responses to shared concerns and to get us responding to our own sense of the appropriate ways to deal with experience.

To put this another way: The pastoral style of As You Like It does not encourage a deep psychological approach to any of the characters, to the logic of their motivation. If that's what we demand from a story to make it interesting, then this play is not going to satisfy us. We are not in that sort of a world. There is far more direct pressure on us to see in the interactions between characters the exploration of some themes, especially issues concerning love. That is not to say that the characters are not theatrically interesting and worth talking about; it is rather to insist that the characters here are serving thematic purposes more obviously than they are in more psychologically plausible plays. So there's little point in seeking to penetrate deeply into the plausibility of the psychological motivation or of the coincidences.

To take one obvious example of a thematic concern, very common in pastoral, we notice in the play a repeated contrast between court and country life. The purpose here is not to provide some naturalistic contrast, for the picture of life in the country is obviously idealised a good deal (although not totally, for there are references to the harsher aspects of life away from the comforts of the court and to the realities of working for an absentee landlord). Nor is the purpose any romantic celebration of the values of country living as somehow more authentic than city life. The pastoral is primarily a vehicle for a (usually) gentle satire on urban values, on some of the corrupting manners of the court (like flattery and excessive attention to clothes or fine language). And we can see this clearly enough in this play. But there is no sense in As You Like It that, given a free choice, any of the principal characters (except Jaques) would actually prefer to live in the country rather than the court.

The other great difficulty with As You Like It for inexperienced readers is much of the humour. Here again, what makes little sense on the page (and doesn't come across as very funny) generally works much better in a production. This point is generally true of all comedy, where the physicality of the human interaction (something not always readily apparent from the text of the play alone) is an essential key to understanding and responding to what is going on. That aspect of comedy, especially Shakespearean comedy, is one reason why, in the curriculum of this course, the comedies are underrepresented. The only quick way to overcome this problem is to focus on seeing the play in production (and there's a useful BBC video version available in the college library).

Q3. The most intriguing aspects of the treatment of love in 'As You Like It" concerns the issue of gender. Justify

One of the most intriguing aspects of the treatment of love in As You Like It concerns the issue of gender. And this issue, for obvious reasons, has generated a special interest in recent times. The principal reason for such a thematic concern in the play is the cross dressing and role playing. The central love interest between Rosalind and Orlando calls into question the conventional wisdom about men's and women's gender roles and challenges our preconceptions about these roles in courtship, erotic love, and beyond.

At the heart of this courtship is a very complex ambiguity which it is difficult fully to appreciate without a production to refer to. But here we have a man (the actor) playing a woman (Rosalind), who has dressed herself up as a man (Ganymede), and who is pretending to be a woman (Rosalind) in the courtship game with Orlando. Even if, in modern times, Rosalind is not played by a young male actor, the theatrical irony is complex enough.

The most obvious issue raised by the cross dressing is the relationship between gender roles and clothes (or outer appearance). For Rosalind passes herself off easily enough as a man and, in the process, acquires a certain freedom to move around, give advice, and associate as an equal among other men (this freedom gives her the power to initiate the courtship). Her disguise is, in that sense, much more significant than Celia's, for Celia remains female in her role as Aliena and is thus largely passive (her pseudonym meaning "Stranger" or "outsider" is an interesting one). The fact that Celia is largely passive in the Forest of Ardenne (especially in contrast to Rosalind) and has to wait for life to deliver a man to her rather than seeking one out, as Rosalind does, is an interesting and important difference between the two friends.

These points raise some interesting issues. If becoming accepted as a man and getting the freedom to act that comes with that acceptance is simply a matter of presenting oneself as a man, then what do we say about all the enshrined natural differences we claim as the basis for our different treatment of men and women? Given that Rosalind is clearly the most intelligent, active, and interesting character in the play and that these qualities would not be likely to manifest themselves so fully if she were not passing herself off as a man, the play raises some interesting questions about just what we mean by any insistence on gender differences as more than mere conventions.

But the issue is much more complicated than that. For Rosalind's assumed name, Ganymede, is a very deliberate reference to the young male lover Zeus carried up to Olympus, and it points us to what might be a very strong element in the courtship game between Orlando and Rosalind and in the feelings Phoebe has for Rosalind, namely homoerotic desire. There's little in the play to suggest this explicitly, but a production which showed, say, that Orlando's feelings were becoming involved with Ganymede, so that the pretend courtship has a strongly erotic undercurrent, would not be violating the text. Perhaps it's hard to distinguish totally between Orlando's feelings for Rosalind and Orlando's feelings for Ganymede. And that challenges all sorts of conventional expectations about erotic love, in order to "probe the surprisingly complex issue of what is natural in matters of love and sexual desire" (Jean Howard, Introduction to As You Like It in The Norton Shakespeare).

That's why the play wedding ceremony that Rosalind and Orlando go through with Celia playing role of officiating minister is, for all the acting going on, quite powerfully charged. Celia, who loves Rosalind, supervises the wedding of the two people presenting themselves as men, and under the obvious fun of the make believe there's a powerful sense of the sexual attraction the two have for each other. It's worth asking at this point just how much Orlando might know or suspect or what feelings are keeping him in this game. There seems little doubt that underneath his play acting he is experiencing a strong bond with Rosalind/Ganymede, something which emerges as even more ironic if we sense (from the style of the production) that part of him either recognises Rosalind or is responding to the same characteristics in Ganymede that make him so in love with Rosalind.

This point is underscored by the very strong instant desire that Phoebe finds for Rosalind/Ganymede, which seems at first not unlike the feelings Orlando has for Rosalind. Phoebe, of course, abandons her love as soon as she learns that Rosalind is a woman, but the play confronts us with the question about the validity of those feelings. If a set of men's clothes is the only thing distinguishing conventional sexual arrangements from alternatives, we are invited (at least) to wonder somewhat about the extent to which conventional arrangements do not exhaust the erotic possibilities.

The play, of course, in its closing scene celebrates conventional heterosexual marriages. But by that time it has offered us, at least by powerful suggestions, some erotic alternatives, without condemning such possibilities as inherently unnatural. And, depending upon how some of these key scenes are played, a production of As You Like It can evoke in the audience some very interesting and (perhaps) ambivalent feelings about mature sexuality.

This point seems to be emphasised in the epilogue spoken by the newly married Rosalind, where the boy actor playing the role calls attention to the fact that he is not a woman, as if to remind us (maybe) that the happy union of Orlando and Rosalind in which we take such delight has explored other possibilities than heterosexuality. This point can be underscored strongly if Orlando is present with Rosalind during this epilogue (say, holding her in his arms) and the actor playing Rosalind is removing his make up (e.g., wig). And, of course, if the actor playing Rosalind has made some erotic connections with the audience, then his final revelation in the Epilogue will force the audience member to confront some of his own feelings about gender attachments.

As I say, it's rare to see Rosalind nowadays played by a boy, although there have been all-male productions in modern times. And so the epilogue is often omitted or edited. As it stands, the boy actor's offer to kiss the desirable grown men in the audience ("If I were a woman") gives the last words of the play an ironic and erotic resonance that challenges gently the heterosexual weddings we have just celebrated.

Q4. The Philosophy of Jaques in As You Like It .Elucidate.

Jaques is one of the characters in Shakespeare's comedy As You Like It. We- as audience and readers- learn that although he was previously a libertine, he now seems to have turned to philosophy in his quest for a new identity. As a philosopher he questions much of what he sees around him.

At one point Jaques analyses what it is to be a man. He sees the world as a stage wherein men and women are players, and their different ages represent different acts and scenes in the play. His descriptions suggest that the roles are largely beyond the players' control; that a script for the play has already been written by an exterior force. But there is a sense of contradiction in all this; the stages Jaques outlines for us (presented to his audience as universal) do not account for his own role. Since this is the case we must either presume that Jacques is somehow exceptional or that the roles are not as fixed as people imagine. One can always argue that Jaques is an outcast of some sort. On the other hand, the Duke Senior is eager to offer him a position at court, thereby giving him an opportunity to obtain an acceptable role within the framework of a hierarchical, society, but Jaques turns down the offer. He needs to widen his horizon, and is so impatient about learning more that he does not even stay to celebrate with the rest of the uke's men."To see no pastime, I.". Instead he wants to go to Duke Frederick: "Out of these convertites,/ There is much matter to be hear'd and learned".

Jaques has no particular interest in being part of an established society. He creates his own role and his own destiny. By his mere presence in the play we are made aware of the infinite choices that confront human beings in their lives. Rosalind is the only other character in As You Like It who really challenges established roles, but whereas she (in all likelihood) returns to court and is satisfied with the new development (after all, she brought it about), Jacques is unwilling to let go of his freedom and independence introduced to him in the green world.

Jaques first attempts to challenge established norms by putting on a fool's appearance: "O that I were a fool!/ I am ambitious for a motley coat.". He further announces: "Give me leave to speak my mind".In this way he can serve as a cleanser of "the foul body of th'infected world". He knows that at "the pompous court" he can only speak his mind if people think him a fool, whereas here in the woods, in the green world, he is free to say and do as he chooses. He seems to have no wish to be bound by courtly rules or any other rules for that matter. Jaques is on the whole very much a contrast to the other characters in the play, what they take seriously he does not, what they think is funny, he does not. He fascinates as well as annoys his companions; among other things he ridicules Orlando's infatuation with Rosalind, showing a very cynical side of himself. But he too can on occasion be happy and agreeable.

Jaques's main concern seems to be freedom to say and do what he wants. He is not willing to compromise as he must do if he returns to court. He sticks to his principles and is not overly concerned with what other people think of him. In this sense he is very much like *"The Contrary Woman",a woman who never gives in. He goes in the opposite direction of his friends, both physically and spiritually. They follow the roles as set up for them in Jaques's speech about a man's seven ages, he proves their potential invalidity.

"The Contrary Woman" is a Norwegian folktale about a woman who even floats upstream.

Q5. Discuss the Character of Touchstone in As You Like It.

As You Like It features, like so many of Shakespeare's plays, a professional clown, Touchstone, and it's worth paying some attention to his role for what it contributes towards establishing and maintaining the upbeat comic spirit of the play. For the jester is the constant commentator on what is going on. His humour, pointed or otherwise, thus inevitably contributes to the audience's awareness of what is happening, and the way in which other characters treat him is often a key indicator of their sensibilities.

Touchstone is one of the gentlest and happiest clowns in all of Shakespeare. He comments on the action, makes jokes at other people's expense, and offers ironic insights about their situation. But throughout As You Like It, such traditional roles of the fool are offered and taken with a generosity of spirit so that his remarks never shake the firm comic energies of the play. When he ridicules Orlando's verses, Rosalind laughs along with him. When he points out to Corin that the shepherd must be damned for never having lived at court, Corin takes it as good natured jesting (which it is). When Touchstone takes Audrey away from her rural swain, William, there are apparently no hard feelings (although much here depends on the staging). In this play, the professional jester participates in and contributes to a style of social interaction which is unqualified by any more sobre and serious reflections. This makes Touchstone very different from the bitter fool of King Lear or from the most complex fool of all, the sad Feste of Twelfth Night, both of whom offer comments that cast either a shrewd, melancholy, or bitter irony on the proceedings.

Touchstone himself becomes the target of much humour by his immediate attraction to Audrey, the "foul" country lass.

There is something richly comic here, seeing the staunch apologist for the sophisticated life of the court fall so quickly to his animal lust. But the satire here is very good humoured. Touchstone himself acknowledges the frailty of his vows and does not attempt to deceive anyone about his intentions. He knows he is serving his lusts and that that is no good basis for a lasting and significant marriage. But the play builds up no severe indictment against what he is doing, and Audrey herself makes no protest. So this most unlikely of unions becomes part of the celebration of love at the end of the play, an expression of the comic variety of the experience, rather than offering any ironic commentary.

Q6. Bring out the element of pastoral setting in As You Like It.

Central to the pastoral vision of As You Like It is the setting in the Forest of Ardenne, especially the contrast between it and the ducal court. In the former, there is a powerful political presence which creates dangers. Deception lurks behind many actions, brothers have secret agendas against their brothers, and people have to answer to the arbitrary demands of power.

In the Forest of Ardenne, however, life is very different. For one thing, there is no urgency to the agenda. There are no clocks in the forest, and for the exiled courtiers there is no regular work. They are free to roam around the forest, prompted by their own desires. There is plenty of food to eat, so the communal hunt takes care of their physical needs. That and the absence of a complex political hierarchy creates a much stronger sense of communal equality hearkening back the mythical good old days. The exiled Duke himself attests to the advantages of living far from the court, free of the deceits of flattery and double dealing and welcomes Orlando to the feast without suspicion.

And, most important here, especially in comparison with the history plays, is the importance of singing. As You Like It is full of songs-not performances by professional court musicians, but impromptu group singing which expresses better than anything else the spontaneous joy these people derive from life in the Forest and the joy they give back to others. The songs indicate clearly the way in which in the Forest people can shape their actions to their moods-a situation totally unlike the court where one has to consider one's actions much more carefully.

Hence, the Forest of Ardenne provides for the exiled courtiers an important freedom to experiment with their lives, to discover things about themselves. In the Forest people can talk openly with whoever they might happen to meet on a stroll through the trees, and that might be anyone, given that in the Forest no one owns any particular territory (there are no rooms, palaces, roads-unlike the court where there is a preoccupation with property) and thus one might well meet and have to deal with a person whom one would never get close to in the court (that can have comic results, of course, as Touchstone's conversations with Audrey and William demonstrate). In the Forest life is, as I have observed, lived more immediately in the moment with whatever life presents at the moment. Such an approach to life is impossible in the politically charged world of the court.

That freedom makes possible Rosalind's transformation and her taking charge of the courtship and makes an interesting contrast between Rosalind and Viola (in Twelfth Night)-the latter is not nearly so free to take charge, because she is still operating in a social environment with a clear structure of authority, which she has to respect. Hence, the fortunate outcome of that play relies upon her patience and luck far more in the case of Rosalind, who is the driving force in her courtship (Viola's desires very nearly are unfulfilled).

We should note, however, that the Forest of Ardenne is not an entirely idyllic setting. The Duke pays tribute to the often brutal weather, and there are some dangerous animals lurking in the underbrush. Corin, the shepherd, informs us that he works for another man-a slight but significant reminder that even in this pastoral setting the realities of power are not entirely absent.

And, of course, there is never any sense here (as there might be if this were a Romantic vision of life) that the Forest is a suitable place to live on a continuing basis. Given the opportunity to return to the court, all the exiles (except, significantly, Jaques) seize the chance. The Forest has done its work-it has educated some, repaired fraternal relationships, brought the lovers to a fuller awareness of their own feelings. Now, they can return to what will be, we sense, a much better and fuller life in the court.

Q7. Comment on the role of Jaques in "As You Like It".

The essentially healthy emotional intelligence of Rosalind and Orlando and their suitability for each other emerge from their separate encounters with Jaques (in some editions Jacques), the melancholy ex-courtier who is part of Duke Senior's troupe in the forest. Both Rosalind and Orlando take an instant dislike to Jaques (which is mutual). And in that dislike we are invited to see something vitally right about the two of them.

For Jaques is, in effect, the opposite of everything Rosalind stands for. He is a moody cynic, who likes to look at life and draw from it poetical contemplations at the generally unsatisfactory nature of the world. He is, in a sense, an initial Hamlet-like figure (the comparison is frequently made), someone without any motivating erotic joy, who compensates for his inadequacy by trying to drag everything down to the level of his empty emotions and by verbalizing at length in poetical images. He takes some pride in what he calls his very own brand of melancholy which can suck the joy out of life as a weasel sucks the protein out of an egg (an interesting image of the destruction of new living potential), and he spends his time wallowing in it. His own social desire seems to be to find someone else to wallow in the same emotional mud as he does. But the spirits of the other characters, especially of Rosalind and Orlando, are too vital and creative to respond favourably to Jaques's attempts to cut life down to fit his limited moods.

That judgment no doubt sounds quite harsh. And perhaps it is, for Jaques is a relatively harmless person, who deceives no one (nor does he try to), and his poetical reflections, like Hamlet's, are often seductive. But we should not let the fame of some of his utterances (particularly the famous "Seven Ages of Man" speech a frequently anthologised piece of so-called Shakespearean "wisdom") conceal the fact that his approach to life is thoroughly negative. He sees no value in anything other than calling attention to the world's deficiencies. He does not recognise in the fellowship, music, and love all around him any countervailing virtues.

This point is made really explicit at the very end of the "Seven Ages of Man". As Jaques concludes his cynical evaluation of the emptiness of human life by talking about how in old age men become useless lumps of flesh ("Sans teeth, sans eyes, sans taste, sans everything"), Orlando enters carrying Adam. The latter is the living denial of everything Jaques has just said, for Adam is very old, but has actively striven to help Orlando with generosity, love, and a sense of duty, qualities which confer upon him an emphatic and obvious value. The dramatic irony in that entrance points us to the severely limited and limiting understanding of the world which Jaques has just uttered.

[As an aside, it might be worth remarking that this habit of excerpting speeches of Shakespeare and setting them up as "gems" outside of their immediate dramatic context has the unfortunate tendency to immortalise a passage as some special insight into the nature of life when it is, in fact, quite the reverse. The speech of Jaques is, along with the advice of the Polonius to his son, the most famous example of this problem. Far from being a particularly mature earned insight into anything important, Jaques's speech is an indication of his limited and unwelcome sense of the unsatisfactory nature of life. The entrance of Orlando and Adam underscores this point.]

Oscar Wilde, in one of his most famous apophthegems, once defined a cynic as one who knows the price of everything and the value of nothing. That definition applies very well to Jaques, and it helps us at once understand why Rosalind and

Orlando will have nothing to do with him. Rosalind understands that love comes at a price. Time will change things, and a commitment in love brings with it the risk of infidelity (and there is much talk of that in the play). But she will not therefore deny its value or refuse to take the risk. On the contrary, she determines to extract the full value from her excited feelings for Orlando, not by freezing those feelings in some sour poetical reflections but by experiencing them moment by moment, no matter what the future may bring. Orlando also is too full of the spirit of life to find anything in Jaques's gentle but persistent pessimism at all worth bothering about.

I don't mean to over-emphasize the kill-joy quality of Jaques. He is generally harmless enough, particularly in this play where everyone recognises him for what he is and where he has no particular interest in pulling others down to his level against their will. If they don't want to sit down with him and rail against the first born of Egypt, he's content to move away on his own. But it's significant that he's not a fully participating member of the final celebrations and that he is going to remain in the forest. He has learned nothing and, indeed, is incapable of learning anything, simply because he is not open to experience (in terms of the earlier analysis I offered of Richard II and Hamlet, Jaques is a "chatterer"). He's made up his mind what life is all about, and he is seeking confirmation of a pre-set attitude.

Traversi's summary comment on Jaques hits the mark precisely:

Jacques' motive is, in the last analysis "observation," the gratifying of a self regarding curiosity based on a kind of personal impotence, an inability to participate fully and naturally in the processes of life; and, since his attitude is one which implies throughout an incapacity for genuine giving, for the positive acceptance of an order, at once natural and distinctively human, beyond the isolated self—the acceptance by which, in love or otherwise, the self is at last justified—he remains a mere marginal presence in the process by which that order is finally... consummated.

Q8. Mention The Transformation of Rosalind in As You Like It.

Many characters undergo a change in William Shakespeare's play, As You Like It. Duke Senior goes from being a member of a court to being a member of a forest. Orlando changes from a bitter younger brother to a love-sick young man. But the most obvious transformation undergone, is done by Rosalind. Her change from woman to man, not only alters her mood, candor, and gender, but allows her to be the master of ceremonies.

Celia and Rosalind are fairly happy in the court of Celia's father, Duke Frederick. However, much to her surprise, the Duke banishes Rosalind from his court. Celia, not allowing her beloved cousin to "go it alone", decides to accompany her to where ever she may roam. They decide to search out Rosalind's father, Duke Senior, in the forest of Arden. Before they depart, Rosalind decides that for both her and Celia's safety, she will dress herself as a man, saying,

"Were it not better,
Because that I am more than common tall,
That I did suit me all points like a man?
A gallant curtal ax upon my thigh,
A boar spear in my hand, and- in my hear
Lie there what hidden woman's fear there will-
We'll have a swashing and a martial outside,
As many other mannish cowards have
That do outface it with their semblances.

At first glance, this transformation is a mere change of clothes and the addition of weapons, but it goes much deeper.

To Rosalind, the taking on of a man's appearance requires certain things. She believes that while dressed as a man, she cannot bring shame to the image of a man. A good example of this is in Act 2, Scene 4, where she says, *"I could find in my heart to disgrace my* man's/ apparel and to cry like a woman;

but I must comfort/ the weaker vessel, as doublet and hose ought to show/ itself courageous to petticoat.This is not the only time she mentions a doublet and hose. It seems almost that the doublet and hose are the actual source of strength for a man, as in the next example when Rosalind is begging Celia for an answer, saying, "Good my complexion!

Dost thou think,/ though I am caparisoned like a man, I have a doublet/ and hose in my disposition?".

Q9. Comment on the title of As You Like It.

Shakespeare's As You Like It is a good play for anyone to read or see. Some readers would enjoy one aspect of it, some would enjoy another. But all would, in general, enjoy the play. Albert Gilman says that Shakespeare intended to imply that all that people need to live together in harmony is "good sense, love, humour, and a generous disposition." (Gilman) This play is deeper than the surface, and that is part of its appeal to every kind of person.

As its title declares, this is a play to please all tastes. ".For the simple, it provides the stock ingredients of romance....For the more sophisticated at d, it p propounds...a question which is left to us to answer: Is it / better to live in the court or the country?....For the learned and literary this is one of Shakespeare's most allusive plays, uniting old traditions and playing with them lightly... (Gardner)

The title of the play came from a note to his "gentlemen readers" in Thomas Lodge's book, Rosalynde, in which he said, "I f you like it, so." (Lodge) People interpret different lines and actions of the characters as they wish, and we know Shakespeare would not object; it says so right in the title of the play! Actors and Directors have taken this literally, and have made various changes to the script, such as having Phebe gnaw on a turnip or an apple between her lines and having Rosalind kiss the chain before giving it to Orlando.

The characters in As You Like It are easy to understand because they follow their simple wishes; they do something because it suits them. For example, Oliver hates Orlando because he wants to. There is no reason for him to resent him, none at all: "... for my soul, though I know not why, hates nothing more than he." (Shakespeare) Duke Frederick banishes Rosalind because people felt sorry for her for her father's sake. Finally, Rosalind herself had no other reason than a simple whim to not tell Orlando who she really was.

Touchstone added the humour to the story, and Jacques added the melancholy. Shakespeare entered both of these characters into the play to balance each other. He also added Audrey and William to give all of the characters someone to love. Because they don't add anything to the plot, these two are not mentioned much. Jacques, because he has the same name as Orlando's brother, was probably meant to be the "Second Brother." But because of his attitude and his outlook on life, Shakespeare realised that "the born solitary must have no family." (Gardner)

Because Duke Frederick had banished the whole court, there was no one left. So he went to the Forest to "seek the enemies so necessary to his existence." (Erickson 189) While he was there, he was changed by a religious old man, popularly thought to be a hermit, and gave the crown back the Duke Senior. He realised that he was wrong in banishing everyone to the Forest of Arden. It wraps up the play very well and adds to the public appeal more than merely killing the tyrant.

Silvius and Phebe were not as big a part of As You Like It as Montanus and Phoebe in Rosalyade. Play-goers would be more interested in the main love-afTair, rather than spending a lot o f time on those two. Silvius thought he loved Phebe, where he probably really loved love itself. "He's fall'n in love with your foulness, and she'll [Phebe] fall in love with my [Ganymede's] anger." (Shakespeare) Phebe did not treat him with respect and was not worthy of his love. Joseph Locket says "Silvius' longings for Phebe show...a losing of the self rather than finding of the lover, and more worthy of mockery than respect." (Locket)

Orlando is the "handsome, well-mannered, young hero" (Gardner) necessary to a good romance. His whole sense of self came from his heritage. He saw himself as the son of Sir Rowland de Boys. When he won the wrestling match, he won the right, in his mind, to claim his father's name. When Oliver came into the forest to find his brother and was attacked by the lioness, Orlando saved him. The kindness he showed to Oliver started with the willingness of Duke Senior to share his meal with Adam and Orlando.

Rosalind, under the disguise of being Ganymede, could get away with a lot more than she could as herself. As Rosalind, Ganymede could not te11 Phebe to "sell when you can, you are not for all markets." (Shakespeare) She could "spoof love and yet be a lover," (Gilman) Through the tool of Ganymede, Rosalind was acting out "parts scripted for women by her culture." (Howard) She used the laws of society to achieve her own ends.

Rosalind's disguised love-play is not merely a game with hapless Orlando, but an education: he must care enough to keep his promises and appointments, and respect her enough to speak as well as kiss.

She is "teaching her future mate how to get beyond certain ideologies of gender to more enabling ones." (Howard) Through her interactions with Orlando as Ganymede, Rosalind is accomplishing much. Her ultimate end is a "rational relationship," rather than one of "heady emotionalism." (Locket) She wished to keep her intelligence and dignity instead of having a relationship such as Audrey and Touchstone (based on lust) or Silvius and Phebe (based on his love of her "foulness"), but she still wanted the bliss of romance. "No wonder she seems so modern, and pleases so many modem audiences." "...Rosalind does not so much woo Orlando as educate him in the proper way to love." (Locket)

Shakespeare crams his first act with incident in order to get everyone to the forest as soon as he possibly can and, when he is ready, he ends it all as quickly as possible. (Gardner)

Shakespeare begins the play in the court, then quickly goes to the Forest. He spends little time in the court because not much happens there, and Shakespeare leaves no room for boredom here. As You Like It is a play based on place, as opposed to time. This comedy, like most of Shakespeare's other works, was taken from another source. Shakespeare took Rosalyade and "stripped Lodge's plot down to the bare bones and added no subplot of his own." (Gardner)

Shakespeare's tragedies are violent and merciless, but he omitted much of the violence from As You Like It that was included in Rosalynde. The wicked uncle was converted in the Forest instead o f being killed in the battle at the end o f the story, and, at the wrestling match, Charles was thrown, but his neck was not broken. Shakespeare made his villains not quite so villainous, "in the spirit of a playful comedy." (Locket) Charles, who wrestled Orlando, was not as evil as in Rosalynde, as he did not do it for money but was deceived by Oliver. Even Oliver does not treat Orlando as badly as Saladin treated Rosader, and Duke Frederick did not banish his own daughter like Duke Torismond did.

Shakespeare made his characters more equal in character value; not only did he make his villains better, he also made his heroes worse, with the exception of Rosalind and her father, Celia was not thrilled at the opportunity to play the priest and "marry" Rosalind/Ganymede and Orlando, as she was in Lodge's version, and Celia was in a bad mood far the remainder of that scene. Orlando, when he disrupted the Duke Senior's dinner, was much more harsh, abrupt, and forceful than Rosader in the same situation. Duke Senior was the same as Gerismond in showing kindness to Orlando/Rosader when the latter demanded food. Shakespeare's Rosalind was better than Lodge's Rosalynde, for when they gave Orlando/Rosader the necklace, Rosalynde gave it to him to toy with his emotions. Rosalind had honest intentions in that action. "Shakespeare's people are more human, with virtues and flaws for all." (Locket) This made the play more lifelike, adding to its charm.

Unlike his other comedies, As You Like It did not have the "broad humour." This might have been because of their recent loss of the company's funnyman, Kempe. Out of this, however, Shakespeare has created "the most re6ned and exquisite of the comedies." This is probably why Audrey's former lover, William, makes such a short appearance. He is the closest of all the characters in the play to a "gross clown." (Gardner)

When someone first sees or reads this play, it is just a cute story with romance, nature, and some violence; what else could one want? This is for the "simpler" play-goer. However, if someone who is more "sophisticated" read up on the characters and studied their motivations and personalities, the whole play would become real and much more interesting because the audience/reader would understand more how they feel. The "learned and literary" would study and analyse each sentence and phrase and research why Shakespeare used certain words or referred to a specific person or event. As You Like It can be read, studied, and/or ana1ysed, depending on the tastes o f the readers and actors. Someone might not like a story because it is too light or too complicated, but a different person might enjoy it for the same reason. As You Like It appeals to all tastes, for it can be whatever the reader wants it to be.

Q10. The Romantic Love of Silvius and Phebe has been portrayed in a beautiful manner in As You Like It .Discuss.

There are several types of love depicted in Shakespeare's As You Like It. One variety of love portrayed in this comedy is romantic love, the romantic literary ideal which became popular in the Middle Ages. According to the courtly love tradition a lover worships his lady and serves her, suffers all sorts of indignities for her sake, and thinks only of her. He must be loyal to her for life, no matter how badly she treats him, or how much he suffers for unrequited love. A true lover never ceases to adore his lady, and when he speaks of her he only uses poetic language and style. These conventions of courtly love are clearly exemplified in As You Like It in the romantic attachment of Silvius and Phebe.

When Rosalind, Celia and Touchstone arrive in the forest of Arden they meet Silvius and Corin, an old shepherd, who are engaged in a conversation about love. Corin is advising his friend on how to treat the woman he loves. However, Silvius doubts the old shepherd's authority in such matters, for although Corin admits having been drawn into acts of madness for the sake of love during his youth, he cannot recall any of them. Silvius clearly manifests that if Corin has forgotten even the most insignificant detail of the actions love made him run into, then he has never been truly in love. Even more, Silvius also explains that a true lover never ceases to adore his lady in speech, even if this moves his listener to discomfort, and further explains that sincere love may drive a lover to interrupt a conversation out of passion. To prove this last point, Silvius suddenly interrupts his speech passionately crying the name of Phebe, his beloved, several times.

Silvius reflects the behaviour of the courtly lover, who is capable of the most foolish actions for the sake of his beloved, and who suffers the pangs of unrequited love and the abrupt separation from his lady. His only concern is love and, although he is uneducated, his language is lofty, poetic, and artificial when he speaks in praise of Phebe. Indeed, both Phebe and Silvius speak in elaborate verse in order to comply with the courtly love conventions. In their courtship, Silvius praises her virtues and begs for the slightest sign of affection, and Phebe scorns and rejects him all along. This romantic and artificial attitude towards love was often portrayed in pastoral romantic literature, and Silvius an Phebe were names often given to the lovers in such genre. Thus, it may be said that Silvius and Phebe represent stock characters, the typical characters in pastoral romances who acted out the conventions of the courtly love tradition.

It may further be argued that As You Like It presents a parody of romantic love, achieved mainly through the character of Touchstone, who constantly mocks Silvius's behaviour. When Silvius speaks of the follies a lover may run into, Touchstone, who is more practical rather than romantic, humourously mocks him by listing the foolish actions he has been capable of out of love. He even claims having once kissed the udders of a cow just because his beloved had milked them.

Some of conventions of romantic love are also acted out, at least at a certain point, by other characters in the comedy. As mentioned before, all four couples fall in love at first sight, an unavoidable tradition in the romantic ideal. Rosalind and Orlando feel infatuated when they first see each other. Later, Orlando continues his courtship in the manner of a courtly lover, writing love poems in praise of Rosalind and feeling lovesick for being separated from her. Despite the fact that Orlando has seen Rosalind only once before, he quickly adopts her as the object of his adoration and devotion. Rosalind, for her part, adopts the same attitude and goes into exile with the image of Orlando as the perfect lover, enough reason to feel lovesick. Celia and Oliver also fall in love at first sight, and although very little can be seen about the nature of their love, for it is not so clearly analysed in the play, they soon join the other couples in the wedding ceremony.

Q11. Rosalind seems to think a mannish outside sufficient to convince the world at large. Comment

Rosalind's - or rather Ganymede's - preoccupation with the outward show of things. Whether this is a result of her cross-dressing, the reason for the same, or the playwright's way of revealing his presence is not as yet clear to me, but Rosalind's constant insistence on the truth of masks and on the other hand her readiness to doubt this same truth fascinates me.

When she decides to dress up as a boy, Rosalind seems to think a mannish outside sufficient to convince the world at large. She is "more than common tall" and therefore all she needs is a "gallant curtle-axe", a "boar spear" and a "swashing and a martial outside" to hide her feminine anxiousness. Taking it for granted that noone will have the hunch to look beyond her male costume, she reasons that since cowardly men are able to hide these feminine qualities, she should be able to pass off as a man, simply by behaving mannishly.

Being so totally dependent on her own disguise not being found out, it is funny how she proceeds to doubt anyone who does not put on an outward show fitting to their claims to feeling. The first to be put on the stand in this fashion is Orlando. As Ganymede Rosalind refuses to accept Orlando's claim to being the desperate author of the love-verses she has found hanging on the trees on the grounds that he has no visible marks of love upon him.

A lean cheek, which you have not; a blue eye and sunken, which you have not; an unquestionable spirit, which you have not; a beard neglected, which you have not (...) Then your hose should be ungartered, your bonnet unbanded, your sleeve unbuttoned, your shoe untied, and everything about you demonstrating careless desolation.

He is, in other words, not exactly the picture of the despairing suitor. Neither does Jaques measure up to Rosalind's expectations of the melancholy traveller. She greets him with a "they say you are"), and sends him off with the order of:

Look you lisp, and wear strange suits; disable all the benefits of your own country; be out of love with your nativity, and almost chide God for making that countenance you are; or I will scarce think you have swam in a gondola.

She seems thus constantly disposed to put emphasis on the exterior show of feelings. At the times when her own disguise falters for a moment, however, she very soon draws the fixity of other people's assumed identity into question. This is perhaps most clear in the scene where Orlando has failed to turn up the first time. Her anxiety - assisted by the fact that she is alone with Celia - compels her to lower her defences for a moment. Her instinctive attack on Orlando is against his semblance: "His very hair is of the dissembling colour." One moment later she seems to cancel this with her "I'faith his hair is of a good colour." Either she is now very confused, or she is saying that the ability to dissemble is a good thing.

Had Rosalind been a human being, we might have seen this preoccupation with people's appearance as an expression of an insecurity towards her own identity, conscious or unconscious. An insecurity that would be quite natural in her situation of displaced heir and disguised female. Seen in this light she is either consciously playing with the identity of others in order to be more at ease with her own, or she is unconsciously expressing an anxiety as to whether she will really be able to carry off the act, without being exposed and without loosing her sense of self in the process.

"My way is to conjure you" says Rosalind in the epilogue, and as she has conjured her fellow characters throughout the play, so has she conjured the audience. But as the audience is fully aware this is "only a play," and Rosalind only a character on stage. The perpetual reminders of the Act as opposed to the Real Thing can readily be seen - in cooperation with the epilogue - to express the playwright's warning against accepting as real the illusion he has created, in the twentieth century we would call it meta-fictionality.

Q12. Compare the element of Time in Macbeth and As You Like It

In Shakespearean drama, a dynamic and explosive fusion of jealousy, pride, anger and ambition is characteristic for heroes' behaviour. The tragedy was caused by the excessive flaw in character - self-respect and dignity combined with the feelings of hate and revenge. A disaster usually occurred to lead to destruction of the protagonist. Due to divine justice, punishment is inevitable and therefore no happy ending is possible. Therefore, time is the hero's main enemy, mercilessly working against him. The mystery of tragedy is that once the protagonist has learnt a lesson of how to renew the order in himself, death is the only outcome /no memento mori, however/.

Comedy differs in the mood it approaches and addresses life. It presents situations which deal with common ground of man's social experience rather than limits of his behaviour – it is not life in the tragic mode, lived at the difficult and perilous limits of the human condition.

In "Macbeth" the first scene presents a meeting of three witches during stormy weather. Shakespeare shows disturbed, angry nature - thunder and lighting represent light - daytime and dark – night-time. Light is the metaphor for innocence, purity, truth, and goodness as opposed to dark - evil. It is also a suggestion that the innocent will suffer as well as the guilty. The fog and filthy air signify moral and spiritual obscurity and "the set of sun" means the end of the reign and kingship. The sun appears only twice – when Duncan sees the swallows flying around the castle of death and during the army gathering to purify the earth of its shame (traitors).

There is very strong sense of predestination ('when' instead of 'if') while in "As You Like It" Orlando's flight is pathless and the meeting of lovers – an act of Fate. In both plays the succession of the scenes is very swift; in tragedy the impression is that longer time elapsed than provided for because passage from thought to a critical resolution is difficult. The outcome of the comedy is obvious while Macbeth enters the spiral of decline within his imagination. Sleep has been banished – the protagonist is aware of the nightmare; his only one dream is the murder which would break the cycle and show the way out of the nightmare – liberation. But the world is a nightmare; "to be" means to escape to live in another world where:

" Rebellious dead, rise never...
... and our high-placed Macbeth
Shall live the lease of nature, pay his breath
To time and mortal custom" /IV.i.98/

Therefore, in tragedy there is conflict of two realities – not only opposed but irreconcilable; illusory freedom and the main outlined goals in life are lost in the past or asserted before their time. In comedy, on the contrary, the heroes' ideals are real and the power of the opposing forces – illusory.

All is left is contempt – the concept of man was crumbled to pieces in "Macbeth":

"Time and the hour runs through the roughest day" / I.iii.146/

While in "As You Like It" time was the main factor which contributed to a resolution of all the problems posed and overcoming the difficulties.

Further study questions

- What are the two main settings of the play? What symbolic functions do they have? Where are most characters happiest? Why do the inhabitants of the forest go back to the city at the end of the play? Is "reality" affected by the characters' sojourn in the idealised "Green World" of the forest? Compare/ contrast with *A Midsummer Night's Dream*.
- Definition: a *dramatic foil* is a minor character who resembles or is in parallel circumstances to a central figure in the play. Foils are similar enough to the main character(s) to provide a useful basis of comparison, but different enough that the comparison is meaningful: they enhance our understanding of the main character's personality traits or actions. Which characters in *As You Like It* function as foils to which other characters? What does the comparison of these parallel characters (or sets of characters) bring to our understanding of the play as a whole?
- In I.i. we learn that two sets of brothers are in a state of contention. What causes their quarrels and hatred? Why is Rosalind banished? Why does Celia go with her? Is their behaviour "natural"? Note use of the words "nature," "natural" and "unnatural" (and instances of "unnatural" behaviour) throughout the play. Like *A Midsummer Night's Dream, As You Like It* ends with multiple weddings. Consider the symbolic function of the final celebration. What

initial conflicts are harmoniously resolved by the marriages? What breaches are healed? Is love the "natural" antidote to "unnatural" hatred?

- Consider the various depiction(s) of love represented by Rosalind and Orlando (the central couple) and their foils, Phebe and Silvius, Touchstone and Audrey, and Celia and Oliver. How does Orlando show he is in love? What kind of lover is he? (realistic, idealistic, sad, silly, etc.?) How does Rosalind react to his behaviour? Why does "Ganymede" tell Orlando he needs a "love-cure"? What traits does Orlando share with Silvius? Why does Phebe reject Silvius? Why (other than the obvious reason!) does Rosalind reject Phebe? What kind of love is Touchstone most interested in? Why does he choose Audrey? Are they well matched? And what about Celia and Oliver? Keep in mind that women's parts were played by men in Shakespeare's time. What humour is derived from the sexual ambiguity of Rosalind/Ganymede's interaction with Orlando and Phebe? (For a similar case of gender-bending, compare Viola/Cesario in *Twelfth Night*.)
- Until the multiple weddings with which it ends, *As You Like It* does not follow the conventional plotline of a romantic comedy, which typically involves the ups and down of a couple working toward a mutual acknowledgement of affection while tormented by uncertainty concerning the other's affections. By contrast, in *As You Like It*, Rosalind learns that Orlando loves her early in the play. So why doesn't the story end there? (Since it is likely that her father would approve their marriage, why doesn't she reveal herself to Orlando and to Duke Senior immediately?) What is the purpose of her continued testing of Orlando? How does Rosalind differ from a conventional romantic heroine? Who is in control

of the love story between Orlando and Rosalind? Why might Shakespeare have given Rosalind the play's epilogue? Compare/contrast Rosalind with Puck, who delivers the Epilogue of *A Midsummer Night's Dream*. To what extend are they analogous? How do they differ?

- Jaques is a conventional stereotype of the melancholic in Renaissance literature, a thoughtful, moral, serious type with a satiric wit and a tendency to moroseness (Hamlet is another famous melancholic figure). How does Jaques relate to Duke Senior, to Orlando, and to Rosalind? Touchstone represents another Shakespearean convention: the court jester as wise Fool, who speaks truth through apparently nonsensical utterances (like Feste in *Twelfth Night* or the Fool in *King Lear*). Why is Touchstone's role so attractive to Jaques?
- Note the way in which Shakespeare plays with pastoral conventions. Is the pastoral life meant to seem ideal? Why or why not? While clearly a pastoral comedy, *As You Like It* still has much in common with Shakespeare's "romantic comedies" — not just the prominent role played by love and love relationships, but the presence of fantastic, magical or improbable elements. What magical or fantastic events occur in the play (although the fantastical elements are less pronounced than in *A Midsummer Night's Dream*)?
- *As You Like It* is a very talky play. After Act I, not much actually *happens* (a violation of conventional plot structure), but the characters *talk* incessantly. To what extent is *As You Like It* a play *about*language? Note in particular conversations or statements *concerning* language: how ideas are, can or should be expressed; a given character's difficulty in understanding language (or in being understood); the tension between literal and figurative speech; the

importance of saying what one means. Note also the presence of several poetic debates (another conventional feature of pastoral poetry). What does Shakespeare seem to be saying by this emphasis on language? Is there a connection with what Rosalind wants to teach Orlando?

Chapter 19

Critical Essays on "As You Like It"

Orlando and the Golden World: The Old World and the New in *"As You Like It"*

Although it is one of the few Shakespeare plays not mentioned in Charles and Michelle Martindale's *Shakespeare and the Uses of Antiquity,As You Like It* does, I shall argue, show a considerable interest in the classical past. Moreover, it does so, paradoxical though this may seem, specifically in the context of the New World. In Shakespeare's play, a setting which hovers with suggestive indeterminacy between England and France holds up a mirror in which the audience can see itself facing both a newly discovered continent in relation to which early modern Europe is the old world, and a classical past in relation to which it is itself new. In this confusing slippage of newness and oldness, Shakespeare seems to introduce a comforting absolute by his repeated references to the concept of a golden age.

However, disturbing ironies and instabilities accrue to the word "gold" as the quest for the ideological 'gold standard' proves to be fissured by a conflict between the classical definition of the golden age as a time of spiritual excellence, and the far more materialistic lust for the literal gold of the new world. At the same time as it shows how European attempts to establish dominance in the New World of the Americas are underpinned by pride in a classical heritage, *As You Like It* thus also charts a growing gulf between the values and attitudes of early modern Europeans and that authorising classical culture.

In the second half of the 1590s, much gossip and several significant texts were generated by the 1595 expedition of Sir Walter Ralegh to Guiana, in search of the mythical city of El Dorado. These range from Ralegh's own account, which presents itself as insistently factual, to George Chapman's *De Guiana Carmen Epicum*, which harnesses the full representational armoury of poetry, and by its Latin title and use of the epic form deliberately presents itself as hymning the English colonial enterprise in the Americas in much the same spirit as Virgil had chronicled Aeneas's forays into Africa and Italy. *As You Like It*, I think, also forms part of the collective cultural response to Ralegh's journey, and develops Chapman's classicising impulse into a double imaging of liminality which focuses not only on the encounter of Europeans with the New World but also, as an inseparable corollary, on the encounter of modern Europeanness with its own formative past. This play which is so full of doubles, with two characters called Oliver, two called Jaques, and (in the Folio) even two dukes called Frederick, offers a further doubling of old world and new in which each finds its features reflected in those of the other. It thus explores a dual pressure being exerted on notions of what it means to be a member of civilised European society and on what the practices, ideals, and the collective memory of such a society should be.

Much has been written about the ways in which expectations formed by classical texts conditioned what Europeans thought they saw in the New World. Aristotle in particular provided a paradigm influential in structuring explorers' experiences, but many other writers were also drawn on, and the phenomenon was a wide-ranging one. Neil Whitehead discusses its presence not only in European writing in general but in that of Ralegh in particular, and interestingly argues that it was not a simple case of imposition of a pattern of expectations, but that the myths which acquired most currency were those which chimed in with something pre-existent in native thought: the relative importance of *Sciopodi* and *Acephali* in the European writing on the New World is directly connected to the relative importance of those icons in native thought. The dog-headed people, centaurs, and minotaurs do not appear with the same frequency as other monstrous / marvellous motifs in the colonial records because they were not part of the native repertoire. The extent to which the process was a two-way one is also clearly indicated by the ways in which discoveries about the New World led Renaissance writers to reassess their conceptions of the old. Garcilaso de la Vega saw the Inca empire in terms of the Roman one, and Las Casas's comparison of the Indians with ancient Britons is emblematic of an increasing move away from accepting the romanticised account of early British history offered by Geoffrey of Monmouth to a view that the pre-Roman inhabitants of Britain were, in a popular pun, little more than brutish. This was a particular historiographical change with which, as has recently been traced, Shakespeare was later to engage in *Cymbeline,* but the climate of thought which gave rise to it, and which allowed the discovery of the New World to interrogate the certainties of the old, is already incipient in *As You Like It*.

Shakespeare's source for *As You Like It,* Thomas Lodge's *Rosalynde, or Euphues' Golden Legacy* (1590), was written during a voyage to the Canaries. Both the subtitle of Lodge's work and the unusual circumstances of its composition may alert us to an important aspect of Shakespeare's play: its interest in the idea of a golden world, and the ways in which that has been imagined in both classical and New World contexts. (And as Keir Elam ingeniously suggests, Shakespeare's use of the word "lodging" in his play points up the debt.) In both cases, the idea of the Golden Age represents a lost past from which the present is painfully conscious that it has declined, but the two are rather differently envisaged. For the Renaissance, the 'golden age' of the classical past was experienced primarily as a time of supreme achievement in writing, with Virgil

standing as perhaps the ultimate exemplar of attainment. The classical conception of the golden age, however, was by no means centrally constructed as literary. Ovid specifically says that "no bronze tablets were erected," and the "golden race" of Hesiod would hardly have had time to write, since "with legs and arms never failing they made merry with feasting beyond the reach of all evils." (Ironically, Peter Martyr compared the Indians' own fables, orally transmitted, with Ovidian narrative.) In Hesiod's schema, it is not until the fourth separate race of men that we come to named individuals who have left any written record, in the shape of the Homeric heroes.

The exiled Duke in *As You Like It* is notably attuned to the former ideal: he praises his environment because it offers him "books in the running brooks." Jaques, however, sees in the same brooks the tears of a wounded deer whose distress offers sharp experiential proof that this is *not* a peaceful pastoral paradise just as the wind and hunger do. Even as we take our first step into "the golden world" which Charles has described the forest as being, an ideological fissure opens up at our feet. Moreover, the concept of 'the golden age' not only differs from period to period, but is also subject to retrospective revision. The discovery of the New World itself changed the idea of the classical period as a golden age, since "the very fact of the discovery of America meant that the moderns had achieved something that had not been achieved by antiquity," and thus led Bodin to conclude that "the age which they call golden...if it be compared with ours, would seem but iron." Ironically, however, the New World which thus undid the goldenness of antiquity was itself golden only in the most problematic of senses. Golden worlds are repeatedly evoked in *As You Like It*, but they are also shadowed by equally insistent references to a very un-golden dystopia, Ireland, which was often figured as the prototype and testing-ground of England's New World colonisation projects. Moreover, as in Guiana, what eventually proves to lie at the heart of the mystery in *As You Like It* is not a golden world at all, but a

golden man, and this in turn raises the whole question of whether a golden world ought ideally to be so in the spiritual or the material sense. What does it mean to be golden, and how can society aspire to such a condition?

Although the actual temporal setting of *As You Like It* is never made clear, and its affiliations are indeed poised almost as ambiguously as its twin geographical allegiances to Warwickshire and the Ardennes, it is heavy with references to the past. The opening lines, with their 'once upon a time' feel, create a rich sense of nostalgia and of the backward glance to a dimly-recalled past: "As I remember, Adam, it was upon this fashion". Quite apart from their evocation of the founding father of the human race, Orlando's words here establish a sense of people ruled and configured by their awareness of an authorising past which, however, they are not sure they can fully know or remember - apt image indeed of the relationship of the Renaissance to that of which it purports to be a rebirth. Orlando is again associated with remembrance of things past when he tells Adam,

O good old man, how well in thee appears
The constant service of the antique world,
When service sweat for duty, not for meed!
Thou art not for the fashion of these times,
Where none will sweat but for promotion,
And having that do choke their service up
Even with the having; it is not so with thee.

(II.3.55-62)

Shakespeare's use of "antique" here serves to align Adam not only with the Christian but also with the classical past, which is, as so often, specifically characterised as morally better than the degenerate present. Suggestively, when Adam disappears without explanation half-way through the play it is almost certainly because he is required to double first the classically-named Corin and then the god of marriage, Hymen. Whether we are to interpret Hymen as an actual supernatural presence or as being obviously Corin dressed up remains

unclear, nicely figuring an ambiguity about how real and how enduring the classical past is.

The same note of praise of antiquity is sounded when Orlando's later praise of Rosalind takes the form of comparisons to the great beauties of the classical past:

Nature presently distilled
Helen's cheek, but not her heart,
Cleopatra's majesty,
Atalanta's better part,
Sad Lucretia's modesty.

(III.2.141-4)

Moreover, as well as being a character who alludes to and is associated with the past, Orlando's very name encodes a lost era of chivalric glory and values, for, together with the presence of two Olivers in the play, it surely prompts us to remember that behind the name Orlando lies the French hero Roland, most recently brought to prominence in Sir John Harington's 1591 translation of *Orlando Furioso*. This is a text which in turn intersects once again with the history of South American exploration: it contains a passage describing Amazons, and when Ralegh was imprisoned in 1592 Sir Arthur Gorges told Elizabeth's chief minister Cecil that "Sir W.R. will shortly grow to be Orlando Furioso if the bright Angelica persevere against him a little longer." (It is notable that the names of both Orlando and his brother are Shakespeare's own additions, since Lodge's equivalent characters are called Rosader and Saladyne.)

Other characters also refer to the past. We hear of Troilus and Leander (IV.1.88-96), celebrated classical lovers whose stories had, in turn, become a fundamental part of the English literary tradition: Shakespeare himself would shortly follow Chaucer in writing of Troilus and Cressida, and Chapman, author of *De Guiana Carmen Epicum*, had recently completed Marlowe's putatively unfinished *Hero and Leander*. We are reminded, too, of other pasts in Jacques' "'Tis a Greek invocation, to call fools into a circle. I'll go sleep, if I can; if I cannot, I'll rail against all the first-born of Egypt" (II.5.56-8), his "My lungs began to crow like Chanticleer" (II.7.30), and Celia's "You must borrow me Gargantua's mouth first: 'tis a word too great for any mouth of this age's size" (III.2.218-9). Gargantua and Chanticleer take us out of the classical era and into the Middle Ages and the Renaissance, and classical and Christian rub shoulders again in Rosalind and Celia's discussion of Orlando: told that Orlando was seen under an acorn, Rosalind exclaims, "It may well be called Jove's tree, when it drops such fruit" (III.2.229-30), while Celia associates him with the age of chivalry when she says, "There lay he, stretched along like a wounded knight" (III.2.233-4), imagery which will be echoed later in the description of the serpent and the lioness (IV.3.99-121).

The past, however, is not simply evoked; we are also reminded of the ways in which it may be posthumously reconstructed. A Renaissance audience invited to think of Leander would remember that Chapman had not only supplied a conclusion to Marlowe's poem, but had also coined the name "Sestiad" (from the fact that the poem is set partially in Sestos) for its verse units - a retrospective appropriation, indeed a virtual colonisation, of the authentically classical "Iliad." The way in which classical authors may find themselves received in Christian times is even more directly recalled in the jokes about "elegies on brambles" (III.2.347-8) and "honest Ovid" (III.3.6), which appear to allude to the recent public burning of Marlowe's pioneering translation of *All Ovid's Elegies*. Just as in Bodin's rejection of classical authority, we are reminded here of how hard classical values and allegiances may find it to survive in a modern, Christian age. Appropriately, too, the play ends with an invocation of both classical and Christian forms of closure, which may indeed be seen as virtually in competition: Jacques jokes that "There is sure another flood toward, and these creatures are coming to the ark" (V.4.35-6), but, after marriage by the Christian priest Sir Oliver Martext has earlier been dismissed as a possibility, it is the classical god Hymen who presides over the closing moments.

Closer and more recent past are also evoked. Charles reports of the old Duke that "They say he is already in the Forest of Arden, and a many merry men with him; and there they live like the old Robin Hood of England: they say many young gentlemen flock to him every day, and fleet the time carelessly as they did in the golden world" (I.1.108-1). When the courtly characters arrive at this modern version of the "golden world," however, they are uncertain whether gold itself is actually current there: Celia begs her companions, "I pray you, one of you question yond man / If he for gold will give us any food; / I faint almost to death" (II.4.58-60. We hear further discussion of the use of gold at II.4.68 and II.4.97). In fact, though, as with so many of the play's confoundings of expectations, there turn out to be very sophisticated and complex economic arrangements operating in the forest, as Corin informs them:

Fair sir, I pity her,
And wish, for her sake more than for mine own,
My fortunes were more able to relieve her;
But I am shepherd to another man,
And do not shear the fleeces that I graze.
My master is of churlish disposition,
And little recks to find the way to heaven
By doing deeds of hospitality.
Besides, his cote, his flocks, and bounds of feed
Are now on sale, and at our sheepcote now,
By reason of his absence, there is nothing
That you will feed on. *(II.4.72-83)*

The golden age envisaged here may, perhaps, be spiritually rich, but it is materially poor.

Alongside this qualified nostalgia for the golden age of the past is a sustained, though equally tempered, interest in the concept of a more contemporary golden world. The play is rich in the language of the English colonial enterprise. Jacques says of Touchstone, "in his brain, / Which is as dry as the remainder biscuit / After a voyage, he hath strange places crammed / With observation" (II.7.38-41), and later prophesies that his "loving voyage / Is but for two months victualled" (V.4.188-9). Rosalind in particular is strongly associated with references to the foreign and the exotic. Orlando's egregious verses declare that "*From the east to western Ind, / No jewel is like Rosalind*" (III.2.84-5), and Rosalind herself tells Celia that "One inch of delay more is a South Sea of discovery" (III.2.190-1). Indeed Rosalind talks a great deal about travel. She says to Jacques, "A traveller! By my faith, you have great reason to be sad. I fear you have sold your own lands to see other men's; then, to have seen much and to have nothing is to have rich eyes and poor hands" (IV.1.19-22). She warns Orlando,

> *I will be more jealous of thee than a Barbary cock-pigeon over his hen, more clamorous than a parrot against rain, more new-fangled than an ape, more giddy in my desires than a monkey; I will weep for nothing, like Diana in the fountain, and I will do that when you are disposed to be merry; I will laugh like a hyen, and that when thou art inclined to sleep.* (IV.1.138-145)

> *She says of Phoebe that*
> *She defies me,*
> *Like Turk to Christian; women's gentle brain*
> *Could not drop forth such giant rude invention,*
> *Such Ethiop words, blacker in their effect*
> *Than in their countenance.* (IV.3.33-7)

And she declares, "my affection hath an unknown bottom, like the Bay of Portugal" (IV.1.192-3). Her reference to "Caesar's thrasonical brag of 'I came, saw, and overcame" (V.2.30-1) further touches on a theme of invasion and conquest also present in Jacques' suggestion "Let's present him to the Duke like a Roman conqueror" (IV.2.2-3) and in her father's remark that "That would I, had I kingdoms to give with her" (V.4.8).

In particular, Rosalind is closely associated with Ireland. Though this may seem a long way from the New World, the two territories were in fact closely associated in the Elizabethan imagination: not only were they both viewed primarily as proposed or actual English colonies, the inhabitants of both were perceived to be equally savage and backward - Dympna Callaghan comments on the extent to which in the Renaissance the Irish were conceived of as being as racially other as blacks. Most directly, perhaps, for any argument which seeks to establish a Guiana context for *As You Like It*, Ralegh had been involved in 'planting' or colonizing both, in ways which may well seem to be remembered in the heady mixture of Irish and New World motifs running through Spenser's work and in Marlowe's interweaving in *Tamburlaine* of images of conquest and what have sometimes been seen as recollections of Ralegh's brutality in Drogheda.

As You Like It as a whole is notably full of references to Irish wolves, Irish rats and Irish music; indeed Sir D. Plunket Barton noted that "Rosalind has so much to say about Ireland that some people have drawn the inference that Shakespeare must have made an Irish tour shortly before the production of the play." She tells Touchstone, "you'll be rotten ere you be half ripe" (III.2.115), touching on an idea often connected with Ireland, where women in particular were considered both to 'ripen' and to 'rot' exceptionally early - Camden remarked in 1586 that "[w]hen their daughters arrive at the age of ten or twelve, they marry them as ripe and capable," and Luke Gernon in 1620 asserted that Irish women were "soone ripe, soone rotten." She also brings together the motifs of both Irishness and classical allusion when she says to Celia, "I was never so be-rhymed since Pythagoras's time that I was an Irish rat, which I can hardly remember" (III.2.171-2).

Most suggestively of all, Rosalind says, "Pray you no more of this, 'tis like the howling of Irish wolves against the moon" (V.2.104-5), which draws on the idea of rebellion against Elizabeth I, often figured as the moon (not least by Ralegh), to point us unmistakably in the direction of the Elizabethan campaign in Ireland. Importantly, though, this is also another instance of the two-way mirroring effect; the site of the encounter between England and its Others is, as so often, a place where the old world as well as the new becomes subjected to scrutiny, for though the wolves may be foolish to howl at that which is so far out of their reach, the queen's own dignity can hardly emerge unscathed from the suggestion of rebellion against her. Further, our registering of this may well alert us to the fact that there are also other possible references to the Virgin Queen in the play, and they too are not entirely flattering. The Duke's declaration that "Sweet are the uses of adversity, / Which, like the toad, ugly and venomous, / Wears yet a precious jewel in his head" (II.1.12-15) may recall the Queen's long courtship by the Duke of Alencon, whom she called her frog; English dislike of the proposed match gave rise to a rich vein of toad jokes. Rosalind's description of "a moonish youth" (III.2.391-2), again recalling the strong association of the Queen with the moon, is also highly satirical. Since the Queen derived her persona as the moon from the classical moon goddess Diana, the image of the Irish wolves howling at the moon very neatly emblematises the onslaught of 'savages' against classical certainties.

The mirror is thus held up to England as well as to America, as the prime emblem of English collective identity, the queen, is examined; just as Orlando finds civility where he expected savagery (II.7.107), so we are led to see the existence of savagery where we might complacently have imagined civility to be. Other cherished institutions come in for similar treatment in the play. *As You Like It* may perhaps have been stimulated to some extent by an upsurge of interest in the figure of Robin Hood, but this is indicative of more than any simple nostalgia for Merrie England: Lois Potter points out that "[a]ll the extant Robin Hood plays belong to the 1590s, a period of uncertainty about the succession to Elizabeth I, and the plays both reflect and displace popular anxiety by dramatizing other periods of instability." Some of these plays, such as *George a Greene*, use the story of Robin Hood to interrogate the concepts of rule and resistance; in the case of *As You Like It*, the evocation of Robin Hood is tellingly juxtaposed with the way the play subjects the hunting of deer - the activity with which Robin Hood is more than any other associated - to a scrutiny which suggests that the Duke's usurpation of the deer in their own forest is no more justifiable than his brother's of the dukedom (II.1.25-7).

In similar vein, Jaques' equation of the horn dance with Roman rites (IV.2.3-4) drains the latter of any sense of sophistication and makes them seem crudely primitive, working in the same spirit of demystification as Garcilaso de la Vega's comparison of the Inca empire with the Roman. (In *Julius Caesar,* a play written probably in the same year as *As You Like It,* Shakespeare shows a strong sense of the relatively crude nature of the fertility practices underpinning much Roman state ritual.) Equally debunking is Rosalind's devastating later coupling of "the fight of two rams, and Caesar's thrasonical brag of 'I came, saw, and overcame"' (V.2.29-31; this again takes the play close to the contested world of Galfridian history which Shakespeare was to explore more fully in *Cymbeline,* where the queen explicitly denies the historicity of Caesar's words).

Moreover, not only does Celia as Aliena literally become the Other, but when Rosalind adopts "no worse a name than Jove's own page" (I.3.122), her new appellation of Ganymede, as Marlowe's *Dido, Queen of Carthage* had so strongly pointed out, irresistibly evokes sodomy, something often thought to be prevalent amongst the Indians, but here again, by the use of classical allusion, located as a product of the Old World rather than the New. And another controversy associated with the New World is evoked when Rosalind asserts that "The poor world is almost six thousand years old" (IV.1.85-6); this was precisely what was contested by Thomas Hariot, who argued that the existence of the America Indians proved the world to be more like *sixteen* than *six* thouand years old, and thus disproved the Bible. (It is notable that Rosalind passes on immediately from this remark to reminiscences of the verse of Marlowe, said to have been the friend of Hariot and to have shared both his heretical opinions and the alleged sodomitical tendencies of the Indians.)

Much of the language of *As You Like It,* then, conspires to remind its audience that the penetration of new lands may both prove more problematic than anticipated and also have unexpected consequences for the denizens of the old, and it does so by drawing on images which, for contemporaries, seem resonantly to recall the actual difficulties of the Elizabethan colonial enterprise and the problems of trying to achieve a settlement in Ireland. Other elements of the text also combine to underline the force of these echoes: Jaques' travel leaves him poor, echoing the failure of Ralegh and others to bring back vast sums from the Americas, and suggesting, ultimately, that the English colonial venture may not only be attended with difficulties, but may not even be worth the candle. Nevertheless, the text also insists that there is still gold to be struck, even if not of the sort that might have been expected.

Orlando's name begins with the French word for gold, *or* (derived ultimately, as Shakespeare would have known, from the Latin *aurum*), and his first speech reinforces the association, as he says, "My brother Jaques he keeps at school, and report speaks goldenly of his profit" (I.1.4-6). The idea is also present in the dual association of Orlando with Atalanta, both in his own poem and in his exchange with Jaques. Jaques says scornfully, "You are full of pretty answers: have you not been acquainted with goldsmiths' wives, and conned them out of rings?," to which Orlando replies, "Not so; but I answer you right painted cloth, from whence you have studied your questions," and to this Jaques responds in turn, "You have a nimble wit; I think 'twas made of Atalanta's heels" (III.2.262-8). Jaques accuses Orlando of associating with goldsmiths' wives; Atalanta was running after a golden apple. There may be no golden land, but there is a golden man, who like a noble savage is "never schooled and yet learned" (I.1.135), and Rosalind, who is, after all, accompanied by a Touchstone, appropriately finds him.

This was the quintessential ambiguity at the heart of all English attempts to strike it rich in South America. The Spanish name El Dorado, which actually means a golden man, and seems to represent a genuine indigenous concept of a golden king, was insistently misinterpreted as a golden *land*. Even where the etymology was understood or the concept it signified fully grasped, a slippage - slippages being an essential characteristic of almost everything associated with the idea of El Dorado - occurs, as when Sir Robert Dudley, illegitimate son of the Earl of Leicester, who mounted an expedition shortly before Ralegh's first foray, noted that "I was told of a rich nation, that sprinkled their bodies with the powder of golde, and seemed to be guilt, and that farre beyond them was a great towne called El Dorado, with many other things." (The richly suggestive pun of 'guilt' with 'gilt' is of course another issue, but speaks too loudly to be ignored totally.) Above all, the determination to read El Dorado as a country instead of a person is the central feature of the quest of Sir Walter Ralegh, whose title-page of *The Discoverie of the Large, Rich and Bewtiful Empire of Guiana* (first published in 1596, two years before the probable date of *As You Like It*) quite erroneously refers to "the great and Golden Citie of Manoa (which the Spanyards call El Dorado."

As You Like It shares many notable features with the *Discoverie*. This is perhaps unsurprising, since Thomas Lodge, author of *Rosalynde,* Shakespeare's source for the play, seems to have been personally connected both with Ralegh and with the Guiana voyage: his captain on the voyage to the Canaries during which he wrote *Rosalynde* was probably a captain on the Guiana expedition, and the ship in which Lodge sailed was owned by Ralegh. And Shakespeare, who so frequently recalls Marlowe elsewhere in the play, was hardly likely to overlook the fact that Chapman, author of the continutation of Marlowe's *Hero and Leander* (from which Shakespeare quotes directly in the play), had also written an epic poem, *De Guiana,* in response to Ralegh's voyage, in which he specifically speaks of the proposed second Guiana voyage as creating "A golden world in this our iron age." (Ralegh's reply to Marlowe's "The Passionate Shepherd to his Love" had of course already established the two men as the proponents of two opposing attitudes in the Renaissance's interrogation of the pastoral ideal.) If, however, as many critics have suggested,

Shakespeare did indeed feel some sympathy for the Essex / Southampton faction, this would automatically tend to make him less well-disposed than Chapman towards Essex's chief enemy Ralegh. (There are some suggestive possible parallels between Essex and Anthony Munday's reworking of the Robin Hood figure as the exiled Earl of Huntingdon.) Though Shakespeare may echo the discourse of the *Discovery* just as Chapman does, his attitude towards it seems considerably less eulogistic.

There are a number of signs of intersection between *As You Like It* and the *Discoverie*. The strangely composite nature of the geography of Arden, in which France interpenetrates Warwickshire and is home to lions and serpents, may be seen almost as an inversion of Ralegh's Guiana, since "[i]t has been suggested that Ralegh's reportage of the landscapes of Orinoco was so strongly influenced by his desire to make it seem a favourable place for settlement, and to make the exotic acceptably familiar, that he was led into projecting an English landscape on to an American wilderness," describing the land as being "as full of deare, as any forrest or parke in England," although he maintained, in defiance of all other authorities on natural history, that there were lions there too (*Discoverie,*) - and was also careful to stress that though the landscape might resemble England, it was pointedly unlike Ireland, since there were no bogs (*Discoverie*). Ralegh tends only to discuss those features of Guiana which he regards as familiar and assimilable within an English context, such as the woman who reminds him of someone back home, rather than anything new - as Charles Nicholl observantly points out (*Discoverie*), he does not even mention tobacco. When Ralegh looks at an American waterfall, he fancies the peaceful and benevolent sight of church towers (*Discoverie*); similarly, Orlando conjures the inhabitants of the forest by their memories of "where bells have knolled to church" (II.7.115). As well as travelling to America himself, moreover, Ralegh had also supported the expedition of the Frenchman Jacques Morgue (*Discoverie*), whose name may be echoed in *As You Like It*'s Jaques. Equally the fratricidal urges of Oliver and the Duke parallel those of Atahualpa

(Atabalipa in Ralegh), who killed his elder brother, while one of his younger brothers fled with his men, like Duke Senior (*Discoverie*).

Brotherhood is a crucial trope in the history of the settlement of the New World, and a theory of the universal brotherhood of man was indeed the reason supplied to the Indians to persuade them to desist from sodomy: Cortés explain[ed] to Montezuma "how we are all brothers, sons of one father and one mother who were called Adam and Eve," and the 'place of a brother' is not to sodomise brother. Cortés further explained that that was why Charles V had sent him, though it is presumably implicit here that the Spaniards enjoy the privileges of the elder brother. Echoing his rhetoric, Ralegh specifically recommends the settlement of Guiana as a way for the queen to "employ all those souldiers and gentlemen that are younger brethren" (*Discoverie*), and the question of younger brothers is seen by Louis Montrose as one crucial to *As You Like It*. When Orlando tells Oliver that "[t]he courtesy of nations allows you my better, in that you are the first born, but the same tradition takes not away my blood, were there twenty brothers betwixt us" (I.1.43-46), his militancy is certainly lent a new piquancy in the light of the abuse of the language of brotherhood to legitimise the Spanish colonisation of America.

It has recently been suggested that although gold was valued by indigenous South Americans, this was less for its worth than for its appearance and symbolic value (*Discoverie*). Given the extent to which it, too, presents its golden world as a locus of spiritual peace rather than exploitable economic wealth, *As You Like It* would seem both to mock Ralegh's obsession with plunderable riches - which could even, perhaps, have been why it was initially 'stayed' by the Master of the Revels - and, by valuing the golden man Orlando more than gold itself, to sound the same note of valuing the human more than the material as is found in indigenous attitudes, and indeed in the classical idea of the Golden Age, since, as Charles Nicholl notes, "the plenty of the Golden Age was a *freeing* of man from the search and scrabble for wealth," just as Orlando extols "The constant service of the antique world, / When service sweat for duty, not for meed!" (II.3.57-8). (Though Shakespeare himself need not have had quite so rosy-tinged a view of classical disdain of gold: the first remark addressed by Geoffrey of Monmouth's Cassivelaunus to Julius Caesar, in the section which would become a principal source for *Cymbeline*, is "The cupidity of the Roman people, my dear Caesar, is really quite beyond belief. They have an insatiable thirst for anything made of gold or silver.") Ralegh enthused that in Guiana "all the rockes, mountaines, all stones in the plaines, in woodes, and by the rivers sides are in effect thorow shining, and appeare marveylous rich," but the gold which he brought back was pronounced worthless (*Discoverie*); Arden, by contrast, may not be paved with gold, but it offers, more educatively, books in its brooks, and, more humanistically, an aesthetic which seeks its goldenness more in the spiritual than the material sense.

At the same time, though, the play shows itself acutely aware that the very fact of encounter with the outside world changes what is inside. Just as both Oliver and the Duke find that the entire basis of their lives is transformed on the borders of the forest, so Phoebe, Silvius, Audrey and William all find that they have unexpectedly found or been deprived of marriage partners by the advent of the courtly party. (Given the insistent sexualising of the language applied to the 'penetration' and 'husbanding' of the maidenheads of 'cuntries' like Guiana, not to mention the prominence of real-life relationships like that of Cortés and Doña Marina, it is particularly appropriate that it is in the arena of sexual partnerships that the indigenous inhabitants' lives are most dramatically transformed; moreover, the Robin Hood element of *As You Like It* chimes eerily with the link recently postulated between Doña Marina and Maid Marian.) Shakespeare's play never lets us forget that the cutting edge of encounters with the New World has cut both ways, and has forced the old world to re-evaluate its whole notion of goldenness and value. Equally, though, he does not agree that the best of the old world has thereby been entirely vitiated. Though a distinctly mocking eye may be turned on its ganymedes and on its pretensions to totality of knowledge, classical civilisation is still looked on with affection in this play in which books are still valued and a classical, spiritual idea of the golden, as found in the old world, is presented as preferable to the more mercenary ideologies fostered by the material wealth of the new.

Instruction Versus Deception: from 'Rosalynde' to 'As You Like It'

Thomas Lodge's *Rosalynde* is an unwieldy pastoral, overladen with classical allusions and Latin aphorisms for courtier and shepherd alike. The romance is thick, heavy, and conventional. Yet when Shakespeare took it in hand, to rework the tangled web of disguise and romance into *As You Like It*, he changed much of the emphasis, by both altering and adding characters. *Rosalynde* is a celebration of love; *As You Like It*, a philosophical discourse on love, for Rosalind does not so much woo Orlando as educate him in the proper way to love.

Shakespeare cuts to the chase, eliminating much of the prologue to *Rosalynde*. We hear of old Sir Roland de Boys (Lodge's John of Bordeaux) only through Orlando's opening speech, not the extended deathbed collection of aphorisms Lodge provides (though this shade of Polonius perhaps influences old Adam's long-winded style). Likewise, the extended ruminations are cut entirely or, for the forest scenes, condensed into tighter dialogue. Lodge's grand tournament, with the jousting prowess of the anonymous Norman (proto-Charles) happens offstage, and we see only a wrestling match. Lodge's usurper favours Rosader after the tournament, but Shakespeare's Frederick spurns Orlando for his parentage and Oliver plots more quickly against his brother, further excising the plot-perambulations of the source and removing the months of tension and reconciliation that plague Saladin and Rosader.

But Shakespeare also takes care to lighten his villains, more in the spirit of a playful comedy than Lodge's sometimes grim pastoral. His Charles is relatively innocent, deceived by Oliver rather than entering willingly into his pay (as the Norman does with Saladin). Oliver, in turn, is not such a relentless foe as Saladin: he has no cronies to assist in binding up Orlando, he does not so mistreat his brother before us as happens in Lodge's pastoral. Even the usurper Duke, Torismond/Frederick, does not exile his own daughter in Shakespeare's play (only remonstrating her with "You are a fool"). And he is not killed in battle at the end of the play, but rather converted to a holy life, in much the same fate that Lodge's Saladin plans for himself in remorse ("[I shall] wend my way to the Holy Land, to end my years in as many virtues, as I have spent my youth in wicked vanities."

In contrast, Shakespeare darkens his heroes: they are not all the blithe, pastoral folk Lodge paints. Celia's single "Is it not a foul bird that defiles its own nest?" early in *Rosalynde* becomes Celia's more extended harangue at the end of IV.i. — unlike in Lodge, Celia does not volunteer to marry Orlando and Rosalind, but is rather shanghaied into the task, to her chagrin. Orlando is not nearly as polite in his first appearance to the exiled Duke: "Forbear, and eat no more!" is rather more abrupt and impolitic than Rosader's polished and chivalric challenge. Shakespeare's people are more human, with virtues and flaws for all.

Amidst this simplification of Lodge's mass of material, Shakespeare also changes many emphases. Lodge's lovers do little but harangue each other about the legendary inconstancy of the other sex: Rosalind performs her share of carping, but also attacks the overwhelming over-romanticism of Orlando's love. Lodge's plentiful sonnets become objects of ridicule in *As You Like It*, material for the doggerel imitations of Touchstone's "Sweetest nut hath sourest rind, / Such a nut is Rosalind" (III.ii.109-110). And Rosalind's lessons to Orlando are meant to make him respect that "sour rind," not to put his love on a pedestal for worship. Touchstone and Audrey present raw sexual love, lust instead of romance; Silvius' longings for Phebe show the foolish extreme of Petrarchan love, a losing of the self rather than a finding of the lover, and more worthy of mockery than respect. Rosalind's disguised love-play is not merely a game with hapless Orlando, but an education: he must care enough to keep his promises and appointments, and respect her enough to speak as well as kiss (IV.i.). Orlando's wound is not merely the delay in the plot that Lodge makes it, but the occasion for his proof that the lesson is learned: Oliver's arrival with the bloody napkin shows Orlando's new-found sensibility.

Lodge's *Rosalynde*'s characters concern themselves greatly with whether to love: Shakespeare's are more worried with the question of how to love. Rosalind strives for the triumph of rational relationships over heady emotionalism, a romance that will allow the woman to keep her intelligence and dignity intact, but still achieve romantic bliss. No wonder she seems so modern, and pleases so many modern audiences.

Relationship to Shakespeare's Other Plays

Measure for Measure was written during the same period as Shakespeare's great tragedies: 1601 to 1608. In this brief time span, he wrote *Hamlet, Othello, King Lear,* and *Macbeth,* as well as *Julius Caesar, Timon of Athens, Coriolanus,* and *Antony and Cleopatra.* Critics frequently point out that *Measure for Measure* could easily have been a tragedy itself. The plot, the characters, and the setting are all potentially tragic. The happy ending is so sudden as to seem contrived, leaving critics to speculate that the play was meant for a tragedy and was turned to comedy at the last moment. Perhaps the poet was so immersed in his tragic masterpieces that their mood was reflected in this work. Or he may have experienced dark and bitter times in his personal life at this period. Audience demands may have influenced him to make comedy of tragic material. Pulled away from his major works to write it, he gave it less than his best. While these variously advanced ideas are no more than speculation, many critics do agree that the play has no consistency of mood, the subject matter is more tragic than comic, and the final scene is jarring.

Measure for Measure is often treated with *All's Well That Ends Well* and *Troilus and Cressida.* Written during the great tragic period, they are often called "bitter" or "dark comedies." They are also known as the "problem comedies" because they examine a grave problem of human existence in a style which is more serious than usual for comedy, yet not strictly tragic either. The play is preceded by Shakespeare's great comedies and is followed by the romances.

All's Well That Ends Well, written about 1598, or six years previous to *Measure for Measure,* turns on the same dramatic device, the substitution of one bed partner for another. Critics point out that while this works well as a part of the plot in *All's Well,* in *Measure for Measure* it seems tacked on. In need of a convenient way to prevent the necessity of Isabella's giving way to Angelo's lewd demands, the author recalled the bed trick from his earlier work and simply inserted it.

Like *Measure for Measure, Othello* found its source in Cinthio's *Hecatommithi.* Written in the same year, it was introduced at court in November 1604, a few weeks before *Measure for Measure.*

The play also bears a noticeable resemblance to *Hamlet* in two of its passages. Angelo's speech on prayers is often compared to that of King Claudius in *Hamlet.* The inability of a conscience heavy with guilt to give sincerity to prayer is expressed by Angelo in Act II, Scene 4:

When I would pray and think, I think and pray
To several subjects. Heaven hath my empty words;
Whilst my invention, hearing not my tongue,
Anchors on Isabel: Heaven in my mouth,
As if I did but only chew his name;
And in my heart the strong and swelling evil
Of my conception.

Angelo's words clearly recall King Claudius' struggle to pray in Act III, Scene 3, lines 97-98 of *Hamlet:*

My words fly up, my thoughts remain below.
Words without thoughts never to heaven go.

Claudio expresses his fears of the unknown in death to his sister Isabella in a speech which clearly echoes Hamlet's famous soliloquy in ("To be, or not to be..."):

Ay, but to die, and go we know not where;
To lie in cold obstruction and to rot;
This sensible warm motion to become
A kneaded clod; and the delighted spirit
To bathe in fiery floods, or to reside
In thrilling region of thick-ribbed ice;
To be imprison'd in the viewless winds,
And blown with restless violence round about
The pendent world; or to be worse than worst
Of those that lawless and incertain thought
Imagine howling: 'tis too horrible!
The weariest and most loathed wordly life
That age, ache, penury and imprisonment
Can lay on nature is a paradise
To what we fear of death.

Chapter 20

"As You Like It" and Various Issues by IAN Johnsons

Dramatic Comedy—Some Observations

Traditional classifications of drama normally started with the basic distinction between tragedy and comedy, a separation common in Greek and Roman drama, and clearly established by Shakespeare's time. Of these two styles, the easiest to define initially was the former. Tragedy was understood as the dramatic portrayal of a great man's suffering and (almost invariably) his death. The hero might be a great villain or famous for virtue (a historical or Biblical character, for example), but the main purpose of the play was to focus on his career, especially the final chapter: the events leading up to his death, his death, and moral reflections upon the story (tragedy lent itself often to fairly orthodox Christian themes: punishments for arrogance, pride, overreaching, and so on).

By common traditions, then, tragedies were serious, involving some ultimate questions about the moral framework of a human life in the face of our common fate, death. Hence, tragedies demanded a formal style in the language (e.g., blank verse), subject matter, and acting: tragedies were, by definition serious and formal—high art, if you will. In addition, the central character had to be, to some extent, larger than life—a suitable focus for our attention on major questions of human existence. Tragic heroes were thus almost invariably people of special social prominence: kings, generals, extraordinarily successful achievers (or over-achievers).

About comedy, however, there was no such general agreement, and in Shakespeare's time there was a fierce competition between rival companies seeking to win over audiences with different brands of comedy. As we shall see, such a competition is still alive in our culture. By way of illustrating this competition, let me list a few of the rival possibilities.

One of the oldest styles of comedy, developed by the Greeks and a staple ingredient of Roman drama, was the so-called New Comedy, or comedy of manners. Here the dramatic focus is squarely on the middle-class urban family, its trials and tribulations, and, in the conclusion, a happy resolution of its problems. This is the sort of drama we are very used to seeing on television in programmes like *All in the Family, Bill Cosby, Malcolm in the Middle, Will and Grace,* and so on, the staple fare of sit-coms.

New Comedy, in other words, presents to its overwhelmingly middle-class audience a image of itself, focusing on their major concerns, especially money, property, quarrels between parents and children, neighbours, husbands and wives·and servants, and so on. It relies heavily on certain stock characters invented by the Greeks and Romans which have not changed all that much—the conniving adulterous husband, the clever servant, the nagging wife, the expensive mistress, the horny son, the boastful soldier, and so on. In many cases, such New Comedy lends itself easily to satire, and so it becomes a favourite vehicle for dramatists who wish to present in their work some lesson for the audience to learn about appropriate conduct (New Comedy is thus a favourite vehicle for those who believe that art should—or must—have a social moral purpose). Since New Comedy is also a common classical form (especially in Latin literature), this form is particularly attractive for any writer who wants to lean on classical models or display his command of classical literature.

New Comedy relies heavily on naturalism—that is, offering a world and characters recognizably similar to the world of the audience, what we would call slice-of-life (again, modern television sit-coms illustrate this quality well). It is predominantly urban in setting, taking place in the street, the market, or in some public space (like a hotel) where the characters can plausibly meet, interact, engage in conflicts, and so on. The source of the conflicts and their resolution rely heavily on things common to the middle-class life of the audience, which may be unexpected but which fit the description of reality defined by the middle-class setting. Hence, there are few violations of the naturalistic basis for the style (no magic, no divine interventions, and so on). There may be many coincidences, but the action never moves to the entirely implausible. In fact, the heart of New Comedy is a tightly constructed and interesting plot. Since the characters are more or less familiar types who don't change very much and since the style is naturalistic, without weird special effects, the major interest in the drama is the way in which the conflict gets increasingly complicated and then resolves itself quickly in a suitably convincing way. The logic of the action must be interesting and plausible within the principles established by the style.

At the other extreme of the spectrum of comic styles is the more anarchic world of Popular Comedy (I use this term for want of a clear label for such a style), a much more free-wheeling affair, closer to a children's pantomime or fairy story than to a naturalistic middle-class life. In many cases, the action is loosely scripted, so as to permit a great deal of improvisation, especially by the clowns, audience interaction, local references, singing, dancing, joke-telling, clowning around of all varieties, and so on. Popular Comedy of this sort respects no particular dramatic rules, and it tends to be much more colloquial, physical, spontaneous, and vulgar than New Comedy. Hence, it often prompts stern criticism from those who believe middle-class drama should observe certain rules about a proper style and subject matter and carry a useful moral lesson.

For instance, an excellent modern example of this Popular Comedy—and the most popular form of live drama in our culture—is professional wrestling. It has a stage, all sorts of props (like chairs, tables), outlandish costumes, continuing audience interaction, and a great deal of on-the-spot improvising as the main actors carry out a loosely scripted performance. It also has no pretensions to any socially redeeming message or any concern for polite taste (as one of its latest wrinkles, the stink fight, where women rub their buttocks in each other's faces, would seem to indicate): its purpose is to give the people a lot of physical entertainment for their money. It also features a great deal of audience participation (as does another very popular form of this style, *The Gerry Springer Show*). Such physical vigour, variety, and spontaneous action are much more important than the plot which (like a wrestling match) may be entirely predictable and thin).

Of course, such Popular Comedy attracts the stern criticism of those who believe that entertainment should pay attention, first and foremost, to public standards of decency and moral purposiveness (or at least naturalistic plausibility). So the sorts of arguments we see about wrestling and Gerry Springer on television are not unlike the sorts of arguments going on in Shakespeare's time about an appropriate style for public dramatic performances (it's all fake, it's too repetitive, crude, predictable, and so on).

In between these two is a style of comedy called pastoral drama. Like New Comedy, pastoral drama tends to avoid the excesses of what I have been calling Popular Comedy and it often has a clear moral purpose. But, unlike New Comedy, it makes no attempt to be strictly naturalistic. Pastoral drama, like pastoral literature generally, usually features an idealised vision of country life, with shepherds and shepherdesses happily united in nature talking all the time about love. But (and this is key to the pastoral convention) the life is typically seen from a city-goer's perspective, a point of view which enables the writer to use the country experience as a means of critiquing urban values in a manner more sophisticated than a point of view defined entirely by the country experience would permit. Pastoral literature, in other words, features an interaction between an urban sophistication and a simplified vision of life away from the city.

Pastoral drama typically features love as its major concern—a romance between country folk, or the love of an urban man for some country lass, or a romance between two urban people who, for some reason or another (frequently implausible) find themselves temporarily in the country, having to deal with country life (i.e., from an unfamiliar perspective). Because pastoral drama takes place away from the city or the palace, it permits the characters to explore life in a totally non-political way, in a setting where their social roles can be momentarily set aside and they can, to some extent, experiment with possibilities not available in the much more restricted world of the city, where they are known, have social and political responsibilities, have to observe much stricter codes of behaviour (e.g., in clothes), and (this is often quite important in the Pastoral style) have to answer to the demands of the clock (i.e., organise their daily schedule more rigorously than in the country).

Also, the pastoral setting often encourages a much less naturalistic style, one in which woodland sprites, fairies, amazing coincidences, enchantment, and so on come with the territory. So pastoral drama, like popular comedy, can routinely violate naturalistic principles in a way which would not be acceptable in the more naturalistic world of New Comedy. Since the action is taking place outside the city, the normal rules of the city do not apply. Thus, anything can happen.

Pastoral comedy, however, is much more sophisticated than Popular Comedy, since it has a potentially important theme (the nature of love) and tries to establish a more or less consistent fictional world (the country setting). While it can often feature the colloquial language of country folk, it also requires a certain sophistication in the exploration of love through poetry and (a very important element in much pastoral drama) music and song.

Shakespeare began his writing career at a time when all these forms of comedy were available, and when companies and playwrights were fighting each other about what the "proper" form of comedy should be. The fight itself is an interesting manifestation of the growing phenomenon of the urban middle-class and the arguments about standards appropriate to its entertainment (things we are still arguing about in our debates over television content).

Leading the charge for a standard of polite comedy were those with a classical education and a preference for New Comedy (e.g., Ben Jonson, Shakespeare's great rival)—particularly because it carried a moral intention of educating the public through satire and because it celebrated the continuing vitality of classical models of drama. These writers often had little use for what they perceived as the crudity and crass appeals to the audience's lowest common denominator of Popular Comedy. In addition, New Comedy was a standard ingredient in the classical education of many young boys, who formed their own companies and generated a popular following for a time.

Early in his career Shakespeare, in response to popular taste, began with New Comedy. His earliest work, especially *The Comedy of Errors*, patterned itself closely on classical models and stuck to the conventions of the style. But he soon began to move towards the pastoral style, taking the urban characters out of their customary setting and putting them into the countryside, shifting the emphasis from the complexities of a plot (quite bewildering at times in *The Comedy of Errors*, with its two sets of identical twins) to the exploration of human relationships in love (the central concern of the pastoral tradition), and relaxing the demands of naturalism appropriate to New Comedy so as to include magical elements. The most famous relatively early example of this shift is *Midsummer Night's Dream*, featuring gods, fairies, magic transformations, and all sorts of implausible occurrences which come about when a few urban characters, including pairs of lovers, wander off into the woods.

One way of appreciating the shift is to attend to the nature of the story. Northrup Frye once observed an important distinction between what he called "Hence" stories and "And then" stories. In the first type, as the label "Hence" suggests, the interest in the story is the logic of cause and effect, how a series of circumstances presents a logical sequence, each stage flowing logically and naturalistically out of the previous situation, as a result of decisions, motives, and so on quite similar to the logic of real life. In "And then" stories, by contrast, events simply follow one after the other, often without any clearly logical link between them (as in many children's stories: "This happened, and then this happened, and then this happened, and so on...."

In New Comedies, like *The Comedy of Errors* (and situation comedies generally), the effect of the play depends upon a tight "Hence" structure, and the audience has to keep close track of the distribution of information so as to understand the various confusions, misunderstandings, quarrels, and so on, each of which makes logical sense once we understand who knows what. But in the pastoral comedies, like *Midsummer Night's Dream* (or a children's fairy story), events tend to follow one another apparently much more casually with no tight logical connection between events (as we shall see in more detail in a few moments).

As You Like It and Twelfth Night: Some Initial Observations

The two comedies we are discussing, both from the late 1590's and early 1600's, illustrate these differing tendencies in comedy. *As You Like It* is clearly a pastoral comedy—with a country setting, much talk of love of all sorts, a story which consists, for the most part, of a series of accidental meetings one after the other, and a resolution involving implausible transformations of character and divine intervention. Although (as we shall see) the Forest of Ardenne is not a completely idealised pastoral setting, we have here all the standard ingredients of pastoral drama.

Twelfth Night is somewhat different. The pastoral element in the play is obviously present in the treatment of love and the leisurely world of Illyria, not quite as pastoral as the Forest of Ardenne, but miles away from the political world of the city. And a good deal of the play follows a loose "And then" plot structure, once again featuring a series of accidental meetings.

However, *Twelfth Night* contains a sub-plot, the tricking of Malvolio, which is clearly drawn from the style of New Comedy, the comedy of manners, the satiric exposure of folly. The characters of the sub-plot, like the foolish knight Aguecheek, the clever servant Maria, the boisterous lay-about Toby Belch, and the self-deceiving Malvolio, are all urban types common in New Comedy, and their plot to trick Malvolio depends, as in almost all New Comedy, on a sequence of events which is plausibly crafted (in "Hence" story tradition). In a sense, *Twelfth Night* is one more experiment, this time combining two distinct styles in a very interesting and dramatically convincing manner.

Preliminary Observations on *As You Like It*

As You Like It will be for many of you a rather difficult play to appreciate and interpret simply on the basis of a reading. The reasons for this are not difficult to ascertain. The play is, as I have observed, a pastoral comedy, that is, a comedy which involves a traditional literary style of moving sophisticated urban courtiers out into the countryside, where they have to deal with life in a very different manner from that of the aristocratic court. This play, like others in the Pastoral tradition, freely departs from naturalism, and in *As You Like It* (certainly by comparison with the History plays) there is little attempt to maintain any consistently naturalistic style.

This can create problems for readers unfamiliar with the conventions of pastoral, especially those who find it just too artificial and incredible to grasp imaginatively. After all, how are we to understand the unmotivated family hatreds which launch the action? We are simply not given any sufficiently detailed look at why Oliver hates Orlando (he himself does not understand the reason) or why Duke Frederick hates Duke Senior and turns on Rosalind so suddenly or, what is most surprising of all, why the nasty people whose animosities have given rise to the plot so suddenly and so conveniently convert and become nice people just in time to wind the plot up happily under the supervision of the goddess Hymen, the Greek deity of marriage, who arrives as an unexpected but welcome guest.

But these features of the plot which we might find unconvincing if we demand naturalism (that is, if we insist on treating the play as a "Hence" story) are little more than standard plot devices in "And then" stories, common in a genre like pastoral, which makes no claims to naturalistic motivation. Such plotting serves to launch and to conclude the comic confusion. The main point of the play here, after all, is not the working out of a carefully constructed plot, but rather the various encounters which take place in the Forest of Ardenne. In fact, the structure of the play is less a carefully complex and unfolding plot than a series of conversations between characters who happen to run into each other amid the trees.

You will notice, for example, that most of the central part of *As You Like It* consists of often random encounters between different characters in the forest. In many cases, they have no particular reason to talk to each other. What these serve to bring out is a series of conversations about life (and particularly about love) in which we witness different attitudes clashing. The effect is to take us through a variety of responses to shared concerns and to get us responding to our own sense of the appropriate ways to deal with experience.

To put this another way. The pastoral style of *As You Like It* does not encourage a deep psychological approach to any of the characters, to the logic of their motivation. If that's what we demand from a story to make it interesting, then this play is not going to satisfy us. We are not in that sort of a world.

There is far more direct pressure on us to see in the interactions between characters the exploration of some themes, especially issues concerning love. That is not to say that the characters are not theatrically interesting and worth talking about; it is rather to insist that the characters here are serving thematic purposes more obviously than they are in more psychologically plausible plays. So there's little point in seeking to penetrate deeply into the plausibility of the psychological motivation or of the coincidences.

To take one obvious example of a thematic concern, very common in pastoral, we notice in the play a repeated contrast between court and country life. The purpose here is not to provide some naturalistic contrast, for the picture of life in the country is obviously idealised a good deal (although not totally, for there are references to the harsher aspects of life away from the comforts of the court and to the realities of working for an absentee landlord). Nor is the purpose any romantic celebration of the values of country living as somehow more authentic than city life. The pastoral is primarily a vehicle for a (usually) gentle satire on urban values, on some of the corrupting manners of the court (like flattery and excessive attention to clothes or fine language). And we can see this clearly enough in this play. But there is no sense in *As You Like It* that, given a free choice, any of the principal characters (except Jaques) would actually prefer to live in the country rather than the court.

The other great difficulty with *As You Like It* for inexperienced readers is much of the humour. Here again, what makes little sense on the page (and doesn't come across as very funny) generally works much better in a production. This point is generally true of all comedy, where the physicality of the human interaction (something not always readily apparent from the text of the play alone) is an essential key to understanding and responding to what is going on. That aspect of comedy, especially Shakespearean comedy, is one reason why, in the curriculum of this course, the comedies are underrepresented. The only quick way to overcome this problem is to focus on seeing the play in production (and there's a useful BBC video version available in the college library).

The Pastoral Setting: The Forest of Ardenne

Central to the pastoral vision of *As You Like It* is the setting in the Forest of Ardenne, especially the contrast between it and the ducal court. In the former, there is a powerful political presence which creates dangers. Deception lurks behind many actions, brothers have secret agendas against their brothers, and people have to answer to the arbitrary demands of power.

In the Forest of Ardenne, however, life is very different. For one thing, there is no urgency to the agenda. There are no clocks in the forest, and for the exiled courtiers there is no regular work. They are free to roam around the forest, prompted by their own desires. There is plenty of food to eat, so the communal hunt takes care of their physical needs. That and the absence of a complex political hierarchy creates a much stronger sense of communal equality hearkening back the the mythical good old days. The exiled Duke himself attests to the advantages of living far from the court, free of the deceits of flattery and double dealing and welcomes Orlando to the feast without suspicion.

And, most important here, especially in comparison with the history plays, is the importance of singing. *As You Like It* is full of songs—not performances by professional court musicians, but impromptu group singing which expresses better than anything else the spontaneous joy these people derive from life in the Forest and the joy they give back to others. The songs indicate clearly the way in which in the Forest people can shape their actions to their moods—a situation totally unlike the court where one has to consider one's actions much more carefully.

Hence, the Forest of Ardenne provides for the exiled courtiers an important freedom to experiment with their lives, to discover things about themselves. In the Forest people can talk openly with whoever they might happen to meet on a stroll through the trees, and that might be anyone, given that in the Forest no one owns any particular territory (there are no rooms, palaces, roads—unlike the court where there is a preoccupation with property) and thus one might well meet and have to deal with a person whom one would never get close to in the court (that can have comic results, of course, as Touchstone's conversations with Audrey and William demonstrate). In the Forest life is, as I have observed, lived more immediately in the moment with whatever life presents at the moment. Such an approach to life is impossible in the politically charged world of the court.

That freedom makes possible Rosalind's transformation and her taking charge of the courtship and makes an interesting contrast between Rosalind and Viola (in *Twelfth Night*)—the latter is not nearly so free to take charge, because she is still operating in a social environment with a clear structure of authority, which she has to respect. Hence, the fortunate outcome of that play relies upon her patience and luck far more in the case of Rosalind, who is the driving force in her courtship (Viola's desires very nearly are unfulfilled).

We should note, however, that the Forest of Ardenne is not an entirely idyllic setting. The Duke pays tribute to the often brutal weather, and there are some dangerous animals lurking in the underbrush. Corin, the shepherd, informs us that he works for another man—a slight but significant reminder that even in this pastoral setting the realities of power are not entirely absent.

And, of course, there is never any sense here (as there might be if this were a Romantic vision of life) that the Forest is a suitable place to live on a continuing basis. Given the opportunity to return to the court, all the exiles (except, significantly, Jaques) seize the chance. The Forest has done its work—it has educated some, repaired fraternal relationships, brought the lovers to a fuller awareness of their own feelings. Now, they can return to what will be, we sense, a much better and fuller life in the court.

The Language of Love

The most obvious concern of *As You Like It* is love, and particularly the attitudes and the language appropriate to young romantic love. This, I take it, is obvious enough from the relationships between Orlando and Rosalind, Silvius and Phoebe, Touchstone and Audrey, and (very briefly) Celia and Oliver. The action of the play moves back and forth among these couples, inviting us to compare the different styles and to recognise from those comparisons some important facts about young love.

Here the role of Rosalind is decisive, and much of one's response to this play (especially in performance) will depend upon our reaction to her. Rosalind is Shakespeare's greatest and most vibrant comic female role, and there's a old saying to the effect that in any successful production of *As You Like It*, the audience members will all leave the theatre in love with her.

She is clearly the only character in the play who has throughout an intelligent, erotic, and fully anchored sense of love, and it becomes her task in the play to try to educate others out of their false notions of love, especially those notions which suggest that the real business of love is adopting an inflated Petrarchan language and the appropriate attitude that goes with it.

Rosalind falls in love with Orlando at first sight (as is standard in Shakespeare), becomes erotically energised, and remains so throughout the play. She's delighted and excited by the experience and is determined to live it to the full moment by moment. One of the great pleasures of watching Rosalind is that she is always celebrating her passionate feelings for Orlando. She does not deny them or try to play games with her emotions. She's aware that falling in love has made her subject to Celia's gentle mockery, but she's not going to pretend that she isn't totally thrilled by the experience just to spare herself being laughed at (she even laughs at herself, while taking enormous delight in the behaviour which prompts the mockery).

At the same time, Rosalind has not an ounce of sentimentality. Her passionate love for Orlando does not turn her into a mooning, swooning recluse. It activates her. She takes charge of her life. She knows what she wants, and she organises herself to seek it out. If she has to wait to pursue her marriage, then she is going actively to enjoy the interim in an improvised courtship and not wrap herself in a mantle of romantic attitudinizing. She initiates the game of courtship with Orlando and keeps it going. She has two purposes here. This gives her a chance to see and court Orlando (in her own name) and thus to celebrate her feelings of love, but it also enables her to educate Orlando out of the sentimental pose he has adopted.

Orlando, too, is in love with Rosalind. But his view of love requires him to write drippy poems and walk through the forest hanging them on trees. He sentimentalises the experience (that is, falsifies it), so that he can luxuriate in his feelings of love rather than focusing sharply on the reality of the experience. In their conversations, Rosalind/Ganymede pointedly and repeatedly deflates his conventional rhetoric. This comes out most clearly in her famous reply to his claim that, if Rosalind rejects him, then he will die.

No, faith; die by attorney. The poor world is almost six thousand years old, and in all this time there was not any man died in his own person, videlicet, in a love-cause. Troilus had his brains dashed out with a Grecian club, yet he did what he could to die before, and he is one of the patterns of love. Leander, he would have lived many a fair year though Hero had turned nun if it had not been for a hot midsummer night, for, good youth, he went but forth to wash him in the Hellespont and, being taken with the cramp, was drowned; and the foolish chroniclers of that age found it was Hero of Sestos. But these are all lies. Men have died from time to time, and worms have eaten them, but not for love.

It needs to be stressed that Rosalind's view of love is highly intelligent (that is, emotionally intelligent) and sensitive.

This is not the statement of a cynic, because we know that Rosalind is very much in love, passionately eager to be with Orlando or to talk about him as much as she can. But the experience is not corrupting her response to life. She will not permit herself or Orlando to be deceived into thinking love is something other than the excitingly real experience she is going through—love is the most wonderfully transforming experience for her but it is not the sum total of everything life has to offer (as Orlando's poems make out). This fusion of passion and intelligence, shot through with a humour which enables her to laugh at herself as much as at other people, makes Rosalind a wonderfully attractive character.

This complex attitude first emerges when she discovers Orlando's poetry. Of course, she knows the poetry is really poor, and she can laugh heartily at Touchstone's damning parody of all the words which rhyme with "Rosalind." But at the same time she is erotically thrilled that Orlando is around and that he is in love with her. Rather than being embarrassed by the wretched sentimentality of her lover, she simultaneously loves the fact that her feelings are returned and can laugh at his attempt to express them. This is not laughter at Orlando, but at the incongruity of the situation and joy at the mutuality of their feelings.

Consider also her sense that the youthful love she is now enjoying will not last. She knows that and is not going to shield herself from that awareness in conventionally romantic platitudes: "No, no, Orlando; men are April when they woo, December when they wed. Maids are May when they are maids, but the sky changes when they are wives" (4.1.124-127). Of course, time will change the passionate excitement she now feels. But she's not going to act like Marlowe's Nymph who denies the passionate shepherd his love because she's afraid of the destructive powers of time. No, she will not let any future fear interrupt or qualify the enormous joy she derives out of being in love right at this moment. What the future will bring will happen. That is no reason not to appreciate the immediate joys of the love she feels for Orlando.

> No, that same wicked bastard of Venus, that was begot of thought, conceived of spleen, and born of madness, that blind rascally boy that abuses everyone's eyes because his own are out, let him be judge how deep I am in love. I'll tell thee, Aliena, I cannot be out of the sight of Orlando. I'll go find a shadow and sigh till he come.

Here she is, in part, laughing at herself as a victim, one more person hit by naughty Cupid. But she's obviously thrilled by the experience and is not going to deny herself one bit of the joy she is feeling.

Rosalind becomes the pivot around whom the other lovers move, because she is the only one with a maturely intelligent sense of the difference between love and sentiment. Thus, she can deliver stern lectures to Silvius and Phoebe about how they are denying themselves the joys that are possible because they have a false sense of love. Silvius's excessively conventional Petrarchan attitudes simply encourage Phoebe to close him out of her feelings and to develop a false sense of her own importance, as Rosalind points out very bluntly: "Sell when you can. You are not for all markets" (3.5.61). She is telling Phoebe, in effect, to wake up to the realities of the world in which she lives and to abandon the sentimental dream in which she has locked herself, thanks to the language in which she and Silvius understand their feelings.

It's significant that throughout much of the play, when Rosalind talks to others about love, she talks in prose, rejecting the formal potential of a more imaginative language, in order to keep the discussions anchored in the reality of everyday life. Rosalind wants love, but she will have it only in the language of everyday speech, without the seductive embellishments of poetical conventions, which corrupt because they take one away from the immediately reality of the experience.

Orlando profits from Rosalind's instructions because he is basically an emotionally intelligent person as well. His commitment to playing the role of the conventional lover is only luke warm; as Rosalind observes, he doesn't have the appearance of such a literary poseur. Significantly, his poetry is very bad, and he's not going to mind acknowledging the fact. He does not love his own words more than his own true feelings and hence does not strive to develop his abilities as a poet and quickly moves into the prose conversations with Rosalind/Ganymede. It's an interesting question whether or not he might recognise or have his suspicions about Rosalind/ Ganymede well before the ending. There's an intriguing possibility that he knows her all along, but recognizing that she is in charge of the game, he is only going to drop the pretense when she gives him the cue. I've never seen this interpretation attempted, but if I were producing the play, I would like to try it.

The Role Of Jaques

The essentially healthy emotional intelligence of Rosalind and Orlando and their suitability for each other emerge from their separate encounters with Jaques (in some editions Jacques), the melancholy ex-courtier who is part of Duke Senior's troupe in the forest. Both Rosalind and Orlando take an instant dislike to Jaques (which is mutual). And in that dislike we are invited to see something vitally right about the two of them.

For Jaques is, in effect, the opposite of everything Rosalind stands for. He is a moody cynic, who likes to look at life and draw from it poetical contemplations at the generally unsatisfactory nature of the world. He is, in a sense, an initial Hamlet-like figure (the comparison is frequently made), someone without any motivating erotic joy, who compensates for his inadequacy by trying to drag everything down to the level of his empty emotions and by verbalizing at length in poetical images. He takes some pride in what he calls his very own brand of melancholy which can suck the joy out of life as a weasel sucks the protein out of an egg (an interesting image of the destruction of new living potential), and he spends his time wallowing in it. His own social desire seems to be to find someone else to wallow in the same emotional mud as he does. But the spirits of the other characters, especially of Rosalind and Orlando, are too vital and creative to respond favourably to Jaques's attempts to cut life down to fit his limited moods.

That judgment no doubt sounds quite harsh. And perhaps it is, for Jaques is a relatively harmless person, who deceives no one (nor does he try to), and his poetical reflections, like Hamlet's, are often seductive. But we should not let the fame of some of his utterances (particularly the famous "Seven Ages of Man" speech in 2.7, a frequently anthologised piece of so-called Shakespearean "wisdom") conceal the fact that his approach to life is thoroughly negative. He sees no value in anything other than calling attention to the world's deficiencies. He does not recognise in the fellowship, music, and love all around him any countervailing virtues.

This point is made really explicit at the very end of the "Seven Ages of Man" speech (2.7.138-165). As Jaques concludes his cynical evaluation of the emptiness of human life by talking about how in old age men become useless lumps of flesh ("Sans teeth, sans eyes, sans taste, sans everything"), Orlando enters carrying Adam. The latter is the living denial of everything Jaques has just said, for Adam is very old, but has actively striven to help Orlando with generosity, love, and a sense of duty, qualities which confer upon him an emphatic and obvious value. The dramatic irony in that entrance points us to the severely limited and limiting understanding of the world which Jaques has just uttered.

As an aside, it might be worth remarking that this habit of excerpting speeches of Shakespeare and setting them up as "gems" outside of their immediate dramatic context has the unfortunate tendency to immortalise a passage as some special insight into the nature of life when it is, in fact, quite the reverse. The speech of Jaques is, along with the advice of the Polonius to his son, the most famous example of this problem. Far from being a particularly mature earned insight into anything important, Jaques's speech is an indication of his limited and unwelcome sense of the unsatisfactory nature of life. The entrance of Orlando and Adam underscores this point.

Oscar Wilde, in one of his most famous apophthegems, once defined a cynic as one who knows the price of everything and the value of nothing. That definition applies very well to Jaques, and it helps us at once understand why Rosalind and Orlando will have nothing to do with him. Rosalind understands that love comes at a price. Time will change things, and a commitment in love brings with it the risk of infidelity (and there is much talk of that in the play). But she will nof therefore deny its value or refuse to take the risk. On the contrary, she determines to extract the full value from her excited feelings for Orlando, not by freezing those feelings in some sour poetical reflections but by experiencing them moment by moment, no matter what the future may bring. Orlando also is too full of the spirit of life to find anything in Jaques's gentle but persistent pessimism at all worth bothering about.

I don't mean to over-emphasize the kill-joy quality of Jaques. He is generally harmless enough, particularly in this play where everyone recognises him for what he is and where he has no particular interest in pulling others down to his level against their will. If they don't want to sit down with him and rail against the first born of Egypt, he's content to move away on his own. But it's significant that he's not a fully participating member of the final celebrations and that he is going to remain in the forest. He has learned nothing and, indeed, is incapable of learning anything, simply because he is not open to experience (in terms of the earlier analysis I offered of Richard II and Hamlet, Jaques is a "chatterer"). He's made up his mind what life is all about, and he is seeking confirmation of a pre-set attitude.

Traversi's summary comment on Jaques hits the mark precisely:

... Jacques' motive is, in the last analysis "observation," the gratifying of a self regarding curiosity based on a kind of personal impotence, an inability to participate fully and naturally in the processes of life; and, since his attitude is one which implies throughout an incapacity for genuine *giving*, for the positive acceptance of an order, at once natural and distinctively human, beyond the isolated self—the acceptance by which, in love or otherwise, the self is at last justified—he remains a mere marginal presence in the process by which that order is finally... consummated. (*An Approach to Shakespeare*, Vol. 1, p. 328)

Perhaps another way of summing up Jacques' is to observe that he's more interested in language than he is in life. His interaction with the world is governed largely by his desire to find occasions to verbalize, to construct poetical reflections on the melancholy state of things. He seems happy enough with this condition not to feel any desire to break out of it, to open himself up to new experience, to listen carefully to others, and thus risk having to adjust his understanding (that is, to learn). In a play that is so centrally concerned with the relationship between language and feelings he may thus stand as an eloquent and charming but ultimately frozen being who has imprisoned himself inside a love of language, perhaps as a protection against the world, perhaps out of a sense of the misplaced importance he gives to a particular form of verbalizing. So his decision to remain in the forest is apt: there he will find plenty of opportunity for gloomy reflections and conversations, without learning from them enough to acquire the civilized intelligence of the newly energized ducal court.

The Question of Gender

One of the most intriguing aspects of the treatment of love in *As You Like It* concerns the issue of gender. And this issue, for obvious reasons, has generated a special interest in recent times. The principal reason for such a thematic concern in the play is the cross dressing and role playing. The central love interest between Rosalind and Orlando calls into question the conventional wisdom about men's and women's gender roles and challenges our preconceptions about these roles in courtship, erotic love, and beyond.

At the heart of this courtship is a very complex ambiguity which it is difficult fully to appreciate without a production to refer to. But here we have a man (the actor) playing a woman (Rosalind), who has dressed herself up as a man (Ganymede), and who is pretending to be a woman (Rosalind) in the courtship game with Orlando. Even if, in modern times, Rosalind is not played by a young male actor, the theatrical irony is complex enough.

The most obvious issue raised by the cross dressing is the relationship between gender roles and clothes (or outer appearance). For Rosalind passes herself off easily enough as a man and, in the process, acquires a certain freedom to move around, give advice, and associate as an equal among other men (this freedom gives her the power to initiate the courtship). Her disguise is, in that sense, much more significant than Celia's, for Celia remains female in her role as Aliena and is thus largely passive (her pseudonym meaning "Stranger" or "outsider" is an interesting one). The fact that Celia is largely passive in the Forest of Ardenne (especially in contrast to Rosalind) and has to wait for life to deliver a man to her rather than seeking one out, as Rosalind does, is an interesting and important difference between the two friends.

These points raise some interesting issues. If becoming accepted as a man and getting the freedom to act that comes with that acceptance is simply a matter of presenting oneself as a man, then what do we say about all the enshrined natural differences we claim as the basis for our different treatment of men and women? Given that Rosalind is clearly the most intelligent, active, and interesting character in the play and that these qualities would not be likely to manifest themselves so fully if she were not passing herself off as a man, the play raises some interesting questions about just what we mean by any insistence on gender differences as more than mere conventions.

But the issue is much more complicated than that. For Rosalind's assumed name, Ganymede, is a very deliberate reference to the young male lover Zeus carried up to Olympus, and it points us to what might be a very strong element in the courtship game between Orlando and Rosalind and in the feelings Phoebe has for Rosalind, namely homoerotic desire. There's little in the play to suggest this explicitly, but a production which showed, say, that Orlando's feelings were becoming involved with Ganymede, so that the pretend courtship has a strongly erotic undercurrent, would not be violating the text. Perhaps it's hard to distinguish totally between Orlando's feelings for Rosalind and Orlando's feelings for Ganymede. And that challenges all sorts of conventional expectations about erotic love, in order to "probe the surprisingly complex issue of what is natural in matters of love and sexual desire"

That's why the play wedding ceremony that Rosalind and Orlando go through with Celia playing role of officiating minister (in 4.1) is, for all the acting going on, quite powerfully charged. Celia, who loves Rosalind, supervises the wedding of the two people presenting themselves as men, and under the obvious fun of the make believe there's a powerful sense of the sexual attraction the two have for each other. It's worth asking at this point just how much Orlando might know or suspect or what feelings are keeping him in this game. There seems little doubt that underneath his play acting he is experiencing a strong bond with Rosalind/Ganymede, something which emerges as even more ironic if we sense (from the style of the production) that part of him either recognises Rosalind or is responding to the same characteristics in Ganymede that make him so in love with Rosalind. The BBC production is worth attending to for its presentation of this complex moment in the play.

This point is underscored by the very strong instant desire that Phoebe finds for Rosalind/Ganymede, which seems at first not unlike the feelings Orlando has for Rosalind. Phoebe, of course, abandons her love as soon as she learns that Rosalind is a woman, but the play confronts us with the question about the validity of those feelings. If a set of men's clothes is the only thing distinguishing conventional sexual arrangements from alternatives, we are invited (at least) to wonder somewhat about the extent to which conventional arrangements do not exhaust the erotic possibilities.

The play, of course, in its closing scene celebrates conventional heterosexual marriages. But by that time it has offered us, at least by powerful suggestions, some erotic alternatives, without condemning such possibilities as inherently unnatural. And, depending upon how some of these key scenes are played, a production of *As You Like It* can evoke in the audience some very interesting and (perhaps) ambivalent feelings about mature sexuality.

This point seems to be emphasised in the epilogue spoken by the newly married Rosalind, where the boy actor playing the role calls attention to the fact that he is not a woman, as if to remind us (maybe) that the happy union of Orlando and Rosalind in which we take such delight has explored other possibilities than heterosexuality. This point can be underscored strongly if Orlando is present with Rosalind during this epilogue (say, holding her in his arms) and the actor playing Rosalind is removing his make up (e.g., wig). And, of course, if the actor playing Rosalind has made some erotic connections with the audience, then his final revelation in the Epilogue will force the audience member to confront some of his own feelings about gender attachments.

As I say, it's rare to see Rosalind nowadays played by a boy, although there have been all-male productions in modern times. And so the epilogue is often omitted or edited. As it stands, the boy actor's offer to kiss the desirable grown men in the audience ("If I were a woman") gives the last words of the play an ironic and erotic resonance that challenges gently the heterosexual weddings we have just celebrated.

A Comment on Touchstone

As You Like It features, like so many of Shakespeare's plays, a professional clown, Touchstone, and it's worth paying some attention to his role for what it contributes towards establishing and maintaining the upbeat comic spirit of the play. For the jester is the constant commentator on what is going on. His humour, pointed or otherwise, thus inevitably contributes to the audience's awareness of what is happening, and the way in which other characters treat him is often a key indicator of their sensibilities.

Touchstone is one of the gentlest and happiest clowns in all of Shakespeare. He comments on the action, makes jokes at other people's expense, and offers ironic insights about their situation. But throughout *As You Like It,* such traditional roles of the fool are offered and taken with a generosity of spirit so that his remarks never shake the firm comic energies of the play. When he ridicules Orlando's verses, Rosalind laughs along with him. When he points out to Corin (in 3.2) that the shepherd must be damned for never having lived at court, Corin takes it as good natured jesting (which it is). When Touchstone takes Audrey away from her rural swain, William, there are apparently no hard feelings (although much here depends on the staging). In this play, the professional jester participates in and contributes to a style of social interaction which is unqualified by any more sobre and serious reflections. This makes Touchstone very different from the bitter fool of *King Lear* or from the most complex fool of all, the sad Feste of *Twelfth Night,* both of whom offer comments that cast either a shrewd, melancholy, or bitter irony on the proceedings.

Touchstone himself becomes the target of much humour by his immediate attraction to Audrey, the "foul" country lass. There is something richly comic here, seeing the staunch apologist for the sophisticated life of the court fall so quickly to his animal lust. But the satire here is very good humoured. Touchstone himself acknowledges the frailty of his vows and does not attempt to deceive anyone about his intentions. He knows he is serving his lusts and that that is no good basis for a lasting and significant marriage. But the play builds up no severe indictment against what he is doing, and Audrey herself makes no protest. So this most unlikely of unions becomes part of the celebration of love at the end of the play, an expression of the comic variety of the experience, rather than offering any ironic commentary.

Bibliography

Bate, Jonathan. *Shakespeare and Ovid*. Oxford: Clarendon P, 1993.

Belsey, Catherine. "The Illusion of Empire: Elizabethan Expansionism and Shakespeare's Second Tetralogy." *Literature and History* 1.2 (1990): 13-21.

Boose, Lynda E. "*The Taming of the Shrew*, Good Husbandry, and Enclosure." In *Shakespeare Reread: The Texts in New Contexts*. Ed. Russ McDonald. Ithaca: Cornell UP, 1994. 193-225.

Bradbrook, M. C. *The School of Night*. New York: Russell & Russell, 1965.

Burgess, Anthony. *A Dead Man in Deptford*. London: Hutchinson, 1993.

Callaghan, Dympna. "Re-reading Elizabeth Cary's *The Tragedie of Mariam, Faire Queene of Jewry*." In *Women, 'Race', and Writing in the Early Modern Period*. Ed. Margo Hendricks and Patricia Parker. London: Routledge, 1994. 163-177.

Canny, Nicholas. *Kingdom and Colony: Ireland in the Atlantic World 1560-1800*. Baltimore: Johns Hopkins UP, 1988.

Cheney, Patrick. *Marlowe's Counterfeit Profession: Ovid, Spenser, Counter-Nationhood*. Toronto: U of Toronto P, 1997.

Curran, John E. "Royalty Unlearned, Honour Untaught: British Savages and Historiographical Change in *Cymbeline*." *Comparative Drama* 31.2 (summer, 1997): 277-303.

Davenport, Edwin. "The Representation of Robin Hood in Elizabethan Drama: *George a Greene* and *Edward I*." In *Playing*

Robin Hood: The Legend as Performance in Five Centuries. Ed. Lois Potter. Newark: U of Delaware P, 1998. 45-62.

Daileader, Celia R. *Eroticism on the Renaissance Stage: Transcendence, Desire, and the Limits of the Visible.* Cambridge: Cambridge UP, 1998.

Dekker, Thomas, and John Webster. *Sir Thomas Wyat.* London, 1607.

Doran, Susan. "Why Did Elizabeth Not Marry?" In *Dissing Elizabeth: Negative Representations of Gloriana.* Ed. Julia M. Walker. London: Duke UP, 1998. 30-59.

Elliott,J. H. *The Old World and the New 1492-1650.* Cambridge: Canto, 1992.

Ferguson, Arthur. *Utter Antiquity: Perceptions of Prehistory in Renaissance England.* Durham: Duke UP, 1993.

Greenblatt, Stephen. *Marvelous Possessions: The Wonder of the New World.* Oxford: The Clarendon P, 1991.

Hall, Kim F. *Things of Darkness: Economies of Race and Gender in Early Modern Europe.* Ithaca: Cornell UP, 1995.

Hunt, Maurice. '"New o'er': mining the veins of Shakespeare's *Cymbeline.*" *English Language Notes* 36.4 (June 1999): 14-27.

Jonson, Ben. *The New Inn.* Ed. Michael Hattaway. Manchester: Manchester UP, 1984.

Jowitt, Claire. '"Monsters and Straunge Births': The Politics of Richard Eden." *Connotations* 6.1 (1996/7): 51-64.

Knapp, Jeffrey. *An Empire Nowhere: England, America, and Literature from* Utopia *to* The Tempest. Berkeley: U of California P, 1992.

Laurence, Anne. "The Cradle to the Grave: English Observation of Irish Social Customs in the Seventeenth Century." *The Seventeenth Century* 3 (1985): 63-84.

Liebler, Naomi Conn. *Shakespeare's Festive Tragedy.* London: Routledge, 1995.

Lim, Walter S. H. *The Arts of Empire: The Poetics of Colonialism from Ralegh to Milton.* Newark: U of Delaware P, 1998.

Lutkus, Alan. "Touchstone." In *Fools and Jesters in Literature, Art, and History*. Ed. Vicki K. Janik. Westport: Greenwood P, 1998. 466-470.

Martindale, Charles and Michelle. *Shakespeare and the Uses of Antiquity: An Introductory Essay.* London, Routledge, 1990.

Monmouth, Geoffrey of. *The History of the Kings of Britain.* Trans. Lewis Thorpe. Harmondsworth: Penguin, 1966.

Murphy, Andrew. *But the Irish Sea Betwixt Us: Ireland, Colonialism, and Renaissance Literature.* Kentucky: UP of Kentucky, 1999.

Nicholl, Charles. *The Creature in the Map.* London: Vintage, 1996.

Plunket Barton, Sir D. *Links Between Ireland and Shakespeare.* Dublin: Maunsel, 1919.

Pong Linton, Joan. *The Romance of the New World: Gender and the Literary Formations of English Colonialism.* Cambridge: Cambridge UP, 1998.

Potter, Lois, ed. *Playing Robin Hood: The Legend as Performance in Five Centuries.* Newark: U of Delaware P, 1998.

Shakespeare, William. *As You Like It.* Ed. H.J. Oliver. Harmondsworth: Penguin, 1968.

Temple Leader, John. *Life of Sir Robert Dudley.* Florence: G. Barbera, 1895.

Waller, Gary. *Edmund Spenser: A Literary Life.* Basingstoke: Macmillan, 1994.

Whitehead, Neil L. *The Discoverie of the Large, Rich and Bewtiful Empire of Guiana.* Manchester: Manchester UP, 1997.

Young, David. *The Heart's Forest: A Study of Shakespeare's Pastoral Plays.* New Haven: Yale UP, 1972.